Austrian Seven Years War Infantry and Engineers
Uniforms, Organisation and Equipment

Dr Stephen Summerfield

Hungarian Fusilier c1760

KEN TROTMAN PUBLISHING

Published in 2011 by Ken Trotman Publishing.
Booksellers & Publishers
P.O. Box 505
Godmanchester
Huntingdon PE29 2XW
England
Tel: 01480 454292
Fax: 01480 384651
www.kentrotman.com

© Dr. Stephen Summerfield

All rights reserved. No part of this publication
may be reproduced, stored in a retrieval system or transmitted
in any form or by any means electrical,
mechanical or otherwise without first seeking the
written permission of the copyright owner and
of the publisher.

ISBN 978-1-907417-15-3

Printed in Great Britain by the MPG Books Group,
Bodmin and King's Lynn

Contents

Contents	3
Tables	4
Order of Battles	5
Acknowledgements	6
Preface	7
Regimental Histories	8
Infantry Uniforms	8
Chapter 1 The Habsburg Lands	**11**
Chapter 2 The Army	**20**
Recruiting	23
Officers	24
Chapter 3 The Seven Years War	**25**
1756 To War	27
1757 The Crisis	36
1758 Rebuilding	43
1759 Offensive	45
1760 Rise of Loudon	46
1761 Army in Crisis	53
1762 Final Stages	54
1763 Peace of Hubertusburg	56
Chapter 4 Regular Infantry	**57**
Garrison Bns	60
Depot Bns	60
Infantry Tactics	61
Chapter 5 German Infantry	**63**
Italian Infantry	113
Netherlands Infantry	116
Inhaber	121
German Infantry Uniforms	122
Chapter 6 Hungarian Infantry	**129**
Hungarian Fusilier Uniform	145
Chapter 7 Grenadiers	**147**
Grenadier Uniform	148
Chatper 8 Infantry Weapons	**150**
Muskets	150
Infantry Swords	153
Polearms	154
Chapter 9 Infantry Colours	**156**
Leibfahne	156
Regimentsfahne	157

Chapter 10 Grenz Regiments	**158**
Croatian General Command – Karlstädt District	162
Croatian General Command – Warasdin District	166
Slavonian District	168
Banal District	171
Grenz Uniform	173
Chapter 11 Jäger Corps and Freikorps	**174**
Deutsches Feld-Jäger Korps	174
German Freikorps	175
Netherland Freikorps	179
Chapter 12 Engineers	**180**
Engineer Corps	180
Miner Corps	184
Sapper Corps	185
Pontoneer Corps	187
Pioneer Corps	189
Jean Baptist Vicomte de Gribeauval (1715-89)	191
Chronology of the Seven Years War	**195**
Glossary	**199**
References	**202**
Regimental Index	**206**
Infantry Regiments	206
Grenz Infantry Regiments	207
Jäger-Korps (disbanded in 1763)	208
Freikorps (disbanded in 1763)	208
Engineering Corps	208

Tables

Table 1: Austrian, British and French officer ranks.	*7*
Table 2: Provincial capital, population, land area and main languages of the different parts of Austro-Hungarian Empire.	*12*
Table 3: Austrian Infantry 1741-64	*57*
Table 4: Organisation of Austrian Infantry 1741-64	*57*
Table 5: Regimental Staff in 1748 [8 officers and 15 NCOs]	*59*
Table 6: Fusilier Company organisation in 1748.	*59*
Table 7: Pre-1760 facing colours for German Infantry musicians.	*127*
Table 8: Grenadier Company organisation in 1748	*147*
Table 9: Infantry small-arms.	*152*
Table 10: Infantry sabres	*153*
Table 11: NCO and Officer pole-weapons.	*155*

Austrian Seven Years War Infantry

Order of Battles

OOB 1: Number of regiments in the Austria Army, 1756.	22
OOB 2: Austrian Army had theoretically 177,444 men in 1756 [Generalstab (1901) I: 133]	23
OOB 3: Regiments in Austria, June 1756.	28
OOB 4: Regiments in the Netherlands, June 1756.	29
OOB 5: Infantry Regiments in Italy, June 1756.	29
OOB 6: Regiments in the Kingdom of Bohemia, June 1756.	30
OOB 7: Regiments in Kingdom of Hungary, June 1756.	31
OOB 8: Regiments in Slavonia, Banat and Transylvania, June 1756.	32
OOB 9: Newly raised Infantry Regiments, 1756-58.	32
OOB 10: Advance Guard and First Line of FM Browne at Lobositz (1 Oct 1756)	34
OOB 11: The Austrian Second Line and the Artillery at Lobositz (1 Oct 1756)	35
OOB 12: Austrian Detachments and Reserve at Lobositz (1 Oct 1756)	35
OOB 13: First Line of the Austrian Main Army at Breslau (22 Nov 1757)	39
OOB 14: Austrian Second Line at Breslau (22 Nov 1757)	40
OOB 15: Austrian Reserve Corps at Breslau (22 November 1757)	41
OOB 16: Austrian Artillery at Breslau (22 Nov 1757)	41
OOB 17: Nádasdy Corps at Breslau (22 November 1757)	42
OOB 18: Austro-Imperial Army at Strehla (20 August 1760) commanded by Karl Friedrich Graf Palatine Zweibrücken-Birkenfeld	48
OOB 19: Austrian Auxiliary Corps at Strehla (20 August 1760) commanded by GFWM von Kleefeld	49
OOB 20: Grenadier and Carabinier Corps at Strehla (20 August 1760) commanded by FML Guasco	49
OOB 21: First Line of FM Daun Main Army at Torgau (3 Nov 1760)	50
OOB 22: Austrian Second Line and Reserve Corps at Torgau (3 Nov 1760)	51
OOB 23: FZM Lacy's Corps at Torgau (3 November 1760)	52
OOB 24: Corps Ried at Torgau (3 November 1760)	52
OOB 25: Austrian Artillery at Torgau (3 November 1760)	53
OOB 26: Adelsbach (6 July 1762) under FML Brentano.	55

Acknowledgements

The informative books of Christopher Duffy upon the Austrian and Prussians Armies have been an inspiration to me. These I would recommend to compliment to this book.

The proof-reading of Mark Webb and Richard Brown have been invaluable to get this book in its final form. The editorial comments of Gerard Cronin of GJM Figurines and Dal Gavin have as ever of great assistance. In addition, this work would have been much harder to put together without the wonderful contributors to the *Seven Years War Project* [www.kronoskaf.com/syw] and Lars-Holger Thümmler of *Generalstad* [www.kuk-wehrmacht.de]. I wish also to thank Hans Karl Weiss, Christian Rogge, Digby Smith and Steven H. Smith for their kind assistance.

I wish to thank NGA Archive, Markus Stein and Dave Hollins for their kind permission to reproduce illustrations from their extensive collections. Especially, wish to acknowledge the kind permission to reproduce the fine illustrations from their edition of Ottenfeld and Teuber (1898 rp2003) of Ken Trotman Ltd. I wish to thank the British Library, *Heeresgeschichtliches Museum* (HGM) in Vienna, the *Landes und Universitatsbibliotek* in Darmstadt, Loughborough University Library, New York Public Library, the Royal Engineers Library and the Royal Armouries at Fort Nelson for their kind assistance.

Preface

This is the companion volume to Summerfield (2011) *Austrian Seven Years War Cavalry and Artillery*. The following conventions have been followed:

- Austrian rank titles and names have been preserved as far as possible.

Table 1: Austrian, British and French officer ranks.

Austrian Army	Prussian Army	British Army
Feldmarschall (FM)	*Feldmarschall* (FM)	General or Field Marshal
Feldzeugmeister (FZM)	*General der Infanterie* (GdI)	Lieutenant General
General de Cavallerie (GdC)	*General der Kavallerie* (GdK)	Lieutenant General
Feldmarschall-Lieutenant (FML)	*General-Lieutenant* (GL)	Major General
Generalfeldwachtmeister (GFWM)	*General-Major* (GM)	Brigadier General
Obrist	*Oberst*	Colonel
Obrist-Lieutenant (Obrist-Lt)	*Oberst-Leutnant* (Oberst-Lt)	Lieutenant Colonel (Lt Col)
Obrist-Wachtmeister / Major	*Major*	Major
Hauptmann / Rittmeister	*Hauptmann / Kapitan*	Captain
Oberlieutenant	*Premierleutnant*	1st Lieutenant
Unterlieutenant	*Sekondeleutnant*	2nd Lieutenant

- The Austrian Infantry Regiments have been numbered IR1-IR57 in accordance to the infantry regimental numbers that were given in 1769. The gaps in the sequence have been noted in the text. Although this was not done in the period, it was considered necessary to show the continuity of the regiments through the changing of their *Inhaber*. This convention is also used by Pengel (1982b) and Duffy (2000 and 2008).
- The Grenz Infantry Regiments are according to their precedence in 1761. The Regimental Index gives a cross reference of Inhaber.
- The Cuirassier [KR], Dragoon [DR], Hussar [HR] and Grenz Hussar [GHR] have been assigned by their seniority in 1761. The Regimental Index in this Volume 2 gives a cross reference to the 1769 Cavalry Numbers used by Pengel (1982) and Duffy (2000 and 2008). See Summerfield (2011) *Austrian Seven Years War Cavalry and Artillery* for more details.
- The Austrians used their own measurements throughout the period and these have been converted to metric.
- The more familiar caisson has been used instead of ammunition wagon, *Munitionwagen* or *Kugelwagen*.
- A glossary of German terms is given in the appendix.

Regimental Histories

The list of Inhaber and regimental histories has been derived mainly from Thürheim (1880) and Wrede (1898-1905) with additional material from Duffy (2000 & 2008) and Thümmler (1993).

References

Duffy, Christopher (2000) *Instruments of War* Volume I of the Austrian Army in the Seven Years War; Emperor's Press

Duffy, Christopher (2008) *By Force of Arms*, Volume II of the Austrian Army in the Seven Years War, Emperor's Press.

Duffy, Christopher (2009) *The Wild Goose and the Eagle: A Life of Marshal von Browne 1705-57*, Tricorne Press, UK. [reprint from the original Chalto and Windus edition]

Hochedlinger, Michael (2003) *Austria's Wars of Emergence 1683-1797*, Longman.

Hollins, David (2005) *Austrian Frontier Troops 1740-98*, Osprey Publishing

Ottenfeld, Rudolf von and Teuber, Oscar (1895 rp 2003) *Die Österreichische Armee von 1700 bis 1867*, Verlag von Emil Berte, Vienna [reprint by Ken Trotman Ltd]

Szabo, F.A.J. (2007) *The Seven Years War in Europe 1756-63*, Longman, London

Thürheim, Andreas (1880) *Gedenkblätter aus der Kriegsgeschichte der k. k. Österreichischen Armee*, Vol I-II, Vienna

Wrede, Alphons Freiherr von (1898-1905), *Geschichte der K. und K. Wehrmacht. Die Regimenter, Corps, Branchen und Anstalten von 1618 bis Ende des XIX. Jahrhunderts*, Volume I-V, Vienna

Infantry Uniforms

There is a considerable amount of conflicting evidence concerning the uniforms for the infantry and there were a number of uniform changes brought about by reforming regiments and the need for economy. At the start of the campaign many of the infantry regiments had coloured waistcoats and the drummers were often in reversed colours. Later in the Seven Years, these distinctions had disappeared probably due to the needs of economy and cost of the dyed cloth. Most of the illustrations are derived from the Albertini and the Raspe Manuscript both dated as 1762 so it is not surprising that none of the German Infantry show colour waistcoats.

The author has decided to present the illustrations and where possible resolve the inconsistencies. The precise details of uniforms are difficult to sort out with the distance of time and these have been highlighted rather than reconciled by the works of Pengel and Hurt (1982 and 1983).

Most of the 19th and early 20th century illustrations follow those of either Albertini, Bautzen Manuscript and Raspe Manuscript both dated as 1762 which differ considerably at times in the details. Their age has meant that there may have been changes in the shade especially of the greens and the reds.

The Albertini (1762) [also spelt Albertina] were first reproduced in 1873 by Kornauth and these delightful full length plates are considered the most reliable by both Pengel (1982) and Duffy (2000). However, the colour has suffered over the last two and a half centuries. A great deal of care has been made by the author to digitally enhance the colour of all the illustrations. Both of Pengel (1983) and Duffy (2000) consider the Albertini (1762) full length plates as being the most reliable.

The Bautzen Manuscript (1762) has been reproduced by Thümmler (1993). They are charming in their naive simplicity but have suffered considerably with age and the yellowing of the paper.

The Brauer Plates (c1930) and the work by Herbert Knötel were based upon the Raspe Manuscript (1762) with some differences. The excellent research of Donath (1970) is more faithful to the Raspe Manuscript (1762) and these have been redrawn by the author to fill out areas that have not been covered by Albertini (1762) or Brauer (c1930). It was felt unnecessary to show examples directly from the Raspe Manuscript as these were well represented by Brauer (c1930) and Donath (1970).

The rarely seen pen and ink drawings have been reproduced from Ottenfeld (1895 rp2003) *Die Österreichische Armée von 1700 bis 1867* by the kind permission of Richard Brown of Ken Trotman Ltd who produced an excellent facsimile in three volumes.

Infantry Uniform Sources

Albertini (1762) *Dessins des Uniformes des Troupes I.I. et R.R. de l'Année 1762*, Vienna [Reproduced in Kornauth, Friedrich (1873) *Das Heer Maria Theresias Faksimile-Ausgabe der Albertina-Hanschrift "Desins des Uniformes des Troupes I.I et R.R. de l'Annee 1762*, Vienna – This shows 102 different uniforms and considered the most reliable of the contemporary sources.]

Bautzen Manuscript (1762) *Die Bautzener Bilderhanschrift aus dem Jahre 1762.* [Reproduced by Thümmler, Lars-Holger (1993) *Die Österreichische Armee im Siebenjährigen Krieg Die Bautzener Bilderhandschrift aus dem Jahre 1762*, Berlin]

Becher, Johann Christian (1757-60) *Wahrhaftige Nachricht derer Begebenheiten, so sich in dem Herzogthum Weimar by dem gewaltigen Kriege Friedrichs II., Königs von Preussen, mit der Königin von Ungarn, Marien Theresen, samt ihren Bundesgenossen zugetragen*, Weimar

Brauer, Hans (1926-62) *Heeres-Uniformbogen*, Uniformbogen No. 7 and No. 23, Heere und Tradition, Berlin. [By Herbert Knötel]

Donath, Rudolf (1970) *Die Kaiserliche und Kaiserlich-Königliche Österreichische Armee 1618-1918*, Simbach [These follow mainly the Raspe Manuscript and more faithfully than Knötel.]

Frederic, Jacques Andre (1759) *Des Troupes de sa Majesté Imperiale Royale comme elles se trouvent effectivement l'an 1759*, Augsbourg

Knötel, Herbert (1890-1921) *Uniformkunde*, Plates: IV:43; V:51; VI:12; VI:13, VI:44; XII:4 and XIV:59.

Ottenfeld, Rudolf von and Teuber, Oscar (1895 rp 2003) *Die Österreichische Armee von 1700 bis 1867*, Verlag von Emil Berte, Vienna [reprint by Ken Trotman Ltd]

Pengel R.D. and Hurt G.R. (1982b) *Austro-Hungarian Infantry 1740-1762*, On Military Matters.

Pengel R.D. and Hurt G.R. (1983) *Austro-Hungarian Hussars, Artillery and Support Troops 1740-1762*, On Military Matters,

Raspe Manuscript (1762) *Der sämtlichen Kayserlich Koeniglichen Armee zur eigentlichen Kentnis der Uniform von jedem Regimente. Nebst beygefügter Geschichte, worinne von der Stiftung, denen Chefs, der Staercke, und den wichtigsten Thaten jedes Regiments Nachricht gegeben wird.*, Nürnberg. [Brauer and the Knötel plates are based upon the Raspe Manuscript]

Schultz, Johann Gottfried (1757-60) *Abbildung Preussischer Kayser und Französischer Soldaten aus dem Siebenjährigen Kriege.*

Dr Stephen Summerfield
Loughborough University
7 January 2011

Chapter 1
The Habsburg Lands

Between 1683 and 1718, Austria rose to European great-power status as a by-product of the struggle of Britain and the Netherlands with France and their success against the Turks. The huge territorial expansion lacked the political, financial and military structures to sustain their new role with its existence threatened in the 1730-40s.

Austro-Hungary encompassed numerous and diverse races. The main political and ethnic components were formed from the *Duchy of Austria, Kingdoms of Bohemia and Hungary, the Austrian Netherlands* and *Austrian Italy*. The Austrian Army was made up of people from many nations with the only commonality being that they were predominately Roman Catholic. Communication was complicated by many languages spoken including German, French, Flemish, Italian, Czech, Hungarian, Serbo-Croat and even Latin. The latter was the official language of the Hungarian government.

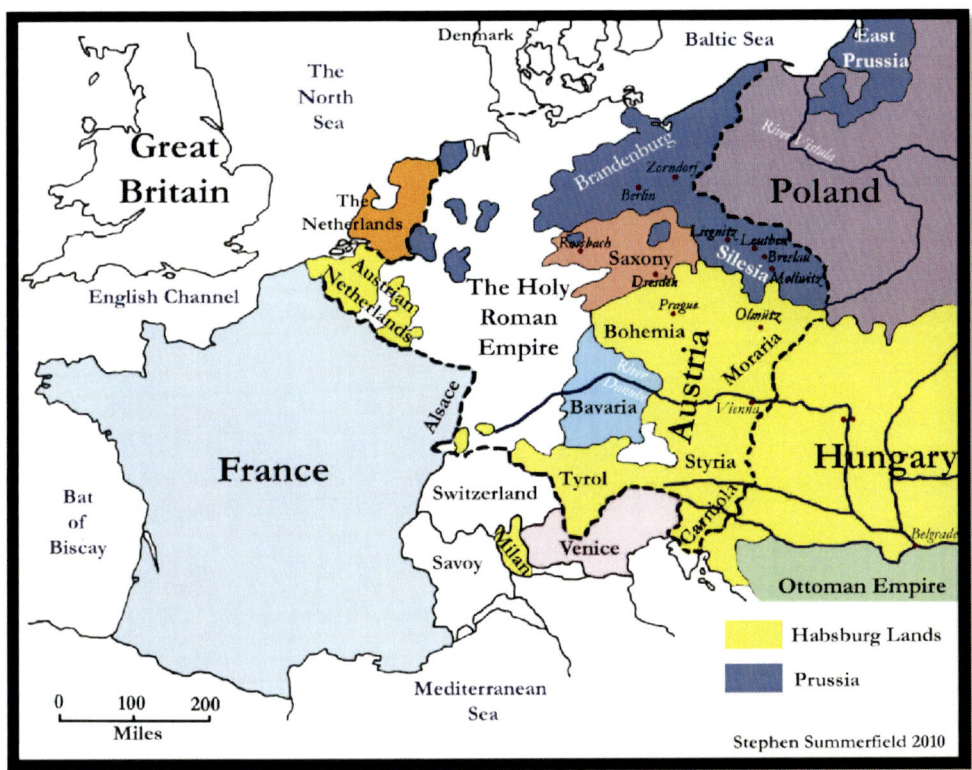

Map 1: Habsburg Lands in 1756

Table 2: Provincial capital, population, land area and main languages of the different parts of Austro-Hungarian Empire.

[Duffy (2000) 40-93 and Hochedlinger (2003) 9-26]

	Year	Capital	Pop. (1754)	Area [km²]	Main Languages
Austrian Hereditary Lands					
Archduchy of Lower Austria	1273	*Vienna*	929,576	31598 km²	*German*
Archduchy of Upper Austria	1273	*Linz*	430,371	11769 km²	*German*
Bohemian Hereditary Lands					
Kingdom of Bohemia	1526	*Prague*	1971613	51,968 km²	*Czech, German*
Marquisate of Moravia	1526	*Brünn*	886,974	22,234 km²	*Czech*
Duchy of Austrian Silesia	1526	*Troppau*	154,782	5,149 km²	*German, Czech*
Hungarian Lands					
Kingdom of Hungary	1526	*Pressburg*	4657503	208,888km²	*Hungarian, German, Romanian, Slovak*
Banat of Temesvár	1718	*Temesvár*	ditto	ditto	*Serbo-Croat*
Transylvania [Siebenbürgen]	1526	*Carlsberg*	1,037,655	54,928 km²	*Romanian, Hungarian, German*
Kingdom of Croatia	1527	*Carlstadt*	465,918	39,266 km²	*Serbo-Croat*
Kingdom of Slavonia	1745	*Peterwardein*	ditto	ditto	*Serbo-Croat*
Inner Austria					
Styria [Steiermark]	1192	*Graz*	696,606	22459 km²	*German*
Carinthia [Kärnten]	1335	*Klagenfurt*	271,924	10376 km²	*German, Slovenian*
Carniola [Krain/Crain]	1335	*Laibach*	344,564	10384 km²	*Slovenian*
County of Görz-Gradisca	1518	*Görz*	102,337	2781 km²	*Slovenian, Italian*
Austrian Littoral					
Fiume [now Rijeka]	1466	*Trieste*	unknown	2166 km²	*Serbo-Croat*
Markgraf of Istria	1382	*Trieste*	unknown	ditto	*Serbo-Croat*
Free City of Trieste	1382	*Trieste*	unknown	ditto	*Italian*
Tyrol and the Vorlande					
County of the Tyrol	?	*Innsbruck*	384,955	20,480 km²	*German, Italian*
Vorlande	1363	*Innsbruck*	299,788	2,849 km²	*German*
Austrian Italy					
Duchy of Lombardy	1713	*Milan*	about 1.3 million	39,255 km²	*Italian*
Duchy of Mantua	1708	*Mantua*	ditto	ditto	*Italian*
Principality of Castiglione	1713	*Castiglione*	ditto	ditto	*Italian*
Principality of Sabbioneta	1713	*Sabbioneta*	ditto	ditto	*Italian*
Austrian Netherlands					
Austrian Netherlands	1713	*Brussels*	about 2 million	18,386 km²	*Flemish and French*
Luxembourg	1713	*Luxembourg*		9,185 km²	*German*

The history of the Austro-Hungarian possessions of the Habsburg is probably the most complex in Europe History. The Habsburgs inherited Aragon and Castile in 1496. Just 60 years later in 1556, *Emperor Charles V* abdicated leaving Spain, the Netherlands and Italy to his son *King Philip II of Spain* who was the husband of Mary Tudor. His Austrian and German possessions were left to his brother *Ferdinand I* (1521-64) who was already King of Hungary and in 1558 he was crowned the Holy Roman Emperor. [Rickett (1983) 32]

The Habsburg link with Spain was only finally broken in 1700 when *Charles II of Spain* died without an heir. He left his dominions to *Philip of Anjou* who was the grandson of the French monarch, *Louis XIV*. Fearing the Bourbon union of France and Spain under a common Bourbon monarch, the Austrian Emperor formed the Grand Alliance with Britain and the Netherlands.

At the Peace of Utrecht (1713) that ended with War of Spanish Succession, Austria was rewarded with the *Spanish Netherlands* [renamed the *Austrian Netherlands*], *Naples, Sardinia* and *Milan*. Austria had triumphed with retaining *Hungary, Croatia* and *Transylvania*, the German Hereditary lands of *Upper* and *Lower Austria, Carinthia, Carniola, Tyrol, Moravia, Silesia* and *Bohemia*. More than a third of the German territory of the Holy Roman Empire was now ruled directly from Vienna. Austria once again ranked with France and Britain as one of the most powerful states in Europe.

Austrian 12-pdr in draft from the War of Spanish Succession

Austrian Hereditary Lands
This consisted of the *Archduchy of Austria* [*Erzherzogthum Österreich*] with the related provinces of *Styria* [*Steiermark/Austrian Alps*], *Carinthia* (*Kärnten*), and *Carniola* (*Krain*). The Austrian Hereditary Lands passed to *Duke Rudolf of Habsburg* (1218-91) in 1283. He had already been elected Holy Roman Emperor in 1273. The Habsburg claim on the Imperial title from 1438 was continuous with the only interregnum of 1745-48. They became Archduchies in 1358.

> **The Archduchy of Lower Austria** was the most prosperous of the German Hereditary Lands benefiting from Vienna being its capital and water routes from Germany, Poland, Hungary, Turkey and Italy.

> **The Archduchy of Upper Austria** extended west on both sides of the Danube towards Bavaria and the independent *Bishoprics of Salzburg* and *Passau*. It was predominately agricultural with the export of iron goods and a growing woollen trade.

Inner Austria
Created in 1564 included the diverse territories of *Styria, Carinthia, Carniola, Görg,* and *Gradisca* plus the Austrian Littoral of *Trieste, Istria* and *Fiume* sprawled across the Alps from the borders of Lower and Upper Austrian, and Hungary to the plains of the Po and the Adriatic coast.

> **Duchy of Carinthia [*Kärnten*]** bordered to the north by the *Hohe Tauern* (the highest range in the Alps east of the Brenner Pass) and the *Niedere Tauern* (in Central Eastern Alps in Austria) ranges and to the south by the *Carnic Alps* in Eastern Tyrol and *Karawanken* (mountain range between Austrian and Slovenia). The *Lower Carinthian Plain* surrounds the provincial capital of *Klagenfurt*. It was a large exporter of wool and mining. From 976 it was part of the Holy Roman Empire and a Habsburg land from 1335.

> **Duchy of Carniola [*Krain/Crain*]** is a traditional and historical region of Slovenia and was particularly exposed to Turkish incursions from the first invasion in 1415. It supplied a large number of the miners, pioneers, and sappers due to their strong mining background despite mining being a reserved occupation.

> **County of Görz and Gradisca** in current north-eastern Italy was acquired in 1518. They spoke mostly Slovenian or Italian.

> **Duchy of Styria [*Steiermark*]** is located in modern-day southern Austria and northern Slovenia. It was well known for the quality of

the iron throughout Europe and was considered to be superior to Swedish iron. The provincial capital of *Graz* with its *Zeughaus* [Arsenal] contained a large number of obsolete weapons due to its decline in military importance. These were lost to Bavaria in 1809.

Regt. Herzog Karl v. Lothringen. Regt. Sachsen-Gotha. Regt. Ahremberg.
Regt. Lascy.   Regt. Ligne.   Regt. Wied.

German Infantry c1762
[Richard Knotel]

The Austrian Littoral comprised the provinces of *Trieste*, *County of Istria* (1382), and *Fiume* (1466) provided very few men for the Austrian Army.

County of Istria is the largest peninsula in the Adriatic Sea located at the head of the Adriatic between the Gulf of Trieste and the Bay of Kvarner. It had been part of the Holy Roman Empire from the late

11th century and a Habsburg possession from 1382. In 1797, with the Treaty of Campo Formio, the Venetian parts of the peninsula passed to the Holy Roman Empire. In 1806, Istria became part of the Kingdom of Italy (1806–1810) and then part of the Illyrian Provinces (1810–1813) before being returned to Austria in 1815.

Free Port of Fiume [now *Rijeka*] became a Habsburg possession in 1466 and was created as a Free Port in 1723.

Free Port of Trieste is in north-east Italy almost surrounded by the Slovenian border at the head of the Gulf of Trieste on the Adriatic Sea. After two centuries of war against the Republic of Venice, the major citizens of Trieste petitioned *Leopold III of Habsburgs Duke of Austria* to become part of his domains which was signed in October 1382. Trieste became an important port and trade hub. In 1719, *Emperor Charles VI* made it a free port within the Habsburg Empire. It was annexed by the French as the Illyrian Provinces (1809-13) before being returned to the Austria in 1815.

Tyrol and Vorlande
Mountainous Tyrol along with the scattered enclaves in southern Germany situated between the Rhine, the Danube and Lake Constance. This region was administered from Innsbruck.

Outer Austria [*Vorderösterreich*] included the Habsburg possessions in the Black Forest and the small possessions along the southern Rhine and Habsburg Alsace.

Swabian Austria [*Schwäbische Österreich*] centred on Markgraf of Burgau.

County of the Tyrol was raised to a county in 1504. Under *Maria Theresa* (r. 1740–1780) it was governed from Vienna.

Vorarlberg: a mountainous region separated *Vorlande* from the Tyrol.

Kingdom of Bohemia
In 1515, *Charles* (1500-58), who became King of Spain in 1516 and Holy Roman Emperor in 1519, married the heir to the Kingdom of Bohemia. As a result on October 1526, *Charles* was elected Kings of Bohemia. King of Bohemia included *Bohemia (Böhmen), Moravia (Mähren),* and *Silesia (Schlesien).*

Most of the latter was conquered by the Prussians in 1740 and ultimately retained by them.

Bohemia: It was in decline disordered by religious intolerance and exploited by German speaking absentee landlords. [Durant (1965) IX: 431]

Moravia (*Morava* [Czech] *Mähren* [German]) is now in the east of the Czech Republic taking its name from the Morava River that rises in the northwest of the region. Until 1641 Moravia's capital was the centrally-located *Olmütz* (German) [*Olomouc* (Czech)] surrounded by marshy land on the Morava river, but after its capture by the Swedes it moved to the larger city of *Brünn* [*Brno* (Czech)] at the confluence of the Svitava River with the Svratka River and resisted the invaders successfully. The town is and was protected (westwards) by the strong fortress of the Spielberg Castle. The Moravians speak various Czech dialects.

Silesia was inherited by the Habsburgs as part of the Kingdom of Bohemia upon the death of the *King Louis II of Bohemia* in October 1526. The two main cities were *Teschen* and *Troppau* [now *Opava*]. Lower Silesia and most of Upper Silesia was lost to Prussia in 1742. *Maria Theresa* fought three wars in an attempt to recover Silesia. The last was the Seven Years War. Austrian Silesia [*Österreichisch Schlesien* (German); *Rakouské Slezsko* (Czech); *Śląsk Austriacki* (Polish)] was only a small part of Upper Silesia and did not conyain any part of Lower Silesia within its borders. The capital of the Austrian Silesia was *Troppau* [*Opava*] on the *Oppa* [*Opava*] *River*.

Kingdom of Hungary

In 1515, Ferdinand (brother to Charles who became Holy Roman Emperor in 1519) married the heir of Hungary. In 1726, Ferdinand became the first Habsburg King of Hungary upon the death of *King Louis II* who was killed at Mohacs (29 Aug 1526) when the Hungarian Royal Army was destroyed by *Sultan Suleiman I of Turkey* (1494-1566). The Kingdom of Hungary was reduced to western and northern Hungary before this was conquered by the Turks in 1541. [Rickett (1983) 23-33] The Kingdom of Hungary included *Hungary, Transylvania (Siebenbürgen), Banat, Croatia* and *Slavonia*.

The Habsburg Kings of Hungary ruled from Vienna through the *Hofrat* [Royal Council]. The *Hofkammer* [Ministry of Finance] in Vienna remained the policy-making body for the government of Hungary through the Hungarian Chancellery. Its executive council in Buda was nominated by the king and had no connection with the diet that was responsible only for the voting of war taxes. The administration of the taxes and all other financial questions were in the hands of the *Kammer* [Treasury] that was answerable only to the Viennese *Hofkammer*.

Hungary suffered from being the main area of contention between the Christians and Turks for centuries. Only in 1699 were the Turks finally driven out of Hungary and Transylvania.

In 1703, the Hungarian rebels under *Francis II Rákóczi* (1676-1735) refused to recognize the Habsburg hereditary claim to the throne of Hungary or the separation of Transylvania from Hungary that was now directly ruled from Vienna. The Treaty of Szatmár (1711) did little to remove the grievances. The Hungarian Diet between 1715 and 1722 established a common Austro-Hungarian standing army to replace the poorly trained and disciplined Hungarian *insurrectio*.

Hungarian Infantry and Hussars c1760

Kingdom of Hungary: The population had fallen, the government was in chaos and the refused to pay Imperial taxes. Only nobles and the church owned land. The *Esterhazy* family held 7 million acres [2.83 million hectares] of land. [Durant (1965) IX: 431]

Kingdom of Croatia following the Battle of Mohács in 1527, the nobles chose *Ferdinand of Habsburg* as their new king.

Banat of Temesvár was a territory north of the Danube in south east Hungary captured from the Turks by *Eugene of Savoy* in 1716 and ceded to Austria in the Peace of Passarowitz (1718). It remained under military administration until 1751 and only became part of Hungary in 1779.

Kingdom of Slavonia was taken from the Ottoman Turks in 1745. The main contribution was the Slavonian Grenz.

Transylvania (*Siebenbürgen*) was lost to Austria in 1809 and regained in 1814.

Austrian Possessions in Italy.
Italy was administered through Italian viceroys. It included the *Duchy of Lombardy*, *Duchy of Mantua* and *Tuscany*.

Duchy of Lombardy became Austrian territory in 1713 with its capital being *Milan*. Napoleon conquered Lombardy in 1796 which became the *Cisalpine Republic* and in 1806, the *Kingdom of Italy*. The Congress of Vienna returned Lombardy to Austria in 1815.

Kingdom of Tuscany was acquired in exchange for Lorraine in 1736 just three months after *Francis Stephen of Lorraine* married *Maria Theresa*.

Austrian Netherlands
The Treaty of Utrecht (1713) that ended the War of Spanish Succession ceded the Spanish Netherlands to Austria. It was only after negotiation with the Dutch Republic was completed with the Barrier Treaty of 15 November 1715 that the greatly reduced *Austrian Netherlands* was handed over. The *Austrian Netherlands* comprised 11 provinces. [Hochedlinger (2003) 222-4]

The principle goal of Habsburg rulers was to exchange the *Austrian Netherlands* for Bavaria that would consolidate the Habsburg possessions in southern Germany. In 1725, the *Netherlands National Regiments* were incorporated into the Austrian army in the Low Countries. In 1788, the Austrian Netherlands rebelled against Austria and only by the end of 1790 was Austrian power restored. In 1794, the entire region was overrun by France and became an integral part of France. Austria confirmed the loss of its territories by the Treaty of Campo Formio (17 Oct 1797).

Chapter 2
The Army

The first regular Austrian standing army was created in 1669 by Italian born *General Raimondo Graf Montecúccoli* (1608-80) who was president of the *Hofkriegsrat* from 1668 until his death in 1680. There was never enough money to fund the army from the estates, imperial diet and other revenues. [Grant (1987) 114]

Old soldiers salute Eugene of Savoy (1663-1736)

The Austrian Army had since the death of *Eugene of Savoy* undergone a severe decline in quality. At the end of the Turkish War of 1737-39, the regular army had 52 infantry regiments and 40 cavalry regiments with paper strength of 160,000 men. The severe financial difficulties led to much discussion in reducing its size but little had been done by the death of *Charles VI* in October 1740. The army now had at the start of the Austrian War of Succession only 107,892 men under arms instead of 141,880. This increased to almost 200,000 by 1743 and sunk to 171,616 in 1748. The effective strength was 40-50,000 men below this mark. [Hochedlinger (2003) 297]

Austrian finances were in a very poor state after the defeats in the War of Polish Succession (1733-35) and Turkish War of 1737-39 in alliance with Russia where Vienna had to cede some of their gains from the Treaty of Passarowitz (21 July 1718). [Scott (2000) 160] The War of Austrian Succession cost 185.85 million florins which were more than eight times the annual state revenue. The occupation of Bohemia and Silesia lost 8 million florins or two thirds of the state revenue. [Hochedlinger (2003) 234 and 280-2]

Even the most conservative elements at the court realised that there needed to be reform. In 1749, *Maria Theresa* started the much needed reform of the administration and finances of the state. The principle architect of the civilian and financial reform was lead by *Friedrich Wilhelm Graf von Haugwitz* (1702-65). In 1744, he led the government of unconquered Austrian Silesian. At this time he became aware that the Prussians raised 7 million florins in taxes from their newly conquered province of Silesia whereas the Habsburgs had only been able to raise 2.1 million florins. His work continued when he transferred to Inner Austria in 1747. In 1749, his reforms were implanted throughout the Habsburg lands except for Hungary, Lombardy and the Netherlands. In May 1749, the Austrian and Bohemian Chancelleries were replaced by the *Directorum in publicis et cameralibus* modelled upon the Prussian General Directory. This was chaired by Haugwitz. In 1757, the special councils of the *Austrian Netherlands* and *Lombardy* were incorporated into the State Chancellery. [Hochedlinger (2003) 269-270]

Empress Maria Theresa and her husband Francis Stephen of Lorraine

FM Leopold Daun was tasked with the improvement of the infantry and cavalry who established greater uniformity in drill and discipline. *Prince Liechtenstein* undertook the staggering improvement in the Artillery that more than made up the shortfall in quality in the rest of the army. [Duffy (2008) 11-12]

The transformation of the Habsburg state had only just started. The problems of lack of geographical continuity, a common language, laws or culture had not been overcome. The lands and provinces could only be governed by consent of the powerful established landowners. This also meant that the Army had to be divided among the divided territories. As Holy Roman Empress, *Maria Theresa* also had the services of the *Reichsarmee* (the Army of the Empire), although this was a fairly small force composed of contingents from a variety of the small (and smaller) entities within Germany.

The much needed *Haugwitz* financial reforms of 1748-49 would produce 110,000 regulars from Austro-Bohemia and Hungary with another 25,000 each from the Netherlands and Italian provinces. This made a total of 160,000 men excluding the *Grenz* and Technical troops. The paper strength at the start of the Seven Years War was 156,750 rising to 197,518 men in 1757. In October 1761, the regular army was reduced to 177,497 men and further to 153,164 at the end of the war in 1764. [Hochedlinger (2003) 298-300]

Friedrich Wilhelm Graf von Haugwitz (1700-65)

OOB 1: Number of regiments in the Austria Army, 1756.
[Generalstab (1901) I: 130]

56 Infantry Regiments
18 Cuirassier Regiments
14 Dragoon Regiments
11 Hussar Regiments
9 Grenz Infantry and 4 Grenz Hussar detachments.
1 German and 1 Netherlands Artillery Corps with miners
1 Engineer Corps
1 Pontoneer Corps

> **OOB 2: Austrian Army had theoretically 177,444 men in 1756**
> [Generalstab (1901) I: 133]
>
> Infantry
>   44 Infantry Regiments with 2,408 men each   105,952 men
>   10 Infantry Regiments with 2,000 men each   20,000 men
>   1 Infantry Battalion   658 men   126,610 men
>   With Grenz Infantry Regiments   15,600 men   15,600 men
>   142,210 men
>
> Cavalry and Hussars
>   18 Cuirassier Regiments with 818 troopers each   14,724 men
>   12 Dragoon Regiments with 817 troopers each   9.804 men
>   10 Hussar Regiments with 615 hussars   6,150 men   30678 men
>   With Grenz Hussars   1,000 men   1,000 men
>   31,678 men
>
> Technical Troops
>   24 German Artillery Companies   2,304 men
>   8 Netherlands Artillery Companies   768 men
>   2 Miner Companies   238 men
>   2 Pontoneer Companies   246 men   3,556 men
>
> TOTAL   177,444 men

Recruiting

This was the responsibility of each regiment. It was not until 1766 that recruiting districts [*Cantons*] on the Prussian model were introduced. Only the Hungarian Infantry and Hussars recruited from within a particular area. The other regiments, termed as "German", recruited throughout Europe especially within the Holy Roman Empire. This is extensively explored by Duffy (2000).

Regimental recruiting parties gave cash bounties to men 18-40 years old and over 5 *Fuss* 4 *Zoll* / 5'6" / 168½ cm who chose to enlist. The cavalryman received double the bounty of the infantryman. Voluntary enlistment was supplemented by a limited conscription in Austria and Bohemia. Enlistment was for life. In May 1757, limited service of six years or the duration of the war was introduced. By the end of the war about a third of the army were enlisted under limited service.

Inhaber

Each regiment had an *Inhaber* [colonel-proprietor or *Chef*] who gave his name to the Regiment. It was not until 1769 that regimental numbers supplemented the name. He enjoyed almost complete control of the finances, discipline, training, uniform and the selection of company grade officers. The latter was normally delegated to the colonel who commanded the regiment. The Inhaber was normally a general or a member of the royal family and many used it as a source of revenue. Considerable differences in Inhaber names especially of Hungarian or Italian origin can be found.

Officers

Despite generous incentives from Vienna, Austria lacked the native nobility to serve in the officer corps unlike Britain, France, Prussia and Russia. The Austrian officer corps remained heterogeneous and cosmopolitan as ever. From 1757, deserving officers with thirty years good service were granted nobility. As this did not come with land, the officer class were even tighter associated with the monarch. [Hochedlinger (2003) 305-6]

Most officers joined their regiments as cadets and received training within the regiment before being promoted to *Fähnrich* in the infantry or *Cornet* in the cavalry. In 1752, education of young cadets was improved by the opening of the Military Academy at Wiener Neustadt for sons of officers, impoverished nobles or civil servants. The first director was *FM Leopold Daun*. This was able to supply a third of the newly commissioned officers. Half the Academy was made up of sons of distinguished officers or officials and the other half from the nobility. The latter had many social advantages and so were fortunate in swifter promotions.

Company officers were promoted by their regimental *Inhaber* and senior ranks by the *Hofkriegsrat* [Council of War] who demanded a payment from the officer for each promotion. There was also an unofficial system of purchase that meant that younger officers could buy out long-serving or wounded officers.

Chapter 3
The Seven Years War

On 12 September 1703, the Pact of Succession signed by *Emperor Leopold I* with his two sons, *Joseph* and *Charles* specified that females could succeed only when all male lines had become extinct and further specified the priorities of the then living Habsburgs. In 1705, *Leopold* died and was succeeded by his son *Joseph I*.

Joseph I died in December 1711 leaving two unmarried daughters and *Joseph* was succeeded by his brother *Charles VI (Charles III of Hungary)* whose will specifying gave his own daughters precedence over his late brother's. In contrast with his predecessors, he showed favour with his non-German subjects particularly the Hungarians. *Charles* required the acceptance of the Hungarians and Bohemians of the 1713 Pragmatic Sanction announced on 1 April that permitted his daughters to inherit the throne. A defensive union was established between Austria and the major powers in Europe.

Empress Maria Theresa (1717-80)

Austria was paralysed by the unexpected death of *Charles VI* on 20 October 1740 without any male heirs. This barred the Habsburg succession to the Holy Roman Empire to which a woman could not be elected. The Pragmatic Sanction provided for the succession of his daughter, *Maria Theresa*. Only Bavaria immediately contested her claim. The Austrian Army was in a wretched condition with the treasury empty and the state now led by the inexperienced *Maria Theresa*. [Scott (2000) 160-2]

In 1740, *Frederick II of Prussia* inherited from his father the best army in Europe. Within days of hearing the news, *Frederick* decided to invade Silesia which was only defended by 8,000 men. [Wilson (1998) 247-8] Most of the Austrian Army was based in Hungary and Transylvania following the recent disastrous war against Turkey. On 16 December 1740, *Frederick* led 27,000 Prussians into Silesia so initiating the First Silesian War. Despite the severe winter and poor state of the roads, Upper and Lower Silesia together with the County of Glatz was under Prussian control by the end of January 1741. The Austrians were defeated at Mollwitz (April 1741) by the superb drill and musketry of the Prussian infantry after the failure of the Prussian cavalry. After Mollwitz, an anti-Austrian alliance was formed called the League. In 1741, the new *Empress Maria Theresa* was barely able to keep the vast Habsburg domains together.

On 24 January 1742, the elective office of Holy Roman Emperor was filled by Joseph's son-in-law, *Charles Albert of Bavaria*, as *Emperor Charles VII* marking the first time in several hundred years that the position was not held by a Habsburg. This reduced *Maria Theresa* to Archduchess of Austria and Queen of Hungary.

Austrian Dragoon c1740

The Peace of Breslau ended the First Silesian War on 11 June 1742. This interlude was used to great effect by *Frederick* to improve his cavalry.

The Austrians were still involved in war against France, Bavaria and Saxony. On 12 March 1743. *Maria Theresa* was crowned Queen of Bohemia. The Anglo-Hanoverian-Austrian Army defeated the French at Dettingen (27 June 1743).

When the Second Silesian War started in 1744, the Prussian cavalry was certainly the equal to the Austrian.

On 20 January 1745, *Emperor Charles VII* died on the eve of the Austrian invasion of Bavaria. On 15 April, *Maximilian III*, the new Elector of Bavaria signed the Treaty of Füssen that exchanged Bavaria for his support for Maria Theresa's husband as Holy Roman Emperor, *Francis I*.

The Treaty of Dresden (25 December 1745) ended the Second Silesian War between Austria, Saxony, and Prussia. *Maria Theresa* recognised *Frederick's* sovereignty over Silesia in return for Prussian recognition of Francis as Holy Roman Emperor. The Austro-Russian Treaty of the Two Empresses of 1746 renewed the alliance that had been first concluded 20 years before. [Scott (2000) 167] The Treaty of Aix-la-Chapelle (18 Oct 1748) finally ended the War of Austrian Succession.

1756 To War

The State Chancellery was established in 1742 as the Austrian ministry of foreign affairs. In 1753, *Wenzel Anton Graf Kaunitz* (1711-1794) became foreign minister [*Staatscanzler*] and believed that it was possible to humble Prussia and regain Silesia. [Hochedlinger (2003) 269]

Wenzel Anton Graf Kaunitz (1711-94)

By the second half of 1755, the balance of power had once again been upset with the start of the undeclared conflict between the British and the French in North America. As a consequence, Britain concluded with Russia the Convention of St Petersburg (30 September 1755) to protect Hanover from Prussia who was allied to France. Russia agreed to supply 55,000 men for a subsidy of £10,0000 with a further £40,000 if these troops operated directly in the defence of Hanover. [Szabo (2008) 13]

Frederick fearing the Russian threat to East Prussia concluded the Convention of Westminster (15 January 1756) with Britain where both parties agreed to keep foreign troops outside the German states.

The French considered this a betrayal of their alliance and had not forgotten Frederick abandoning them in 1745. They chose not to renew their alliance with Prussia that was due to expire in June 1756. This permitted *Wenzel Anton von Kaunitz*, the Austrian foreign minister, to offer a defensive alliance with France. On 1 May 1756, Austria and France signed the First Treaty of Versailles. This defensive alliance provided 25,000 men or the cash equivalent if either came under attack from a third party and Austria would remain neutral in an Anglo-French War. These subsidies for Austrian troops were essential for the much needed improvement of her army.

Austria had already an alliance with Russia since 1726 and renewed in 1746. This was reinforced by *Empress Elizabeth* who had a personal dislike of *Frederick*. Austria began negotiations with Russia in April 1755. The subsidy treaty between Britain and Russia had not yet been ratified.

Austria started mobilising on 18 June but there was a severe lack of men, horses and ordnance. About one third of the infantry were quartered in Bohemia and Moravia but only 9% of the regular cavalry with over 70% quartered in Hungary and distant Transylvania. The contract for the Artillery horses was only signed on 24 July. [Duffy (2008) 15] Finding suitable men for the army was always a problem for Austria. *Daun* estimated that even before the outbreak of the Seven Years War, there was a 38,000 man deficit in infantry in 1755. By June 1756, this deficit had been reduced to 10,000 men.

OOB 3: Regiments in Austria, June 1756.

ARCHDUCHY OF AUSTRIA
Infantry Regiments [I-II, Grenadiers and Garrison Bn]
IR35 Waldeck	2,354	
IR49 Kheul	2,416	
IR59 Leopold Daun	<u>2,401</u>	7,172
Cuirassier Regiments		
KR1 Erzherzog Leopold	<u>809</u>	809

CARNIOLA
Infantry Regiments [I-II, Grenadiers and Garrison Bn]
IR36 Browne	<u>2,444</u>	2,444

CARINTHIA
Infantry Regiments [I-II, Grenadiers and Garrison Bn]
IR47 Harrach	<u>2,371</u>	2,371

STYRIA (AUSTRIAN ALPS)
Infantry Regiments [I-II, Grenadiers and Garrison Bn]
IR13 Moltke	2,372	
IR21 Arenberg	<u>2,469</u>	4,841

TYROL
Infantry Regiments [I-II, Grenadiers and Garrison Bn]
IR46 Maguire	<u>2,322</u>	<u>2,322</u>
		19,959

OOB 4: Regiments in the Netherlands, June 1756.

Walloon Infantry Regiments [I-II, Grenadiers and Garrison Bn]
IR9 Los Rios	2,000	
IR30 Sachsen-Gotha	2,000	
IR38 de Ligne	2,000	
IR55 d'Arberg	<u>2,000</u>	8,000

German Infantry Regiments [I-II, Grenadiers and Garrison Bn]
IR3 Lothringen	2,000	
IR14 Salm	2,000	
IR28 Wied	2,000	
IR40 Jung-(Karl) Colloredo,	2,000	
IR41 Bayreuth	2,000	
IR43 Platz	2,000	12,000

Cavalry Regiments (6+1 depot squadrons)
KR11 Anhalt-Zerbst	800	
DR9 de Ligne	1,000	<u>1,800</u>
		21,800

OOB 5: Infantry Regiments in Italy, June 1756.

LOMBARDY

Infantry Regiments [I-II, Grenadiers and Garrison Bn]
IR15 Pallavicini	2,000	
IR16 Königsegg	2,000	
IR22 Hagenbach	2,000	
IR24 Starhemberg	2,000	
IR56 Mercy	2,000	
IR57 Andlau	<u>2,000</u>	12,000

Infantry Regiments [I-II, Grenadiers]
IR19 Leopold Pálffy	1,570	
IR32 Forgách	1,581	
IR34 Batthyány	1,550	
IR51 Gyulai	<u>1,463</u>	

Dragoon Regiments (6+1 depot squadrons)
DR5 Jung-Modena Dragoons	<u>600</u>	600

FRIULI
IR52 Bethlen	<u>1,548</u>	<u>1,548</u>
		14,148

OOB 6: Regiments in the Kingdom of Bohemia, June 1756.

BOHEMIA
Infantry Regiments

IR1 Kaiser	2,392	
IR8 Hildburghausen	2,408	
IR10 Ludwig Jung-Wolfenbüttel,	2,406	
IR11 Wallis	2,395	
IR17 Kollowrat	2,395	
IR18 Marschall	2,389	
IR20 Alt- (Anton) Colloredo,	2,391	
IR27 Baden-Durlach	2,342	
IR29 Carl Alt-Wolfenbüttel	2,382	
IR50 Harsch	2,367	
IR33 Nicolaus Esterhazy	1,652	
IR37 Joseph Esterhazy	<u>1,652</u>	27,171

Cavalry Regiments

KR2 Erzherzog Ferdinand	824	
KR15 Anspach-Bayreuth	754	
DR1 Erzherzog Joseph Dragoons	815	
DR3 Batthyány Dragoons	<u>813</u>	3,206

MORAVIA
Infantry Regiments [I-II, Grenadiers and Garrison Bn]

IR12 Botta	2,388	
IR25 Piccolomini	2,383	
IR31 Haller	1,840	
IR42 Gaisruck (Gaisrugg)	2,383	
IR53 Simbschen [initially only I Bn]	671	
IR54 Sincère	<u>2,379</u>	12,044

SILESIA
Infantry Regiments [I-II, Grenadiers and Garrison Bn]

IR7 Neipperg	<u>2,393</u>	<u>2,393</u>
		44,814

OOB 7: Regiments in Kingdom of Hungary, June 1756.

HUNGARY

Infantry Regiments [I-II, Grenadiers and Garrison Bn]

IR4 Deutschmeister	2355	
IR44 Clerici [in Hungary and Banat]	<u>1918</u>	4,272

Garrison Battalions

IR2 Erzherzog Karl	430	
IR19 Pálffy, Leopold	431	
IR31 Haller	460	
IR32 Forgách	419	
IR33 Nicolaus Esterhazy	430	
IR34 Batthyány	450	
IR37 Esterhazy, Joseph	430	
IR52 Bethlen	<u>430</u>	3,480

Cuirassier Regiments (6 + 1 depot squadrons)

KR3 Pálffy	771	
KR4 Birkenfeld	806	
KR5 Serbelloni	809	
KR6 Cordova	793	
KR7 Schmerzing	815	
KR8 Trautmansdorff	799	
KR9 Kalckreuth	795	
KR10 Birkenfeld	780	
KR13 Radicati	791	
KR14 Brettlach	780	
KR16 Gelhay	749	
KR17 Lucchesi	<u>782</u>	9,470

Dragoon Regiments (6 + 1 depot squadrons)

DR2 Liechtenstein	809	
DR4 Savoyen	807	
DR7 Hessen-Darmstadt	806	
DR8 Sachsen-Gotha	801	
DR10 Kollowrat	806	
DR12 Porporati	<u>783</u>	4,812

OOB 8: Regiments in Slavonia, Banat and Transylvania, June 1756.

SLAVONIA AND BANAT
Infantry Regiments [I-II, Grenadiers and Garrison Bn]
- IR23 Baden-Baden   2,350
- IR48 Luzan (Banat and Slavonia)   1,940   4,290

Cavalry Regiments
- KR12 Emanuel Infant von Portugal [in Banat]   782
- DR13 Koharn   759   1,541

TRANSYLVANIA
Infantry Regiments
- IR26 Puebla   2,388
- IR45 Heinrich Daun   2,263   4,651

Garrison Battalion
- IR51 Gyulai   537   537

Cavalry Regiments
- KR18 Herzog (Alt-) Modena   822
- DR11 Württemberg Dragoons   809   1,631

OOB 9: Newly raised Infantry Regiments, 1756-58.

Newly Raised Infantry Regiments
- IR39 Johann Pálffy [raised 1756-7]   2,000

Newly raised Dragoon Regiments (No Grenadier company)
- DR6 Löwenstein Chevauleger [raised 1759]   800

Staff Regiments (for the protection of the HQ)
- IR Stabs-Infanterie-Regiment [raised 1758]   2,732
- DR Stabs-Dragoner-Regiment [raised 1758]   465

Prussian Invasion of Saxony

On 29 August 1756, the Prussians invaded Saxony whose borders were only 50 miles from Berlin. [Showalter (1996) 132] This started the Seven Years War commonly referred to the Third Silesian War by the Austrians. The war soon became a continental war due to the alliances. The wife of the *Dauphin of France* was a member of the ruling house of Saxony so France was naturally affronted by the Prussian invasion. The Saxon Army of 19,000 men under *General Friedrich August von Rutowski* withdrew into a defensive camp at Pirna. This ultimately like a prison to them rather than retire into Poland or Bohemia. [Szabo (2008) 36-40]

Austria's Response

FM Maximilian Ulysses Browne commanded the Austrian Army of 32,465 men in Bohemia. He had only received 40x 3-pdr regimental guns, 6x 6-pdrs and 4x 7-pdr howitzers on 30 August which was 98 pieces short of the complement plus inadequate reserves of musket cartridges. There were no field guns to spare for *FM Octavio Piccolomini* in Moravia.

Maximilian Ulysses Browne (1705-57)

Despite grave concerns, *Browne* left Kolin on the 14 September and led his army into Saxony along the west bank of the Elbe. On 1 October 1756, he encountered the Prussian Army at Lobositz in northern Bohemia numbering 18,000 infantry, 10,500 cavalry and 97 pieces. This was the first major test for the new Austrian Army that performed far better than in the previous Silesian Wars. The Austrians were outnumbered in guns and cavalry. At about 7:30 am, the 18 squadrons of Prussian cavalry were repulsed by heavy Austrian fire and the Austrian cavalry defeated a subsequent general attack by the Prussian Cavalry. It took the Prussian infantry six hours of fighting to dislodge the Austrians who withdrew in good order to a strong position just 8 km south at Budin leaving the Prussians to claim victory as they had control of the battlefield. The Austrians lost 2,873 men and the Prussians much the same. This was not the same Austrian Army that had been so easily beaten during the War of Austrian Succession. [Duffy (2008) 19-31: Szabo (2008) 42-4]

The breakout of the Saxons in Pirna was scheduled for the 11 October by a pontoon bridge across the Elbe, with a relief corps of 9,000 men marched east from Budin. The Saxons finished the pontoon bridge one day late on the 12th and almost starving established a bridgehead across the Elbe. The Austrians under *Browne* were only 6 miles away. He had done all that could be done but let down by his subordinates and the Saxon failure to contact him, [Duffy (2009) 221] on 14 October, the 18,000 Saxons at Pirna capitulated. The Austrians returned to winter quarters in Bohemia and forced Frederick to return to Silesia. The Elector of Saxony was permitted to retire to his Polish Kingdom and 17,000 Saxons were forcibly incorporated into the Prussian Army. [Szabo (2008) 45]

The conquest of Saxony had given a 150 km buffer zone and swelled the Prussian treasury by an estimated 70 million Taler. Yet the continuation of the war was a strategic miscalculation and the need to blockade the Saxons in Pirna had robbed *Frederick* of the opportunity to make a decisive strike into Austrian territory again the unprepared army of *Browne*. [Duffy (2008) 38]

**OOB 10: Advance Guard and First Line of
FM Browne at Lobositz (1 Oct 1756)**
34 bns, 34 grenadier coys, 69 squadrons, 12 combined elite squadrons
[After Project 7YW (Aug 2008)]

Advance Guard (*GFWM Hadik*) – In front of Lobositz
    8 coys/Combined Carabiniers,
    4 coys/Combined Horse Grenadiers
    I-IV/HR6 Baranyay Hussars
    I-V/HR12 Hadik Hussars
    I-IV/Combined Grenadiers (34 coys)
    Detachment of Grenz from GIR Karlstädt & GIR Banal (100 men)

First Line (*General Lucchesi* assisted by *GL E. Kollowrat*)
  Right Wing Cavalry (*GL Radicati* & *GFWM O'Donnell*) deployed in the centre
    I-VI/DR1 Erzherzog Joseph Dragoons
    I-VI/KR6 Cordova Cuirassiers,
    I-VI/KR15 Ansbach-Bayreuth Cuirassiers

  Centre Infantry (*General C. Kollowrat* assisted by *GL W. Starhemberg*)
  GFWM Wied Infantry Brigade
    I-II/IR1 Kaiser Franz I,
    I-II/IR10 Jung-Wolfenbüttel,
    I-II/IR50 Harsch
  General Perony Infantry Brigade
    I-II/IR29 Alt-Wolfenbüttel,
    I-II/IR27 Baden-Durlach
  General McGuire Infantry Brigade
    I-II/IR11 Wallis,
    I-II/IR47 Harrach

  Left Wing Cavalry (*GFWM Löwenstein*)
    I-VI/KR5 Serbelloni Cuirassiers, I-VI/KR8 Trautmansdorff Cuirassiers,
    I-VI/DR2 Liechtenstein Dragoons

OOB 11: The Austrian Second Line and the Artillery at Lobositz (1 Oct 1756)

Second Line

Right Wing Cavalry (*GFWM Lobkowitz*) deployed in the centre
- I-VI/KR1 Erzherzog Ferdinand Cuirassiers,
- I-VI/KR4 Stampach Cuirassiers

Infantry Centre
GFWM Krottendorf Brigade
- I-II/IR8 Hildburghausen,
- I-II/IR17 Kollowrat
- I-II/IR33 Esterhazy, Nicolas,
- I-II/IR37 Esterhazy, Joseph

GFWM Wolfersdorff Brigade
- I-II/IR49 Kheul, I-II/IR35 Waldeck

Left Wing Cavalry (*GFWM Hedwiger*)
- I-VI/KR3 Carl Pálffy Cuirassiers,
- I-VI/KR14 Brettlach Cuirassiers

Artillery (*General Feuerstein* with 94 pieces and a pontoon train)

Position batteries	6x 12-pdrs guns,
	12x 6-pdrs guns,
	6x 7-pdr howitzers
Battalion guns	70x 3-pdrs battalion guns

OOB 12: Austrian Detachments and Reserve at Lobositz (1 Oct 1756)

Detachments (Graf von Lacy) along the Elbe up to Schreckenstein
- 4 coys/Converged Horse Grenadiers
- DR1 Erzherzog Joseph Dragoons,
- DR2 Liechtenstein Dragoons,
- DR3 Batthyányi Dragoons,
- DR10 Kollowrat Dragoons,
- GIR Karlstädt Grenz (400 men) [Oguliner or Ottochaner]
- I-II/IR36 Browne,
- I-II/IR20 Alt-Colloredo

Corps de Reserve (GFWM Draskovich)
- I-II/GIR Karlstädt [Oguliner or Ottochaner]
- I-II/GIR Banal

1757 The Crisis

By the Treaty of St Petersburg (11 January 1757), the Russians signed a defensive alliance with Austria and France. On 21 March 1757, Sweden joined the alliance against Prussia with 20,000 men. On 1 May 1757, *Louis XV* signed the second Treaty of Versailles that bound him to put 105,000 men in the field against Prussia and subsidise Austria with 12 million florins as well as payments to Sweden and the friendly German states. [Duffy (2008) 38-39]

Bohemia

On 18 April, *Frederick* once again took the initiative by a large scale offensive into Bohemia with 113,000 men at four points hoping to inflict a decisive defeat on the Austrian forces who were still in winter quarters. At Reichenberg (21 Apr), the *Duke of Bevern* defeated Königsegg's Austrians before joining *FM Schwerin*.

On 6 June, the 62,000 Austrians under *Prince Charles of Lorraine* and *FM Browne* were soundly defeated at Prague losing 13,400 men and the remaining 49,000 retired into the city. The Prussians left 20,000 men to besiege the city. The remaining 30,000 men under *Frederick* set out to find *Daun's* Austrian Army of 55,000 men that was forming in eastern Bohemia. At Kolin (18 June) about 50 km east of Prague, *Frederick* received his first defeat and the rout was only prevented by the I Bn/Prussian Garde. The Prussians gave up their blockade of Prague when they retreated back into Saxony on 20 June. *Daun* reached Prague on 23 June.

Prussia assailed from all sides.

In July, the Russians invaded East Prussia and defeated a smaller Prussian force at Gross-Jägersdorf (30 Aug). Prussia was now threatened by the Austrians (south), French (west), Russians (east) and the Swedes (north). This was compounded by the defeat of the *Duke of Cumberland* in Hanover that removed both Brunswick and Hanover from the war after the signing of the Convention of Klosterzeven (8 Sept 1757). In September 1757, Russia withdrew from East Prussia into winter quarters so permitting Frederick to move the bulk of his eastern forces to Pomerania to repel a Swedish invasion and subsequently occupied most of Swedish Pomerania.

Reichsarmee and defeat at Rossbach

Very little was expected of the *Reichsarmee* under the Austrian *FM Sachsen-Hildburghausen* who had reformed the *Grenz*. Mobilisation started in February 1757 but only 25,000 men of the planned 120,000 had been raised. These were joined in Franconia by 24,000 French. In June, Vienna urgently requested that these would be sent eastwards after their dramatic defeat at Prague. Threatened by invasion from Austria and the French army under *Soubise* from the west, the prospects for Prussia seemed grim.

Frederick with an army if only 22,000 men, marched west to Thuringia to deal with the French and the *Reichsarmee* despite being hampered by *Hadik's* raid and temporary occupation of Berlin (Oct 1757). Frederick routed the French and *Reichsarmee* at Rossbach on 5 November, which is 40 km south-west of Leipzig. This allowed *George II of Britain* to revoke the Convention of Klosterzeven and Hanover re-entered the war on the Prussian side.

Andreas Graf Hadik (1710-90)

Silesia

The *Duke of Bevern* with 43,000 men at Bautzen covered Brandenburg and Silesia. On 7 September, the Prussians under *GL Winterfeldt* (who was killed) were defeated by *GdC Nádasdy*. The *Duke of Bevern* ordered a Prussian withdrawal being severely outnumbered by the Austrians.

The town of Schweidnitz in the recently acquired Prussian province of Silesia (now *Swidnica* in south-west Poland) was constructed from 1747 to 1756 to secure his hold upon Silesia. *Frederick* had instructed *Oberst von Sehrs* to fortify the town of Schweidnitz with a girdle of detached forts and lunettes. The Austrians considered it little more than a fortified camp rather than a fortress. The town was defences were feeble with a low rampart that was against the medieval wall and so was not designed to give supporting fire to the outer wall. The five detached star-forts and seven redoubts were up to 500 m from the town wall that they were supposed to be mutually supporting but according to Duffy (1975: 68), they were not successful in this as their faces were too low. On 30 September 1757 it was invested by the Austrians and it was captured on 13 November 1757. After the capture of Schweidnitz, the Austrians joined up the works by continuous entrenchments. [Duffy (1985) 139]

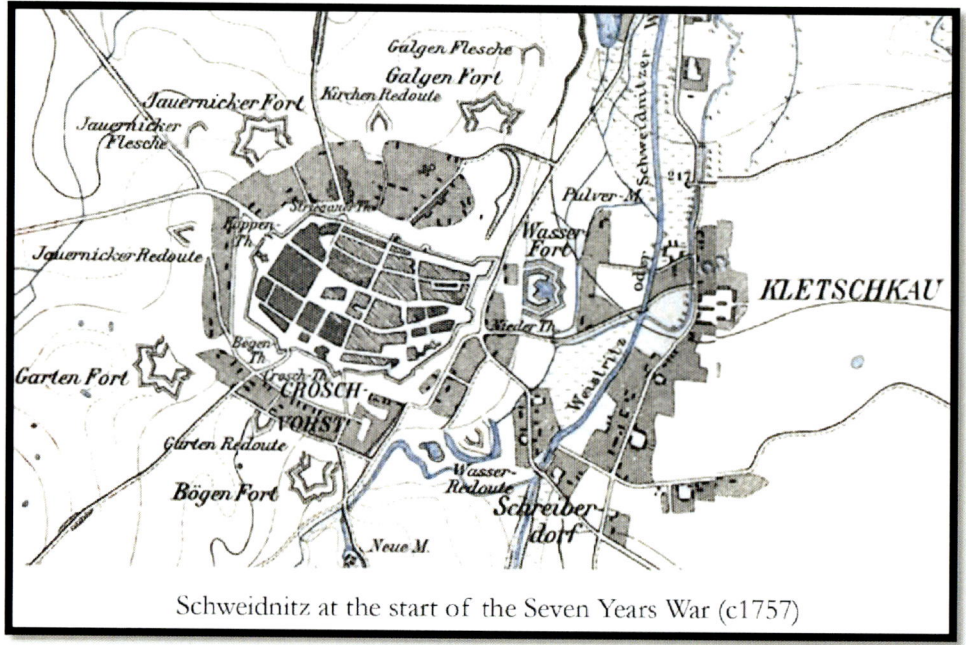

Schweidnitz at the start of the Seven Years War (c1757)

These and other defeats forced the Prussians back into Prussian territory. On 22 November, the over-extended Prussian line of earthworks and villages in front of Breslau was successfully attacked by *Charles of Lorraine* causing the *Duke of Bevern* to abandon his siege. [See OOB 10 and 11]

Frederick hurried back east to join his shattered Silesian Army. At Leuthen (5 Dec) just a few kilometres from Breslau, the superior Austrian Army of 65,000 men under *Charles of Lorraine* was routed by *Frederick's* 33,000 Prussians. The Austrians lost 3,000 dead, 7,000 wounded, 21,000 POW and 116 guns to fewer than 7,000 Prussians. This redressed the balance in the Prussian favour. *Charles of Lorraine* was replaced by *FM Daun*. On 20 December, Breslau surrendered with a loss of 17,600 men as prisoners.

OOB 13: First Line of the Austrian Main Army at Breslau (22 Nov 1757)

Commanded by *Prince Charles of Lorraine* assisted by *Graf Leopold Daun*
56 bns, 67 grenadier coys, 103 squadrons, [38,276 infantry and 8,292 cavalry]
[After Project 7YW (Aug 2008)]

First Line

Right Wing Cavalry
(*GdC Graf Lucchesi* assisted by *Marquis de Spada*)
    Marquis de Ville Brigade
        I-VI/DR1 Erzherzog Joseph Dragoons,
        I-VI/KR1 Erzherzog Leopold Cuirassiers
    Graf Aspremont Brigade
        I-VI/KR17 Lucchesi Cuirassiers

First Line Infantry *(General Kheul)*
Andlau Division
    Duke d'Ursel Brigade
        I-II/IR1 Kaiser Franz I, I-II/IR7 Neipperg
    Unruhe Brigade
        I-II/IR12 Botta, I-II/IR59 Leopold Jung-Daun
Graf Macguire Division
    Marquis Los Rios Brigade
        I-II/IR26 Puebla, I-II/IR21 Arenberg
    Graf Browne Brigade
        I-II/IR29 Alt-Wolfenbüttel, I/IR37 Esterhazy, Joseph
Graf D'Arberg Division
    Graf Lacy Brigade
        I/IR33 Esterházy, Nicolaus, I-II/IR25 Thürheim,
        I/IR49 Kheul

Left wing cavalry (*GdC Graf Serbelloni*)
    Prince Hohenzollern Brigade (assisted by Graf Stampach)
        I-V/KR15 Ansbach-Bayreuth Cuirassiers,
        I-VII/KR16 Gelhay Cuirassiers
    Buccow Brigade (assisted by *Hedwiger*)
        I-VI/KR9 Kalckreuth Cuirassiers,
        I-VI/KR2 Erzherzog Ferdinand Cuirassiers,
        I-IV/DR7 Hessen-Darmstadt Dragoons

Extreme Left Wing Infantry (Graf Puebla)
    von Mayern Brigade
        I-II/IR47 Harrach, I-II/IR13 Moltke
    Marquis d'Aynse Brigade
        I/IR8 Hildburghausen, I-II/IR2 Erzherzog Carl

OOB 14: Austrian Second Line at Breslau (22 Nov 1757)

Second Line
  Second Line Right Wing Cavalry (*Prince Esterházy*)
    Graf Benedict Daun Brigade
      I-V/DR9 Benedict Daun Dragoons (*Graf Lanthieri*)
      I-IV/DR11 Herzog Württemberg Dragoons (*Graf Argenteau*)
    Graf Trautmansdorff Brigade
      I-VI/KR5 Serbelloni Cuirassiers,
      I-VII/KR11 Anhalt-Zerbst Cuirassiers

  Second Line Infantry (*General Kheul*)
  Graf Starhemberg Division
    Wulffen Brigade
      I/IR3 Carl von Lothringen,
      I/35 Waldeck
    Buttler Brigade
      I/IR11 Wallis
      I/IR15 Pallavicini
  Haller Division
    Graf Kinsky Brigade
      I-II/IR17 Kollowrat
    Graf Siskovics Brigade
      I/IR27 Baden-Durlach,
      I/IR4 Deutschmeister,
      I/Rot Würzburg
  Angern Division
    Graf Würben Brigade
      I/IR36 Browne
      I/IR52 Bethlen
  Marquis de Clerici Division
    Baron Gemmingen Brigade
      I-II/IR50 Harsch
      I/IR23 Baden-Baden
    O'Kelly Brigade
      I/IR42 Gaisruck
      I-II/IR10 Jung-Wolfenbüttel

  Second Line Left Wing Cavalry (*GdC Graf Stampach*)
    Graf Ludwig Starhemberg Brigade (assisted by *Graf Martigny*)
      I-VII/KR6 O'Donnell Cuirassiers,
      I-VI/KR7 Schmerzing Cuirassiers
    Graf Kollowrat Brigade
      I-VI/KR10 Birkenfeld Cuirassiers (*Lefebvre*)
      I-IV/DR10 Kollowrat Dragoons (*Prince Lobkowitz*)

OOB 15: Austrian Reserve Corps at Breslau (22 November 1757)

Reserve Corps
- *Graf Nicolaus Esterházy Division*
  - *Otterwolf Brigade*
    - I/IR57 Andlau,
    - I/IR28 Wied,
    - I/IR22 Sprecher,
    - I/IR56 Mercy
  - *Graf Wied Division*
    - *Blanquet Brigade*
      - I/IR9 Los Rios,
      - I-II/IR20 Alt-Colloredo,
      - I/IR55 d'Arberg,
      - I/IR31 Haller
    - *Wolff Brigade*
      - I/Kurmainz IR,
      - I/IR16 Königsegg,
      - I/IR30 Sachsen-Gotha,
      - I/IR36 de Ligne
  - *Grenadiers and Carabiniers Corps (Sprecher)*
    - *Prince Löwenstein Brigade*
      - 4 coys/Converged Horse Grenadiers,
      - 8 coys/Converged Carabiniers
    - *Reichlin Brigade*
      - 35 coys/Converged Grenadiers

OOB 16: Austrian Artillery at Breslau (22 Nov 1757)

Artillery (220 artillery pieces and a Pontoon train)
- Position batteries
  - 14x 12-pdrs,
  - 32x 6-pdrs,
  - 14x 7-pdr howitzers
- Battalion guns
  - 160x 3-pdrs battalion guns

OOB 17: Nádasdy Corps at Breslau (22 November 1757)
[24,205 infantry and 8729 Grenz (40 Bns + 26 grenadier coys)
and 4,198 cavalry and 2,696 hussars (38 sq)]

First Line
  Right Wing Cavalry
  Batthyányi Dragoons,
  Zweibrücken-Birkenfeld Dragoons

  Infantry Centre (Austrian)
  FML Prince von Arenberg Division
  I/IR2 Erzherzog Carl,
  I-II/IR45 Alt-Daun, Heinrich,
  I/IR12 Botta, I/IR48 Luzan,
  I/IR25 Thürheim, I/IR44 Clerici,
  I/IR32 Forgách, I/IR34 Batthyány,
  I/IR39 Johann Pálffy, I/IR31 Haller,
  I/IR59 Leopold Daun, I/IR13 Moltke,
  I/IR7 Neipperg, I/IR55 Arenberg,
  I/IR46 Maguire, I/IR19 Leopold Pálffy
  Grenz Light Troops [Nádasdy]
  Grenz (8,729 men) and Hussars (2,696 men)
  Württemberg Corps (GL von Spiznass) of 5,237 men
  I-II/*Truchsess Fusilier Regiment*,
  I-II/*Roeder IR*, I-II/*Spiznass IR*
  I-II/*Prinz Louis*,
  I-II/*Leib-IR*, 1st-3rd *Grenadier Battalions*

  Left Wing Cavalry (Saxon Cavalry)
  I-IV/*Prinz Albrecht Chevauleger*,
  I-IV/*Prinz Karl Chevauleger*

Second Line
  Right Wing Cavalry
  I-VII/DR5 Jung-Modena Dragoons
  I-VII/DR8 Sachsen-Gotha Dragoons,

  Infantry Centre
  Bavarian Corps (GFWM Graf Seyssel d'Aix) of 5,119 men
  II-III/*Leib-Regiment*,
  I/*Preysing IR*, II/*Kurprinz IR*
  I-II/*Herzog Clemens IR*,
  I-II/*Minucci IR*,
  I-II/*Morawitzky IR*

  Left Wing Cavalry (Saxon Cavalry)
  I-VI/*Graf Brühl Chevauleger*

1758 Rebuilding

This was the last year that *Frederick* went on the offensive in Austrian territory. Austria was confined to the defensive to build a new army. On 26 December 1757, *Daun* reported that the Austrian Main Army had only 17,000 effectives. By March 1758, the Austrian Army in Bohemia had grown to 63,000 men. [Szabo (2008) 126-7]

Silesia
On 18 April 1758, Schweidnitz fell and so Austria lost their last foothold in Silesia. [Duffy (1974) 180]

Moravia
Frederick once more took the offensive and at the end of April invaded Moravia. On 31 May, he laid siege to Olmütz garrisoned by 8,500 men on 3 May with the first batteries opening fire. On 21 June, a Prussian convoy of 4,000 wagons and caissons departed from Neisse in Silesia for Olmütz to resupply the siege army that had almost consumed its supplies. On 22 June, *Daun* was able to reinforce the garrison with 1,200 men.

On 28 June, GFWM *Loudon* with a mixed force of 6,000 infantry and 3,500 cavalry attacked the Prussian supply column at Gundersdorf. Then the next day Siskovics with 4,000 Grenz and Hussars joined *Loudon* near Domstadtl where they captured 3,000 wagons of the siege column. Only 100 wagons and the remnants of the Prussian forces escaped. The Prussians lost 3,000 men with 1,500 captured to only 600 Austrians. On 2 July, *Frederick* abandoned the siege and withdrew from Moravia into north-eastern Bohemia and then Silesia. This was his final attempt to invade Austrian territory. [Szabo (2008) 149-152]

Raid on the Elbe
On 5-8 June, GdC *Andreas Hadik* with 2,000 grenadiers, Hungarian Fusiliers and Grenz raided the Elbe.

Saxony
By brilliant movements, the Austrians had forced *Frederick* out of Habsburg lands for the last time. From now on the major area of the campaign was Silesia and Saxony. [Duffy (2000) 10] By August the Austrian Main Army had grown to 84,000 men. *Daun* moved into Saxony. On 11 September, *Daun's* Army took up position at Stolpen, east of Dresden and on the night of 5-6 October, *Daun* reached Kittlitz with 80,000 men.

After the battle of Hochkirch
[After La Pegna]

On 10 October, *Frederick* arrived at Hochkirch with 30,000 men. On 14 October, *Daun* surprised the main Prussian army at Hochkirch just east of Bautzen in Saxony. *Frederick* lost most of his artillery and heavy casualties but retreated in good order, helped by the densely wooded landscape.

Frederick retired into Silesia to relieve Niesse that was invested by the Austrian Corps of *FZM Ferdinand Philip Graf Harsch*. The key position was the modern star-fort named Fort Preussen. On the night of 28-29 October, the Austians dug the first parallel only 325m from the fort rather than the usual 500-800m to Fort Preussen. In the darkness, the Prussian gunners fired ineffectually over the Austrian sappers heads due to their expectations that the attackers would be further away. Only two Austrians were injured despite the volume of fire. However, the approach of *Frederick* caused the siege to be abandoned the siege on 6 November. [Duffy (2008) 148-9]

Daun then moved back to Dresden and attempted to take the city. He had to abandon his attempt when *Frederick* arrived after relieving Niesse and withdrew into Bohemia for the winter in late November.

Reichsarmee
An Austrian corps assisted the *Reichsarmee* in their objective to liberate Saxony.

1759 Offensive

Austria put more than 160,000 men into the field and this was a severe strain upon her economy and resources. The pace of the previous year had taken its toll upon Austria and Prussia. The campaign was slow in starting. The Allied plan was for the Austrian Main Army under *Daun* to invade Silesian, a smaller Austro-*Reichsarmee* to operate against Leipzig to the west, Swedish troops to advance through Pomerania to occupy the mouth of the River Oder and the powerful Russian army to join *Daun* in Silesia.

Silesia and the Main Army

The Corps of *FZM Harsch* at Náchod (19,000), *FML Beck* at Braunau [*Broumov*] (7,000) and *FML Loudon* at Trantenau (10,000) protected the passes into Silesia. These three advanced corps amounted to 92,000 men by March 1759. [Duffy (2008) 156] On 26 June, *Daun* with 60,500 men moved into Upper Silesia and reached Reichenbach. *General Saltykov* commanding 70,000 Russians reached the Oder and defeated the Prussians at Kay (23 July).

In early August, *Loudon* with 24,000 Austrians joined 36,000 Russians and were planning to march south to Silesia to join *Daun*. On 12 August, at Kunersdorf near Frankfurt they were attacked by 50,000 Prussians. Frederick suffered a crushing defeat. The Austrians and the Russians failed to grasp the opportunity to end the war. The days of the Hohenzollern state seemed to be beyond repair.

Battle of Maxen (20 Nov 1759)
[after Franz Paul Findenigg]

Meanwhile, *Daun* reached Triebel about 80 km away. The Russians advanced up the Oder River to invest Glogau but abandoned this upon the approach of *Frederick*. *Daun* returned to Saxony upon hearing of the capture of Dresden by the Reichsarmee of *General Maguire* on 4 September. With control of Dresden, *Daun* had a useful foothold in southern Saxony for his winter quarters.

Moravia
GdC de Ville had 28,000 men in Moravia. On 17 April, *GL Fouqué* commanding 25,000 Prussians invaded Austrian Silesia. *De Ville* fell back to Hermannstadt [*Sibiu*] where he held them at bay until the Prussians retired back across the border. On 16 July, the combined army of 38,500 Austrians under *de Ville* and *Harsch* invaded Silesia.

Bohemia
FML Gemmingen and *FZM Arenberg* with 17,000 men guarded the Bohemian-Saxon border.

Reichsarmee
FM Serbelloni commanded 20,000 Austrians and 20,000 men from the *Reichsarmee* in Franconia and Thuringia. In early September, they captured Dresden. The campaign year ended with another military disaster for Prussia. On 20 November, the Austrians and part of the *Reichsarmee* attacked *General Finck* commanding 15,000 Prussians at Maxen just south of Dresden. The next day, he was compelled to surrender his whole army. *Frederick* could not afford another loss in manpower.

1760 Rise of Loudon
The survival of Prussia through the catastrophes of 1759 was miraculous and said much upon the resilience of the state structures. The Austrian plan was to leave their main army in Saxony to tie down the *Frederick* while 50,000 under the recently promoted *FZM Loudon* joined the Russians.

Loudon in Silesia
In spring 1760, *Loudon* invaded Silesia and started preparations to lay siege to Glatz. The siege guns had to be brought up from Olmütz.

Meanwhile, in the early hours of 23 June, the 30,000 men under *Loudon* brushed aside and destroyed the 11,500 Prussians under *Fouqué* from the long ridge of Landeshut and by 9am the last Prussian battalion surrendered due to lack of ammunition. The Prussians lost 2,000 killed, 8,000 captured with 68 pieces and only 1,500 managed to escape.

Now *Loudon* could concentrate upon the siege of Glatz starting on the night of 20 July when the trenches were opened. Glatz was captured on 26 July after a couple hours of bombardment followed by a storm. The Prussian commander, *Oberst-Lt Bartholomew d'O* surrendered his garrison of 2,500 men and 200 pieces. For this act, he was later court-martialled and executed. [Szabo (2008) 279-283]

Ernst Gideon Freiherr von Laudon (1717-90)

On 30 July, *Loudon* surrounded Breslau and attempted by bluff to take the city. However, with the approach of *Prince Henry* whose Prussians had covered 100 km in just 3 days, *Loudon* was forced to abandon the blockade. On 13 August, he was was defeated at Liegnitz by *Frederick* despite the Russian advance guard of *Chernyshev* with 25,000 men being only a few miles away. The Austrians lost 4,000 men with a further 4,700 men captured. The Prussians lost less than 3,400. [Szabo (2008) 284-8]

Reichsarmee in Saxony

In August, the *Reichsarmee* of 16,000 men under *Prince Zweibrücken* was joined by 15,000 Austrians under *General Hadik* after the departure of Frederick with the main Prussian Army from Saxony. On 20 August, *Zweibrücken* attacked a smaller Prussian Army under *Hülsten*. Rather than undertake a second assault, the *Reichsarmee* marched around the Prussian right flank causing them to retreat to Torgau. On 27 September, Torgau surrendered and by 14 October so did Wittenberg after a siege. Saxony was now liberated from Prussian occupation. [Szabo (2008) 312-3]

OOB 18: Austro-Imperial Army at Strehla (20 August 1760) commanded by *Karl Friedrich Graf Palatine Zweibrücken-Birkenfeld*
9,500 Austrians [10 bns, 12 grenadier coys and 26½ sq] and 16,000 Reichsarmee [27 bns, 20 grenadier coys and 12 sq] Austrian allies in ITALICS.

Main Corps [*Palatine Zweibrücken-Birkenfeld*]
[13,000 men in 22 bns, 18 sqns]
    Kreis Infantry
    I-II/*Mainz Lamberg,*
    I-II/*Rot Würzburg,*
    I-II/*Kreis IR Baden-Baden,*
    I-II/*Kreis IR Fürstenberg,*
    I/*Kreis IR Württemberg,*
    I-III/*Kreis IR Kurbayern,*
    I-II/*Kreis IR Kurpfälzisch Effern,*
    I/*Kreis IR Kurkölnisch Nothaft,*
    I/*Kreis IR Kurkölnisch Wildenstein,*
    I-IV/*Kreis IR Kurmainz,*
    I/*Kreis IR Hessen-Darmstadt,*
    II/*Kurpfalz Garde zu Fuss*

    Cavalry [*Obrist Zettwitz*]
    I-V/*Kreis Bayreuth Cuirassiers,*
    I-III/*Kurpfalz Cuirassiers*
    Austrian I-V/Brettlach Cuirassiers
    Austrian I-V/De Ville Cuirassiers

Reserve Corps [*Prince Stolberg*]
(4,000 men in 7 bns, 1 grenadier Bn, 10 sqns)
    Austrian Infantry [*GFWM Würzburg*]
    I/IR46 Maguire,
    I-II/IR33 Nicolaus Esterházy,
    I/IR48 Luzan
    Grenadier Bn (4 coys) [Luzan/Maguire/N. Esterházy]
    I-II/*Kreis IR Pfalz-Zweibrücken,*
    I/*Kreis IR Kurtrier*

    Cavalry Brigade
    Austrian I-V/Zweibrücken-Birkenfeld Chevauleger
    I-V/*Kurpfalz Leib-Dragoner*

    Austrian Artillery
    2x 6-pdr guns

OOB 19: Austrian Auxiliary Corps at Strehla (20 August 1760) commanded by *GFWM von Kleefeld*
(3,000 men in 4 bns, 1 grenadier Bn, 5 hussar sq)

Austrian and Allied Infantry
I-II/*Blau Würzburg*,
I/GIR1 Banal,
I/GIR Karlstädter-Szluiner
Converged Grenadier Bn (4 coys from *Blau Würzburg* and Grenz)

Attached Cavalry
Austrian I-V/Baranyay Hussars

OOB 20: Grenadier and Carabinier Corps at Strehla (20 August 1760) commanded by *FML Guasco*
(5,000 men in 4 bns, 6 grenadier bns and 5½ sq)

Austrian Infantry
Austrian I-II/IR30 Sachsen Gotha,
Austrian I-II/IR15 Pallavicini
6 Bns of Converged Austrian Grenadiers

Cavalry Brigade
I-IV/*Kreis Hohenzollern Cuirassiers*,
I-III/Converged Horse Grenadiers and Carabiniers

Austrian Main Army
Daun followed *Frederick* into Silesia but *Frederick* eluded him when he moved back into Saxony to besiege Dresden on 13 July. The siege was raised when *Frederick* learned that *Loudon* had taken Glatz on the 26th. *Frederick's* foot weary troops joined *Prince Henry* who was holding off the Russian Army. *Daun* joined *Loudon* and the Russians under *General Chernyshev* bringing together 90,000 Austrians and 25,000 Russians. *Daun* advanced as far north as Torgau and Wittenberg so freeing most of Saxony.

Lacy's raid on Berlin
On 26 September, *FML Lacy* (the son of the famous field marshal) with 18,000 Austrians and Saxons as well as 17,600 Russians under *Generals Chernyshev, Panin* and *Totleben* set out on a raid on Berlin which they reached on 7 October. On 9 October, the city was stormed and captured. Berlin was evacuated on 12 October as *Frederick* was threatening and they reached Frankfurt by the 14th.

Defeat at Torgau

On 23 October, *Lacy* rejoined *Daun* who had crossed over to the left bank of the Elbe. *Loudon* remained in Silesia with 30,000 men. On 3 November, the Austrians had 55,460 men [67 bns, 116 sqns, and 8 independent coys] with 275 pieces. They lost 15,000 men and 45 guns at Torgau but were still capable for battle. On 15 November, the Russians withdrew into winter quarters.

OOB 21: First Line of *FM Daun* Main Army at Torgau (3 Nov 1760)

[23,546 infantry (48 Bns), 10,000 cavalry (75 Sq)]

First Line
  Left Wing of Cavalry [GdC. O'Donnell]
  Brigade Lobkowitz
      I-V/KR2 Ferdinand,
      I-V/KR11 Anhalt,
      I-V/DR7 Hessen-Darmstadt

  Infantry Centre
  FZM Herzog von Arenberg
  Brigade Pellegrini
      I-II/IR26 Puebla,
      I-II/IR28 Wied
  Brigade Hartenegg
      I-II/IR1 Kaiser,
      I-II/IR7 Neipperg,
      I-II/IR42 Gaisruck
  FZM Sincère
  Brigade Elmendorf
      I-II/IR17 Kollowrat,
      I-II/IR27 Baden-Durlach
  Brigade Migazzi
      I-II/IR2 Herzog Karl,
      I-II/IR8 Hildburghausen

  Right Wing Cavalry [GdC Buccow assisted by von Schallenberg]
  Brigade Voghera
      I-V/KR1 Leopold,
      I-V/KR13 Benedict Daun,
      I-V/DR4 Savoyen

OOB 22: Austrian Second Line and Reserve Corps at Torgau (3 Nov 1760)

[23,546 infantry (48 Bns), 10,000 cavalry (75 Sq)]

Second Line
  Left Wing of Cavalry [*von Pellegrini*]
    Brigade Zollern
      I-V/KR6 O'Donnell,
      I-V/KR12 von Portugal

  Infantry Centre [*FML Graf Wied*]
    Brigade Browne
      I-II/IR3 Lothringen,
      I-II/IR12 Botta,
      I-II/IR21 Arenberg,
      I-II/IR56 Mercy
    Brigade Brinken
      I-II/IR47 Harrach,
      I-II/IR50 Harsch,
      I-II/IR54 Sincère,
      I-II/IR59 Leopold Daun
  Right Wing Cavalry [*von Schallenberg*]
    Brigade Wiese
      I-V/DR3 Batthyányi,
      I-V/KR17 Buccow

Grenadier Corp [*FML D'Ayasasa*]
  Brigade Ferrari
    I-III/Grenadiers,
    I-V/Converged Carabiniers/Horse Grenadiers
  Brigade von Normann
    I-III/Grenadiers,
    I-V/Converged Carabiniers/Horse Grenadiers

Reserve Corps [*GdC. Prinz Lowenstein*]
  Brigade Bettoni
    I-V/KR4 Stampach,
    I-V/KR5 Serbelloni
  Brigade St Ignon
    I-V/DR9 St-Ignon
  Brigade Bibow
    I-II/IR36 Tillier,
    I-II/IR40 Jung Colloredo,
  Brigade Dambach
    I-II/IR51 Gyulai,
    I-II/IR41 Bayreuth

OOB 23: FZM Lacy's Corps at Torgau (3 November 1760)
[11,541 infantry (19 Bns) and 6,908 cavalry (41 Sq)]

Corps Lacy: *FZM Lacy*
  Light Troops
    I-VI/HR1 Kaiser,
    I-III/Grenz Hussars
    I-III/GIR Warasdiner-Kreutzer

FML Buttler
Brigade Zigan
    I-II/IR20 Alt Colloredo,
    I-II/IR22 Lacy,
    I-II/IR45 Daun

FML Meyern
Brigade Pfuhl
    I-II/IR10 Jung-Wolfenbüttel,
    I-II/IR25 Thürheim,
    I-II/IR31 Haller I-II/IR38 Ligne,
    I-II/IR52 Bethlen

FML Zeschwitz
Brigade Lichtenstein
    I-VI/KR10 Birkenfeld,
    I-VI/DR2 Liechtenstein
Saxon Cavalry Brigade [von Goesnitz]
    I-V/Karabiniergarde,
    I-V/Graf Brühl,
    I-V/Prinz Albrecht,
    I-V/Prinz Karl

OOB 24: Corps Ried at Torgau (3 November 1760)
[3,686 men (6 Bns, 10 sqns, 8 independent Coys)]

Corps Ried [*GFWM Ried*]
    I-III/Stabs IR,
    Deutsches Feld-Jäger Corps (8 coys),
    I-III/GIR Slavonische Broder
    I-V/HR7 Széchenyi,
    I-V/Stabsdragoner

> **OOB 25: Austrian Artillery at Torgau (3 November 1760)**
>
> **Artillery** (275 artillery pieces and a Pontoon train)
>
> | | |
> |---|---|
> | Position batteries | 8x 24-pdr, |
> | | 30x 12-pdrs, |
> | | 50x 6-pdrs, |
> | | 20x 7-pdr howitzers |
> | Battalion guns | 167x 3-pdrs battalion guns |

1761 Army in Crisis

In December 1760, *Kaunitz* warned *Maria Theresa* that Austria had the resources for one more campaign without serious cost cutting. In consequence the army was reduced by 20,000 men. Once again, *Daun* was left to hold Saxony while *Loudon* advanced into Silesia with the Russians. *Frederick* was forced onto the defensive by the overwhelming number of men the enemy put in the field.

Saxony

In Saxony, *Daun* commanded about 56,000 Austrians of which most were recruits including 9,233 *Grenz* and hussars. [Duffy (2008) 309] These were used to tie down the Prussians in Saxony.

Silesia

On 23 April, *Loudon* with about 40,000 Austrians invaded Silesia. *Loudon* command rose to 58,000 Austrians on 19 May and 77,400 (supported by 294 artillery pieces) on 17 July. [Duffy (2008) 309]

On 17 August, the 50,000 Russians under *FM Buturlin* joined forces with 70,000 Austrians under *Loudon* in Silesia. The outnumbered *Frederick* with 55,000 Prussians retired into his fortified camp at Bunzelwitz that was supplied from the fortress of Schweidnitz. *Frederick* defied them until Buturlin with most of the Russians retired into Poland on 11 September due to the lack of fodder. This permitted *Frederick* to operate against *Loudon's* communications with Bohemia.

On 1 October, *Loudon* assaulted the strategically important Schweidnitz with 20 Austrian battalions and 8 Russian grenadier companies. Within three hours, he took 3,700 prisoners and 221 pieces for the cost of just 1,767 men. This greatly angered *Frederick* who vowed to retake it the next year. This permitted the Austrians to take up winter quarters in Silesia.

Reichsarmee

GdC Hadik commanded the *Reichsarmee* of about 27,600 men scattered along the upper Main with detachments in Franken-Wald and Thüringen-Wald. These were much troubled by Prussian Raids. The Austrians supported him with little more than a *Grenz* battalion, two Grenadier companies, a dozen squadrons of Hussars and some artillery. On 9 April *Hadik* handed over his command to *FM Serbelloni*. [Duffy (2008) 310-313]

1762 Final Stages

On 5 January 1762, the *Empress Elizabeth of Russia* was replaced by *Emperor Peter III* who happened to be an ardent admirer of *Frederick*. On 16 March, *Peter III* signed an armistice with *Frederick* and this was converted to a peace treaty on 2 May. As a result, Sweden withdrew from the war in May. In June, Russia returned East Prussia that it had occupied since 1758 and Colberg that they had just captured in December 1761 to Prussia. Thus East Prussia, Pomerania and Neumark were free of foreign occupation. In addition, a Russian Corps of 20,000 under *Chernyshev* was put at the disposal of *Frederick*.

In July 1762, *Catherine II* deposed her husband *Peter III* and did not implement the Russo-Prussian alliance. Even so, *Frederick* received a welcome respite to turn his attentions to the Austrians in Saxony and Silesia.

Silesia

Daun resumed the defensive and garrisoned Schweidnitz with 12,000 men under *FML Guasco* while the main army took position on the hills to the south. On 30 June, *Frederick* was joined by 20,000 Russians giving him numerical superiority. Upon the death of *Emperor Peter III* in July, the Russian troops were recalled from Silesia by *Empress Catherine II* and took no further part in the war.

Leopold Josef Graf Daun
(1705-66)

On 21 July, *Daun* was defeated at Burkersdorf forcing him to withdraw to Wüstewaltersdorf [now *Walim*] in Lower Silesia and surrender communications with Schweidnitz. On 8 August, Schweidnitz was placed under siege. On 16 August, *Daun* attacked Reichenbach but once again retired to the mountains.

> ### OOB 26: Adelsbach (6 July 1762) under *FML Brentano*.
>
> **Corps Brentano at Adelsbach**
> **Infantry** (1,800 fusiliers, 900 grenadiers, about 2,750 Grenz, 256 Jäger)
> Converged Grenadiers Bn
> I-II/IR52 Bethlen,
> I/IR55 d'Arberg,
> 2 coy of Jäger
> I-III/GIR Warasdiner-St Georges Grenz
> I-II/GIR Warasdiner-Creutzer Grenz
>
> **Cavalry** (about 2,000 men)
> I-V/HR4 Kálnoky Hussars,
> I-V/DR9 St-Ignon Dragoons,
> I-V/HR7 Hessen-Darmstadt Dragoons
>
> **Reinforcement under Soutien**
> **Infantry**
> Converged Grenadiers Bn
> I-II/IR23 Baden-Baden,
> I-II/IR27 Baden-Durlach,
>
> **Cavalry**
> I-V/KR1 Erzherzog Leopold Cuirassiers
> I-V/*Prinz Albert Chevauleger* (Saxon)
> I-VI/HR1 Kaiser Franz I Hussars

Defence of Schweidnitz (8 Aug-1 Oct 1762)

In August 1762, *FML Franz Guasco* commanded the Austrian garrison of 23 senior officers, 612 grenadiers, 7,507 fusiliers, 130 cavalry, 1,512 Grenz and 441 technical troops (artillerymen, artillery fusiliers, engineers, miners and sappers). The defence of Schweidnitz was prolonged as long as it was by the miners under *Captain Pabliczek* from Bohemia who displayed a clear superiority over the Prussians in the counter-mining war. [Duffy (2008) 300] Little headway could be made against the pressure mines that had been invented by French Engineer *Bernard Forest de Belidor* (1698-1761) and used to great success by *Gribeauval*. [Wurzbach (1859) 333]

Frederick was determined to re-take Schweidnitz. He gave command of the mining operations to French renegade Engineer *Simon Deodat Lefebvre* who was a disciple of *Belidor*. Trenches were opened on 7-8 August about 900 paces from Fort Jauernicker. [Duffy (1985) 127] On 22 August, *Guasco* offered to surrender if he could withdraw his command to Austrian lines, but *Frederick* refused. On 1 September, the first Prussian mine of 2 tonnes of gunpowder exploded. On 8 September, *Frederick* threatened to put the whole garrison to the sword if they did not surrender. *Daun* abandoned the relief of Schweidnitz on the 18 September due to the impassable roads caused heavy rain.

On 8 October, either a mortar bomb or the Prussian 2 tonne mine exploded the powder magazine of the Jauernicker Fort. [Duffy (1975) 140-3] The next day the garrison surrendered. The siege had lasted 63 days and cost 3,000 lives. *Guasco* was promoted to FZM [lieutenant general] with the Grand Cross of Maria Theresa Military Order in his absence. [Szabo (2008) 413-4]

Reichsarmee in Saxony

The *Reichsarmee* of 45,000 men commanded by *Serbelloni* was in Saxony operating against *Prince Henry* who took the offensive in May driving the Austrian corps back to Dresden away from the *Reichsarmee* and forcing it to retire through Franconia. *Serbelloni* was replaced by *Hadik*. On 29 October, *Hadik* was surprised by *Prince Henry* at Freiburg just west of Dresden and the Austrians were defeated. This was the last major battle of the war.

1763 Peace of Hubertusburg

Kaunitz's mighty anti-Prussian alliance had failed to defeat *Frederick*. Even his contemporaries were greatly surprised by this. The Prussians had not only withstood seven years of war against a superior enemy but had maintained themselves as one of the five great powers in Europe and avoided any territorial losses. [Hochedlinger (2003) 343]

The Peace of Hubertusburg was signed on 15 February 1763. This restored the boundaries of Prussia, Austria and Saxony as they had been before the war started. This left *Frederick* as master of Silesia much to the frustration of *Maria Theresa*. The Austrians lost 303,595 men with 32,622 killed in action and 93,404 men dead of disease or wounds. A total of 89 infantry colours, 23 cavalry standards, 397 cannon, 46 howitzers, 31 mortars and 554 caissons had been captured by the Prussians during the war. [Woods (2008) 14]

In 1765, *Emperor Francis Stephen* died and was succeeded by *Joseph II*, Maria Theresa's eldest son, who became joint ruler with her until 1780 when she died.

Chapter 4
Regular Infantry

Upon the accession of Maria Theresa, there were 51 infantry regiments of which three were Hungarian, two Italian, three Walloon from the Netherlands and one Tyrolean (Battalion). The remainder drew recruits from the other Habsburg territories including Austria, Bohemia, Moravia, and Austrian Silesia plus other states in the Holy Roman Empire. Each regiment had three battalions of five companies plus two grenadier companies. [Ottenfeld (1895) 117-8]

Table 3: Austrian Infantry 1741-64
[Hochedlinger (2003) 301]

Year	Infantry Regiments	Nationality
1741	51	43 German, 3 Hungarian, 2 Italian and 3 Walloon
1742	59	43 German, 9 Hungarian, 2 Italian and 5 Walloon
1742	60	43 German, 9 Hungarian, 3 Italian and 5 Walloon
1748	54	39 German, 9 Hungarian, 2 Italian and 4 Walloon
1750	56	39 German, 11 Hungarian, 2 Italian and 4 Walloon
1757	56	39 German, 11 Hungarian, 2 Italian and 4 Walloon
1764	57	39 German, 11 Hungarian, 2 Italian and 5 Walloon

Table 4: Organisation of Austrian Infantry 1741-64
[Hochedlinger (2003) 302]

Year	Fusilier Bns	Coys of men	Gren Coys	Total Coys	Regimental Strength
1740					2,016
1741-43	3 Bns	5 coys of 120	2 coys of 100	17	2,007
1744-48					2,307
1749-55	4 Bns	4 coys of 136	2 coys of 100	18	2,408
1756	2 Field Bns 1 Garrison Bn	6 coys of 136 4 coys of 136	2 coys of 100	18	2,408
1757	2 Field Bns 1 Garrison Bn	6 coys of 140 4 coys of 140	2 coys of 100	18	2,693
1758-61	3 Field Bns	6 coys of 140	2 coys of 100	20	2,760
1762-63	4 Field Bns	4 coys of 140	2 coys of 100	18	2,427
1764-67	2 Field Bns 1 Garrison Bn	6 coys of 116 4 coys of 116	2 coys of 100	18	2,080
1768-74	2 Field Bns 1 Garrison Bn	6 coys of 113 4 coys of 113	2 coy of 113	18	2,080

In 1748, this was increased to four battalions of four companies plus two grenadier companies. Each Regiment had sixteen fusilier companies (136 all ranks) and two grenadier companies (106 all ranks). In peacetime, this was formed into four battalions of fusiliers (about 550 men each) and two companies of grenadiers (100 all ranks) giving an authorized total of 2408 men.

The *Grefreiter* commanded a *Camaradschten* [section] of 6-7 men. Four *Camaradschten* [sections] were commanded by a corporal. The first company was known as the *Leib-Kompanie* or *Inhaber-Kompanie*.

In 1756, there were 33 German, 2 Italian, 4 Walloon and 16 Hungarian Infantry Regiments. In summer of 1756, two 6-company field battalions of 18 officers and 798 men each were mobilised. The Garrison Battalion of four companies with 12 officers and 532 men remained as the regimental reserve. The two grenadier companies were formed into independent Grenadier Battalions. The eighteen regiments including the two national-Italian regiments in Italy and the four Walloon regiments in the Netherlands both had a lower establishment due to lack of recruits. Their fusilier company mustered only 3 officers and 113 men for a total of 18 officers and 678 men per battalion. [Generalstab (1901) I: 144]

In spring of 1758, each fusilier company establishment was increased to 140 officers and men. Each regiment now had three fusilier battalions of 6 companies giving a total of 24 officers and 816 men per battalion. The two grenadier companies were still combined into Grenadier Battalions. This 1758 organisation remained unaltered until the end of the war. The exception was the four Walloon (Netherlands) regiments organised in 3 battalions with 4 companies each. Severe campaign losses caused out of necessity the field of a reduced number of battalions.
> Note IR5 (1st Garrison Regt) and IR6 (2nd Garrison Regt) were raised in 1766 and 1767 respectively so are outside our period of interest.

In 1767, the Austrian infantry received a new uniform. In 1769, the regimental numbers were introduced and these have been used for clarity in this work as it permits tracing the lineage of the regiments to 1918. The exception being the Netherlands (Walloon) Regiments of IR38 and IR55 in 1796, German Regiments of IR13, IR23, IR43, IR45, IR46 and IR50 were disbanded in 1809, and the Italian regiment of IR44 disbanded in 1809 with these regiments being replaced at a later date. [Pengel (1982b) 1]

Table 5: Regimental Staff in 1748 [8 officers and 15 NCOs]

	Austrian Ranks	Notes
Officers (6 officers 1748-56 and 7 officers 1757-69)		
1	Obrist	Colonel [Oberst in modern German]
1	Obrist-Lieutenant	Lieutenant colonel [Oberst-Leutnant in modern German
1	Obristwachtmeister	Renamed Major in 1757 when the number was raised to two
1	Regiments-Proviantmeister	Regimental Provision-master
1	Regiments-Quartermeister	Regimental Quartermaster who ranked as lieutenant
1	Regiments-Chirug	Regimental Surgeon
Civilian		
	Auditor	Regimental Clerk
NCO		
1	Wachtmeister Lieutenant	Regimental Sergeant-Major
1	Regiment-Pater/ Caplan	Regimental Pastor / Chaplain
1	Regiment-Tambour	Drum-Major,
1	Büchsenmeister	Armourer
3	Fahnenfuhrer / Fuhrer	Colour Sergeant
8	Cadeten	Officer Cadet [Kadetten in modern German]
1	Regiment-Wagonmeister	Regimental Wagon-master (NCO) appointed in wartime
1	Profoss	Provost who was normally a retired NCO

Table 6: Fusilier Company organisation in 1748.

[3 officers, 6 NCOs, 4 Musicians 1 Pioneer, and 99 Grenadiers]

	Austrian Rank	Notes
Officers		
1	Hauptmann / Capitän-Lieutenant	Captain /Captain-Lieutenant (2nd Captain)
1	Lieutenant/ Oberlieutenant (from 1759)	1st Lieutenant [Oberleutnant German]
1	Fähnrich/ Unterlieutenant (from 1759)	Ensign / 2nd Lieutenants
NCOS (7 NCOs)		
1	Feldwäbel	Sergeant-major [Feldwebel German]
1	Fuhrer	Colour Sergeant
4	Corporal	Corporal [Korporal German]
1	Fourier	Company clerk (civilian)
Men (133 men)		
10	Gefreiter	Lance-corporal
110	Fusiliere	Fusilier
2	Fourierschützen	Officer's servants (batmen)
2	Tambour	Drummers
2	Pfeifer	Fifers
1	Zimmerleute	Pioneer/Sapper

Garrison Bns

During 1757, many Garrison Battalions were formed into converged 6-company battalions in response to the Prussian invasion of Bohemia. For example, III/IR13 (Moltke) was formed by four companies of IR13 (Moltke) and two companies of IR49 (Kheul). In spring 1758, the Garrison Battalions serving with the field army were re-raised and organised into six company battalion. These were deployed to escort the transports and other rear activities. In winter 1761-62, overall strength of the regiments had to be reduced as a result of Austria's dwindling financial resources. Each regiments IIIrd (Garrison) Battalion was reduced to four companies to reduce costs.

Depot Bns

In the winter 1757-58, each infantry regiment raised a depot of 1-2 officers and a 100-200 NCOs to operate in the rear areas where the spare regimental baggage was also located. By September 1758, the Depots of 43 regiments had more than 6,900 men located at Prague.

IR18 Marschall c1762

Infantry Tactics

In 1748, the Austrian *Militärkommission* concluded that the superiority of the Prussian infantry in discipline, firepower and drill was the major cause for the victories of Frederick in the two Silesian Wars. As a result, the new drill was introduced in 1749. The new large formation manoeuvres was tested in the summer training camps. However, only in *Reglement 1759* was there a written summary of all innovations issued to the army.

Movement was regulated at the 'ordinary', 'medium', or at the 'double' pace. The latter could also be employed for the attack before closing to small arms fire distance.

Deployed in line of battle, the battalions aligned with 6 pace intervals, with grenadiers present, they likewise formed up with 6 paces intervals with each 1 company deployed on either flank of the regiment.

Fusiliers were deployed in 4 ranks up to the battle of Kolin (18 June 1757) and thereafter in 3 ranks. The regular six company field-battalion was formed in six divisions and the four company Walloon battalions formed into four divisions. The battalion was furthermore divided into 12 (or 8) half-divisions and 24 (or 16) pelotons. Each peloton had 7-8 files if deployed in 4 ranks and 9-10 files if deployed in 3 ranks. Each 3-pdr battalion gun was placed within the battalions intervals.

The battalion could deploy with closed files (touching shoulders) or open files by doubling the intervals (an arms distance). To turn to flank was done by the wheeling of pelotons/half-divisions/divisions or alternatively turning left/right in ranks then marching off. This method was often employed on the battlefield. The extended lines of multiple battalions altered a change of their front by wheeling round their axis.

Deployment from column into line was done by the ordinary quarter wheels of a battalion's sub-divisions [*Einschwenken*] as customarily practiced by basically all contemporary armies. With the deployment, an inversion of the order of ranking was not permitted with the regulations.

The young *Comte Gisors*, son of French *Marshal Belle-Isle* attended a training camp near Kolin in 1754 as part of the staff of *Emperor Francis Stephen* and *Maria Theresa*. He observed the troops being well disciplined and well-clad, but found training of the rank and file rather uneven, the marching step was too short or slow, and pacing was found ill-timed in general. The troops would avoid advancing with extended front but preferred the column, and more often the simple movement by ranks. [Rousset (1868) 83]

Austrian regulations provided a multitude of fire procedures. Musket drill emphasised both speed and aimed fire. The most common was fire by divisions, half-divisions, or pelotons starting from the flanks to the centre. The entire first rank, the two colour pelotons in the centre of the battalion fired only when ordered to do so by the battalion commander. Fire was conducted invariably at the halt, but the regulations permitted fire during a slow advance. A general battalion discharge was recommended only to hasten the retiring or routing opponent during the pursuit.

By the Seven Years War, the Austrian Infantry had matched the Prussian for speed of fire. The Austrian veteran officer *Cogniazzo* of IR2 Erzherzog Karl noted that only when a recruit could perform the musket drill 5 times per minute without powder or word of command would he be permitted to join the peloton or company drill. [Cogniazzo (1780)] A rate of fire of 2 rounds per minute was considered excellent by both the Austrians and Prussians.

Cogniazzo (1780) states that fire by *pelotons* [platoons] was suitable when employed in open terrain, while fire by divisions was capable of creating veritable breeches within the opponent's ranks. He considered firing while advancing by divisions let alone *pelotons* to be unfeasible because they were too apt to lose their distances, hence cause nothing but confusion and disorder within the formation. This observation implies that the Austrian infantry were less capable than the highly practiced Prussians in advancing while firing.

With the bayonet charge, only the first rank levelled their muskets and would fire just before closing with the enemy. On the command of *"Marsch Marsch!"* or *"Hudry Hudry!"* [Hungarian], the infantry would close upon the enemy at the double. The sabre armed Hungarians and grenadiers used their rear rank to either side of their formation to fall upon the opponents flank and rear with drawn sabres. This was rather unusual to European armies and is probably adopted from the much dreaded Turkish Janissaries.

Chapter 5
German Infantry

IR1 Kaiser

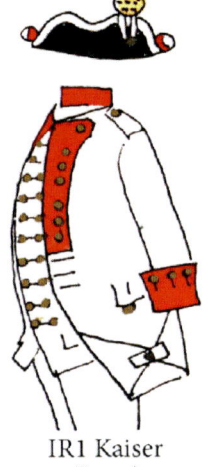

IR1 Kaiser
(Brauer)

It was raised in 1716. In 1918, IR1 Kaiser.

Lapels & cuffs	Red (from 1726)
Turnbacks	White with white turnback tab
Buttons	Yellow
Shoulder straps	White
Pom-Pom	Yellow speckled black

Garrison
Pilsen in Bohemia (1755); Olmütz (1765)

Inhaber
1726 *Crown Prince Francis Stephen Lorraine Duke of Lorraine* (1729), *Maria Theresa's* husband (1737) and *Emperor Francis I* (1745).
1765 *Emperor Joseph II*

Commanders
1752 *Leopold Freiherr von Lagelberg*
1758 *Engelberg Freiherr von Leuven*

Campaigns
[Thürheim (1880) I: 2 & [Wrede I-120]
War of Austrian Succession: Present at Mollwitz (10 Apr 1741). In 1742 it fought at Chotusitz and the siege of Prague. In 1743-44, the regiment was on the Rhine then Bohemia. In 1745 it fought at Hohenfriedberg (4 June) and Soor.

Seven Years War Fought at Lobositz (1 Oct 1756), Prague (6 May 1757), and two companies participated in the siege and storm of Schweidnitz. The regiment suffered heavy

Albertina (1762)

losses at Breslau (22 Nov 1757) and Leuthen. In 1758 at Hochkirch, its commander, Leopold Freiherr von Lagelberg was killed.

Detachments were present at the defence of Olmütz (28 May-2 July 1758) and the whole regiment at Hochkirch (14 Oct 1758). In 1760, the regiment was distinguished in the sorties from Dresden. Thisa regiment was almost wiped out at Torgau (3 Nov) by the Bayreuth Dragoons and in July 1761 it was described as being almost entirely made up of recruits. [Duffy (2008) 428]

Füsilier. Grenadier.

IR1 Kaiser c1756 in pre-1760 uniform
[After Richard Knotel]

IR2 – Hungarian IR

IR3 Carl Lothringen

Raised in 1715 and was also known as Jung-Lothringen. The hardest fighting regiment of the army losing 51.6% in action. [Duffy (2008) 429] In 1918, IR3 Erzherzog Carl.

Tricorn Hat	White scalloped lace
Pom-Pom	Red with white centre
Lapels & cuffs	Red (from 1757)
Turnbacks	White with white edged red turnback tab
Buttons	Yellow
Shoulder strap	White edged red

Garrison
1752 Brussels, 1759 Ghent and 1763 Brussels.

IR3 Carl Lothringen
(Brauer)

Inhaber
1715 *Prinz Franz Stefan von Lothringen*
1726 *Leopold Graf Ligneville* [d. 1734]
1734 *Gottfried Ernst Frhr. von Wuttgenau*
1736 *Carl von Lothringen* (brother of the Emperor) [d. 4 July 1780 in Brussels]

Commanders
1751 *Christian Vogelsang*
1758 *Joseph Graf Ferraris*
1761 *Carl Maximilian Freiherr von Schorlemmer*

Campaigns [Thürheim (1880) I: 12]
War of Austrian Succession: Fought at Mollwitz (10 Apr 1741). In 1742, a Bn was at the siege of Glatz, the grenadiers were at Chotusitz (17 May) then the siege of Prague. In 1744 it was on the Rhine then Bohemia. In 1745 it was present at Hohenfriedberg (4 June) and Trautenau (30 Sept). In 1746, in the Netherlands at Rocoux and Lawfeld (2 July 1747).

Seven Years War In 1757, fought at Prague (6 May), the storm of Gabel (14-15 July), Breslau (22 Nov) and Leuthen (5 Dec) where it suffered the second highest regimental loss in the retreat. At Hochkirch (14 Oct 1758), under *Obrist Graf Ferrarus* captured an 18-pdr battery. In 1759 it was in Saxony and Silesia without participating in any major actions. In 1760, at the siege of Dresden, performed very well in O'Kelly's counterattack at Torgau (3 Nov) and covered the subsequent retreat. Part of Loudon's storm of Schweidnitz (1 Oct 1761).

IR4 Deutschmeister

IR4 Deutschmeister
(Brauer)

The regiment was formed in 1696 by *Grand Master Franz Ludwig of Pfalz Neuberg*. The name of Hoch und Deutschmeister was after the Grand Master [*Hochmeister*] of the Teutonic Order. Recruits came from the Rhineland, Palatinate and the Teutonic Order's numerous dominions in Southern Germany including Swabia. It suffered the third highest infantry desertion of 1169 men. [Duffy (2008) 429]

Lapels & cuffs	Sapphire blue
Turnbacks	White
Buttons	Yellow
Shoulder straps	Blue
Pom-Pom	None

Garrison
1756 Budapest in Hungary. In 1763: Mons in the Austrian Netherlands.

Inhaber
Grand Master of the Teutonic Order
1731 *Clemens August von Wittelsbach, Elector of Cologne,*
1761 *Carl Duke of Lorraine* [d. 1780]
1780 *Maximilian, Elector of Cologne*

Commander
1756 *Carl Mohr v. Wald* [killed at Kolin],
1757 *Franz Graf Callenberg*
1760 *Johann Christoph v. Meichsner zu Adelshofen*

Campaigns [Thürheim (1880) I: 18; Wrede I: 138]
War of Austrian Succession: In 1741-42, part of *Traun's Army*. Fought at Campo Santo (8 Feb 1743) where it captured the standard of the Irlanda Regiment. In 1744, took part in the invasion of Naples and the siege of Genoa (1746-47).

Seven Years War In 1756, the regiment assembled around Königgrätz as part of Corps *Piccolomini*.

In 1757 it distinguished itself at Kolin (18 June) where *Major Johann Graf Soro* who commanded a Grenadier Bn was awarded the first knights cross of the Military Order of Maria-Theresa. The grenadiers took part in the storming of Gabel (15 July). A detachment was in *Corps Nádasdy* at the storming of the Silesian fortress of Schweidnitz (18 Nov). One Bn fought at Breslau (22 Nov) and Leuthen (5 Dec).

In 1758, Hochkirch (14 Oct). The III (Garrison) Bn was with *Corps de Ville* in Moravia and later formed part of the garrison of Olmütz (27 May-2 July).

In 1760, the regiment was part of Loudon's Army at the stormed of Hirschberg at Landeshut (23 June) and Liegnitz (15 Aug). Detachments were part of the defence of Schweidnitz (8 Aug - 9 Oct 1762).

IR5 and **IR6** were formed in 1769 from the Garrison Bns.

IR7 Neipperg

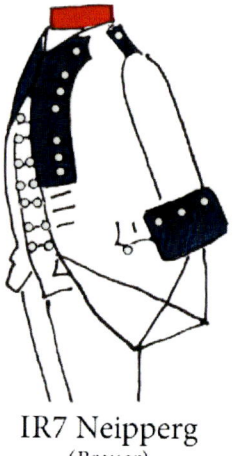

IR7 Neipperg
(Brauer)

The regiment was raised in 1691. The regiment was generally considered unfortunate in combat. [Duffy (2008) 429] In 1918, IR8 Graf Kevenhuller.

Lapels & cuffs	1730 Blue; 1743 Red 1748 Medium Blue
Turnbacks	White
Buttons	Yellow
Shoulder straps	Medium blue
Pom-Pom	None

Garrison
1754 Troppau; 1763 Leipnik [Lipník nad Bečvou]

Inhaber
1691 *Wilhelm Notger Graf von Oettingen-Baldern*
1692 *Johann Ferdinand Frhr. Pfeffershofen*
1700 *Eberhard Frhr. Neipperg*
1740 *Wilhelm Reinhard Freiherr von Neipperg* [Vice-President of the *Hofkriegsrat*] – d. 1774]
1774 *Franz Xavier Graf Harrach* [d. 1781]

Commander
1750 *Heinrich Voith von Salzburg*
1757 *Adolph Frhr. von Pfuhl*
1760 *Wilhelm Frhr. von Schröder*

Campaigns
[Thürheim (1880) I: 29]
War of Austrian Succession: In 1741-42, part of *Corps Khevenhüller* in the winter expedition to Upper Austria and Bavaria then the siege of Prague. In 1744 it was on the Rhine and Bohemia. In 1745 it fought at Habelschwert (1 Feb), Hohenfriedberg (4 June) and Trautenau (30 Sept). In 1747, in the Netherlands at Lawfeld (2 July).

Seven Years War In 1757, fought at Kolin (18 June), Breslau (22 Nov) [I-III Bns] and Leuthen (5 Dec) where it took heavy casualties. In 1758, only the Grenadiers were present at Hochkirch. In 1760, the regiment was ridden down by the Bayreuth Dragoons at Torgau (3 Nov) where it suffered the third highest infantry losses. Re-raised as a result in Moravia in 1761 and later fought at Burkersdorf (20-21 July 1762).

IR8 Hildburghausen

IR8 Hildburghausen
(Brauer)

The regiment was raised in 1647. A consistently good infantry regiment. [Duffy (2008) 429] In 1918, IR8 Erzherzog Carl Stephan.

Lapels & cuffs	Red (From 1732)
Turnbacks	White
Buttons	Yellow
Shoulder straps	White
Pom-pom	Red rosettes

Garrison
1755 Prague in Bohemia; 1763 Gross-Meseritsch [*Velké Meziříčí*]

Inhaber
1647 *Johann Reichardt Graf Starhemberg* [d. 1661]
1661 *Hubert Marchese Pio di Savoya*
1676 *Prosper Graf Arco* [d. 1679]
1679 *Max Laurenz Graf Starhemberg*
1689 *Philipp Frhr. von Chizzola* [d. 1691]
1691 *Leonhard Alexander Frhr. von Lapaczek* [d. 1700]
1700 *Nikolaus Graf Pálffy* [d. 1732]
1732 *Joseph Friedrich Prinz von Sachsen-Hildburghausen*
1787 *Carl Graf Pallavicini* [d. 1789]

Commanders
1752 *Friedrich Freiherr von Bülow*
1758 *Caspar Freiherr von Treys*

Campaign [Thürheim (1880) I: 37]
War of Austrian Succession: In 1742, part of Khevenhüller's winter expedition to Upper Austria and Bavaria. In 1743, at Simbach (9 March). In 1744 it was on the Rhine. In 1745 it was at Pfaffenhofen. In 1746 transferred to Italy where it participated in Graf *Corps Browne* invasion of Provence. In 1747 it was at the siege of Genoa.

Seven Years War Fought at Lobositz (1 Oct 1756). In 1757 it fought at Prague (6 May), Breslau (22 Nov) and received heavy casualties at Leuthen (5 Dec). Good record at Hochkirch (1758). In 1759, transferred to the *Reichsarmee* where it fought at Meissen (21 Sept) and Maxen (20 Nov) and the defence of Dresden. In 1760 it counterattacked together with IR2 Erzherzog Carl at Torgau (3 Nov). In 1761, the three Bns were at the siege of Glatz. In 1762, the regiment was part of the *Reichsarmee* in Saxony and present at Freiberg (29 Oct).

IR9 – Netherlands IR

IR10 Jung (Ludwig) Wolfenbüttel

The regiment was raised on 14 October 1715 as the "*Prinz Heinrich von Württemberg*" Regiment. Recruiting area was southwest Holy Roman Empire.

IR10 Jung-Wolfenbüttel
(Brauer)

Lapels & cuffs	1757 Red
Turnbacks	White with white turnback tab
Buttons	Yellow
Shoulder straps	White with white turnback tabs
Pom-pom	Light blue with white centre

Garrison
Pilsen in Bohemia (1752); Pisek (1763).

Inhaber
1715 *Heinrich Friedrich Prinz Württemberg*
1717 *Friedrich Ludwig Prinz von Württemberg*
1734 *Georg Anton Frhr. Lindermann* [d. 1739]
1740 *Ernst Ludwig von Braunschweig-Wolfenbüttel*
1790 *Carl Frhr. Kheul* [d. 1798]

Commanders
1756 *Carl Graf Alemsloe*
1759 *Friedrich Ferdinand Graf Pappenheim*

Campaigns [Thürheim (1880) I: 52-53]
War of Austrian Succession: In 1743, fought at Dettingen (27 June). In 1745, part of *Traun's Army*. In 1746, in the Netherlands at Rocoux (11 Oct) and Lawfeld (2 July 1747).

Seven Years War Fought at Lobositz (1 Oct 1756). In 1757, at Prague (6 May), Breslau (22 Nov), Leuthen (5 Dec). In 1758, the regiment fought at Hochkirch. In 1759 it was present at Meissen (2-3 Dec). In 1760, one Bn under *Obrist-Lt Frhr. Hasslinger* in the siege of Dresden, at Torgau (3 Nov) where it suffered severely under artillery fire and part of Lacy's raid on Berlin. In 1761 it was in Saxony. In 1762, at Pretzschendorf, and performed very well at Spechtshausen in Saxony where three battalions were present.

> NOTE: Known as *Jung-Wolfenbüttel* to distinguish it from IR29 *Alt-Wolfenbüttel*. In 1918, IR10 Gustav von Schween der Goten und Wenden.

IR11 Wallis

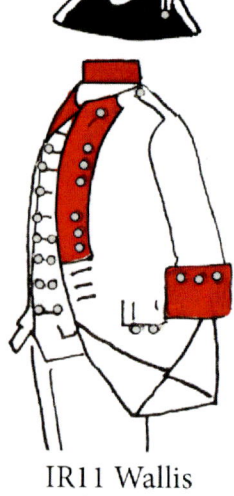

IR11 Wallis
(Brauer)

Very old regiment raised in 1619 by Wallenstein. In 1918, IR11 Georg Prinz Sachsen.

Lapels & cuffs	1740 Red; 1743 Blue 1748 Red
Turnbacks	White
Buttons	White (Brauer)
Shoulder straps	White
Pom-pom	None

Garrison
Prague in Bohemia (1754); Kolin (1763)

Inhaber
1619 *Rudolf Frhr. von Teuffenbac* [d. 1653]
1640 *Ludwig Frhr. von Steinachier* [d. 1673]
1673 *Jobst Hilmar Frhr von Knigge*
1684 *Philipp Emerich Graf Metternich*
1698 *Heinrich Tobias Frhr. con Hasslinger*
1717 *Heinrich Wilhelm Graf Wilczek*
1739 *Franz Wenzel, Graf von Wallis* [d. 1774]
1774 *Michel Graf Wallis* [d. 1798]

Commander
1756 *Philipp Graf Browne de Camus*
1758 *Michael Graf Wallis*
1761 *Michael Ritter von Jeschek*

Campaigns [Thürheim (1880) I: 59-60]
War of Austrian Succession: Fought at siege of Prague (1742), at Ingolstadt (1743). In 1746 it transferred to Italy, fighting at Rottofredo, invasion of Provence and in 1747 at the siege of Genoa.

Seven Years War Fought at Lobositz (1 Oct 1756). In 1757, suffered heavy losses at Prague (6 May), one Bn at Breslau (22 Nov) and Leuthen (5 Dec) where most of the regiment was captured. Distinguished at Hochkirch (14 Oct 1758). In 1760, fought at Landeshut (23 June), Liegnitz (15 Aug) and 3 Bns at the siege of Glatz. In 1761, the regiment was in Saxony. In 1762 it fought at Burkersdorf (20-21 July) and Liegnitz.

IR12 Botta

IR12 Botta
(Brauer)

The regiment was formed as the *Wolfenbüttel Regiment* in 1702 and entered Austrian service in 1712. In 1918, IR12 Parmann.

Lapels & cuffs	1757 Light blue
Turnbacks	White
Buttons	Yellow
Shoulder straps	Light blue
Pom-pom	white

Garrison
Prossnitz [Prostějov], Moravia (1755); Kaurim (1765)

Inhaber
1702 *Duke Adolf August von Holstein-Plön*
1704 *Dominik Frhr. D'Arnant Hubert, Graf de Sain*
1728 *Christof Bernhard Frhr. von Kettler* [d. 1734]
1734 *Franz Ignaz Graf Rumpf* [d. 1745]
1736 *Gottfried Ernst Frhr. von Wuttgenau* [d. 1736]
1739 *Anton Otto Marquis Botta d'Adorno* [d. 1775]
1775 *Johann Josef Graf Khevenhüller-Metsch* [d. 1792]

Commander
1755 *Karl Ulrich Fürst Kinsky*
1757 *Friedrich Freiherr von Elmendorf*
1760 *Franz von Lattermann*

Campaigns [Thürheim (1880) I: 66-67]
War of Austrian Succession: In 1741, there were 10 coys in Neisse Fortress. The Regiment fought at Mollwitz (10 Apr). The III Bn and Grenadiers garrisoned Brieg that capitulated on 4 May. In 1742 it was present at the siege of Prague.

In 1743 it campaigned on the Rhine. In 1745, the regiment fought at Hohenfriedberg (4 June) and Trautenau (30 Sept) before transferring to the Netherlands. The regiment took part in battles of Rocoux (11 Oct 1746) and Lawfeld (2 July 1747). One Bn was at the siege of Maastricht.

Seven Years War In 1757, at Kolin (18 June) held the line against the Prussian breakthrough. The grenadiers were present at the storm of Gabel (14-15 July) and Koischwitz (26 Sept). Four companies were at the siege of Schweidnitz. The regiment fought at Breslau (22 Nov) and Leuthen (5 Dec). The regiment lost 20 officers and 600 men as prisoners on the surrender of Breslau.

In 1758, at Hochkirch (14 Oct) and Dresden (29 Oct). In 1759, large detachments were captured at Pretzch (29 Oct). The grenadiers were present at Maxen (20 Nov). In 1760, the regiment was present at Torgau (3 Nov). In 1761, one Bn was at the storm of Schweidnitz (1 Oct) and participated in its defence the next year. In 1762, the regiment fought at Fischerberg (18 Aug).

IR13 Moltke

IR13 Moltke
(Brauer)

The regiment was raised in 1642 as *Adam Ernst von Traun Regiment*. Lost to Bavaria in 1809 and replaced by a new IR13 in 1814.

Lapels & cuffs	1740 Red 1743 Light blue
Turnbacks	White
Buttons	Yellow buttons
Shoulder straps	Light blue
Pom-Pom	None

Garrison
Graz in Styria (1752); Austrian Alps (Steyr) in 1757; Weisskirchen [Neisse] in Hungary (1763)

Inhaber
1737 *Philipp Ludwig Freiherr von Moltke*,
1780 *Zettwitz*

Commanders
1756 *Vinzenz Graf Migazzi*,
1757 *Ludwig Graf Attems*
1760 *Wolfgang Graf Rindsmaul*

Campaign
Seven Years War In 1757, I-III Bns were present at Kolin (18 June). I bn surrendered at Breslau (22 Nov). II-III Bns fought at Leuthen (5 Dec). In 1758, the II Bn was part of the garrison of Schweidnitz that surrendered. The III Bn garrisoned Olmütz. In 1760, the reformed I-III Bns fought at Hochkirch, at Landeshut (23 June) and at Liegnitz (15 Aug). III Bn participated in Loudon's storm of Glatz (26 July). In 1761, the regiment took part in the second storming of Schweidnitz (1 Oct 1761) and in its subsequent defence (8 Aug-9 Oct 1762).

IR14 Salm

IR14 Salm
(Brauer)

The regiment was raised in 1733.

Lapels & cuffs	1740 Light blue 1748 Black
Turnbacks	White
Buttons	Yellow
Shoulder straps	White
Pom-Pom	None

Garrison
1748 Antwerp; 1763 Roermond

Inhaber
1733 *Nicolaus Leopold Rheingraf von Salm* [d. 1770]
1770 *Franz Joseph Graf Ferraris*

Commander
1752 *Adam Ferdinand Freiherr von Kammer-Obereck*
1757 (ad interim) *Maximilian Prinz zu Salm*
1758 *Christian Freiherr von Bettendorf*
1762 *Maximillian August Zorn von Blowsheim*

Campaigns
[Thürheim (1880) I: 78]

War of Austrian Succession: In 1743, present at Dettingen (27 June). In 1745, the regiment was in Graf Traun's Army on the Main. In 1747 it fought at Lawfeld (2 July) and Bergen op Zoom (18 Sept). A detachment was in Luxembourg.

Seven Years War
In 1754, there were 69% of the regiment recruited from the Holy Roman Empire outside the Habsburg lands and was considered the most German regiment due to the influence of the Inhaber. This was reduced during the course of the war. It suffered the largest infantry desertion of 1779 men. [Duffy (2008) 430: Duffy (2000) 446] In 1918, IR14 Ernst Ludwig von Hessen.

In 1757, distinguished at Kolin (18 June) where it suffered 20 officers and 400 men lost mainly from heavy artillery fire and at Moys (7 Sept).

In 1760, the Grenadiers were at Landeshut (23 June) and the regiment was present at Loudon's storm of Glatz (26 July). In 1761-2, the regiment campaigned in Saxony and was distinguished at Freiberg (29 Oct 1762).

IR14 Salm

IR15 Pallavicini

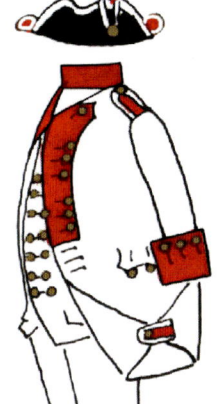

IR15 Pallavicini
(Brauer)

Raised in 1701 for the duration of the War of Spanish Succession and joined Austrian service in 1716. The regiment had rather a poor reputation. [Duffy (2008) 431] In 1918, IR15 Freiherr von Georgi.

Lapels & cuffs	Red
Turnbacks	White with red turnback tab edged white
Buttons	Yellow
Shoulder straps	Red with white edge
Pom-Pom	Red

Garrison
1752 Como (Lombardy); 1763 Chrudim in eastern Bohemia.

Inhaber
1701 *Carl Josef Ignaz Prinz von Lothringen*
1716 *Carl Alexander Prinz von Lothringen*
1736 *Giovanni Lucas Conte die Pallavicini*
1773 *Dominico St Tomiotti de Fabris, Conte di Cassano*

Commander
1755 *Johann Frhr. von Tillier*
1758 *N. von Graevenitz*
1759 *Adolph von Rolshoffen*

Campaign [Thürheim (1880) I: 88]
War of Austrian Succession: In Khevenhüller Corps and in 1742 participated in the Winter Expedition into Upper Austria and Bavaria. In 1743, the regiment was on the Rhine before transferring to Italy where it fought at Rottfredo (1746) and the siege of Genoa. In May 1747, a Bn under *Major Allemann* blockaded Massone Castle.

Seven Years War In 1757, fought at Prague (6 May), Breslau (22 Nov) and Leuthen (5 Dec). In 1758, a Bn was at the siege of Neisse and all three Bns were present at Hochkirch. In 1759, at Maxen (20 Nov). In 1760 it participated in numerous actions in Saxony including Torgau (3 Nov). In 1762, one battalion was distinguished at Teplitz (2 Aug) and the whole regiment was present at Freiberg (29 Oct).

IR16 Königsegg

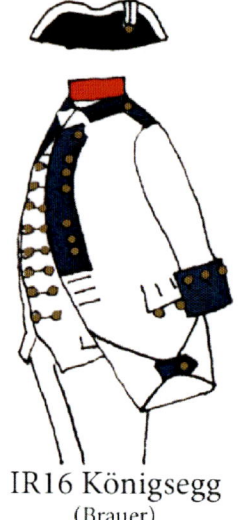

IR16 Königsegg
(Brauer)

It was formed on 23 June 1703 from a cadre of three IR4 Deutschmeister companies, two IR28 Thürheim companies and new drafts. [Thürheim (1880) I: 93] In 1760, *Major Graf Königsegg* was dismissed for corruption. [Duffy (2008) 431] In 1918, IR16 Freiherr von Giesl.

Lapels & cuffs	1740 Dark Blue
Turnbacks	White with blue dart-shaped turnback tab
Buttons	Yellow
Shoulder straps	Dark blue or violet blue
Pom-Pom	None

Garrison
1756 Bozzolo in Mantua; 1763 Como in Lombardy

Inhaber
1703 *Damian Hugo Graf Virmond* [d. 1722]
1722 *Alois Graf von Livingstein*
1741 *Christian Moritz Graf Königsegg-Rothenfels*
1778 *Ludwig Frhr. Terzy* [d. 1800]

Commander
1756 *Franz Graf Königsegg-Aulendorff*
1762 *Joseph Freiherr de Vins*

Campaigns [Thürheim (1880) I: 94]
War of Austrian Succession: In 1742, in the Winter Expedition in Upper Austria and Bavaria before joining the main army in Bohemia fighting at Chotusitz (17 May) and at the Siege of Prague. In 1746, in Italy at the battles of Piacenza and Rottofreddo, siege of Genoa and the invasion of Provence. In 1747, present at the siege of Genoa.

Seven Years War In 1757, fought at Hirschfeld (20 Feb), Reichenberg, one Bn at Prague (6 May), Moys (7 Sept), and Breslau (22 Nov). In 1758, fought at Hochkirch (14 Oct). In 1759 it received heavy losses at Sebastiansberg (31 July). Later fought at Pretzch (29 Oct 1759), Landeshut (23 June 1760) and Liegnitz.

IR17 Kollowrat

IR17 Kollowrat
(Brauer)

The regiment was raised in 1632. During the Seven Years War it suffered the fifth highest infantry desertion of 1099 men. [Duffy (2000) 446] In 1918, IR17 Ritter von Milde

Lapels & cuffs	1740 Red
Turnbacks	White with red tab
Buttons	Yellow buttons
Shoulder straps	Red
Pom-Pom	Yellow with red centre

Garrison
1756 Pilgram [*Pelhřimov*], Bohemia; 1763 Saaz [*Žatec*]

Inhaber
1632 *Melchior Graf Hatzfeld* [d. 1658]
1659 *Antonio Graf Collalto* [d. 1675]
1675 *Friedrich Frhr. von Stadel* [d. 1694]
1694 *Carl Efon Graf Fürstenberg con Mösskirch*
1702 *Carl Emanuel Fürst von Langerval Graf von Buquoi*
1703 *Carl Alexander Prinz Seit.*
1733 *Herzog von Württemberg* [d. 1737]
1737 *Cajetan Graf Kollowrat-Krakowski* [d. 1769]
1769-73 Vacant

Commander
1747 *Franz Aulock*
1759 *Lorenz Freiherr von Rasp*

Campaigns: [Thürheim (1880) I: 101]
War of Austrian Succession: In 1741, at Mollwitz (10 Apr) and the siege of Prague. In 1744, the regiment was on the Rhine then Bohemia. In 1745, at Habelschwert, Hohenfriedberg (4 June) and Trautenau (30 Sept).

Seven Years War In 1756, fought at Lobositz (1 Oct) then on Browne's relief expedition to Saxony. In 1757 it took heavy losses at Prague and Breslau. At Leuthen (5 Dec) the regiment lost the highest percentage of prisoners and missing in the army. In 1758 it fought at Domstadtl (30 June) and was distinguished at Hochkirch. In 1760 it was distinguished at Landeshut (23 June). Also present later that year at Liegnitz (15 Aug) and Torgau (3 Nov). In 1761, participated in Loudon's storm of Schweidnitz (1 Oct).

IR18 Marschall

IR18 Marschall
(Brauer)

The regiment was raised by Patent of 16 April 1682 from five Tyrolean companies and drafts from disbanded regiments. In 1918, IR18 Leopold Salvator.

Lapels & cuffs	1740 Red
Turnbacks	White with red tab
Buttons	Yellow buttons
Shoulder straps	Red
Pom-Pom	None

Garrison
1752 Linz; 1756 Bohemia; 1763 Jung-Brunzlau [Mladá Boleslav]

Inhaber

1682 *Leopold Herzog von Lothringen*
1698 *Josef Herzog von Lothringen*
1705 *Johann Adam Frhr. von Wetzel*
1707 *Franz Xaver Graf Sonnenberg* [d. 1731]
1714 *Damian Frhr. von Sickingen*
1716 *Johann Hermann Franz Graf zu Nesselrode*
1719 *Friedrich Heinrich Frhr. Graf Seckendorf*
1742 *Ernst Friedrich von Marschall auf Burgholzhausen*
1773 *Jacob Friedrich Frhr. von Brinken (or Brincken)*

Commander

1755 *Carl Ludwig Freiherr von Seckendorff*
1759 *Christian Friedrich Freiherr von Leubelfink*

Campaigns [Thürheim (1880) I: 110-111]
War of Austrian Succession: In 1742, fought at Chotusitz (17 May) and the Siege of Prague. In 1743 it was at Simbach. In 1744 it fought at Philipsburg, Germersheim, Lautenberg, Mosheim and the III Bn at the capitulation of Freiburg. In 1745 it fought at Hohenfriedberg and Trautenau (30 Sept). In 1747-48, the regiment was in Italy.

Seven Years War In 1756, the grenadiers fought at Lobositz (1 Oct). In 1757 it was present at Prague (6 May) and Bamberg. In 1758, the III Bn was besieged in Olmütz. In 1759, the regiment was in the *Reichsarmee*, fought at Meissen and notable for its lone stand at Löthain [Korbitz] (21 Sept) and one battalion was present at Maxen (20 Nov). In 1760 it participated at Landshut (23 June), in the storming of Glatz (26 July), at Liegnitz (15 Aug) and the siege of Kosel. In 1761 it was in Saxony. In 1762, the regiment was at Fischerberg. A detachment was besieged in Schweidnitz.

IR19 –Hungarian IR

IR20 Alt-Colloredo

The regiment was raised in 1681. It was known as Alt-Colleredo after 1754 to distinguish it from IR40. In 1918, IR20 Heinrich Prinz von Preussen.

Lapels & cuffs	1740 Blue, 1743 Red 1757 Blue
Turnbacks	White with blue tab
Buttons	Yellow buttons
Shoulder straps	Blue
Pom-Pom	Blue

IR20 Alt Colloredo
(Brauer)

Garrison
1752 Mons; 1763 Loeben

Inhaber
1682 *Prinz Johann Ludwig Anton von Pfalz-*
       Neuburg
1694 *Hans Carl Graf von Thüngen* [d. 1709]
1710 *Friedrich Wilhelm Prinz von Holstein-Beck*
1719 *Johann Friedrich Graf Diesbach*
1744 *Anton Graf Colloredo zu Waldsee*
       [d. 1785]
1785 *Franz Wenzel Graf Kaunitz-Reitberg*
       [d. 1825]

Commander [Wrede I: 257]
1754 *Franz Graf Lacy*
1757 *August Anton Fürst Lobkowitz*
1762 *Blasius Columbanus von Bender*
1769 *Anton Gazzinelli*

Campaigns: [Thürheim (1880) I: 125]
War of Austrian Succession: In 1742, part of the Winter Expedition in Upper Austria and Bavaria. In 1743, transferred to Italy and fought at Campo Santo. On 8 Feb 1744 it was part of the invasion of Naples. In 1746, the regiment fought at Rottogreddo, the expedition to Genoa and the invasion of Provence. In 1747 it was present at the siege of Genoa and action at Exilés.

Seven Years War In 1756, fought at Lobositz (1 Oct). In 1757 at Moys, Prague (6 May), Görlitz, and Breslau (22 Nov). The whole regiment was lost at the surrender of Breslau (Dec 1757). In 1758 it was raised anew and was distinguished at Hochkirch (14 Oct). Took part in Lacy's raid on Berlin, present at Torgau (3 Nov 1760) and Reichenbach. In 1762 a battalion was distinguished in the siege of Dresden and a detachment was at the siege of Schweidnitz.

IR20 Alt-Colloredo

IR21 Arenberg

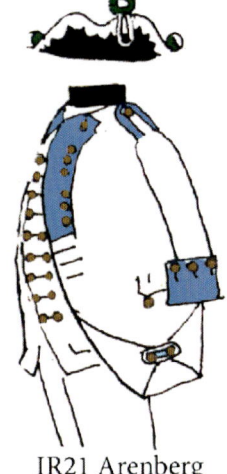

IR21 Arenberg
(Brauer)

Raised in 1733 at the cost of the *Obrist Graf Colmerero* of IR24. [Thürheim (1880) I: 131] In 1918, IR21 Graf von Arenberg und Traun.

Lapels & cuffs	1740 Light blue
Turnbacks	White with light blue turnback tab edged white.
Buttons	Yellow
Shoulder straps	White edged light blue
Pom-Pom	Green with white centre

Garrison: 1755 *Marburg an der Drau* (now Maribor) in Slovenia; 1763 *Königgrätz*

Inhaber
1733 *Ludwig Graf Colmenero de Valderlos*
1734 *Ludwig Ferdinand Graf Schulenburg-
    Oynhausen*
1754 *Carl Raymond Duke von Arenberg* [d. 1778]
1778 *Sigmend Frhr. von Gemmingen-Hornberg*

Commanders
1756 *Silvius Lindainer von Rosen*
1763 *Ernst Freiherr von Normann*

Campaigns [Thürheim (1880) I: 132]
War of Austrian Succession: Winter 1742 campaign in Upper Austria and Bavaria. In 1743 it was in Bavaria. In 1746 it was in Italy at Piacenza and Rottofreddo then the siege of Genoa.

The regiment was recruited from throughout the entire Holy Roman Empire. A report in 1755 stated that the regiment suffered from a high desertion rate due to harsh discipline and drunkenness. The regiment was considered a good fighting regiment. [Duffy (2008) 432]

Seven Years War In 1757, fought at Kolin (18 June), Schweidnitz, Breslau (22 Nov) and Leuthen (5 Dec). In 1758 participated in the successful defence of Olmütz (28 May-2 July) then fought at Hochkirch (14 Oct). In 1759, the regiment was distinguished at Kunersdorf. In 1760, the regiment excelled at Torgau (3 Nov) where it covered the retreat of the army with IR3 Carl Lothringen and IR12 Botta. In 1761 it participated in the second storming of Schweidnitz (1 Oct) and in 1762 at Freiberg (29 Oct).

IR22 Lacy

Formed in 1709. In 1918, IR22 Graf von Lacy.

Lapels & cuffs	Red
Turnbacks	White with red tab
Buttons	Yellow
Shoulder straps	Red
Pom-Pom	Red pom-pom edged yellow and white centre.

Garrison:
1750 *Cremona*; 1756 *Lombardy*; 1763 *Znayn*

IR22 Lacy
(Brauer)

Inhaber
1709 *Engelhart von Plischau* [d. 1717]
1717 *Franz Carl Laimpruch Frhr. zu Eppurg*
1723 *Albrecht Wolfgang Markgraf zu Brandenburg-Culmbach* [k. at Parma (29 June 1734)]
1734 *Heinrich Jakob Frhr. von Suckow* [d. 1740]
1741 *Wilhelm Moriz Frhr. von Roth* [d. 1747]
1748 *Jacob Ignato Freiherr von Hagenbach* [d. 1756]
1757 *Salamon* (or *Simon*) *Sprecher von Bernegg*
1758 *Franz Moritz Graf von Lacy* (*Lascy* or *Lacey*)
1802 *Friedrich Josias Prinz zu Sachsen-Coburg-Saalfeld*

Commander
1750 *Valentin Freiherr von Browne*
1757 *Carl Freiherr von Elrichshausen*
1759 *Joseph Graf Colleredo-Waldsee*

Campaign [Thürheim (1880) I: 140]
War of Austrian Succession: From 1740-43 in Italy. In 1744 it was involved in the enterprise to Naples. In 1746 it fought at Rottofreddo and the siege of Genoa then the expedition to Provence. In 1747, the regiment was at the siege of Genoa.

Seven Years War In 1757, one Bn participated in the raid on Hirschfeld (20 Feb), fought at Prague (6 May), Moys (7 Sept) and Breslau (22 Nov). Captured at the fall of Breslau (Dec 1757). In 1758, the regiment was raised anew and one Bn took part in the siege of Neisse. In 1759, at Dommitzch (25 Oct). In 1760, at Liegnitz, participated in Lacy's raid on Berlin and Torgau (3 Nov). In 1761 it campaigned in Saxony. In 1762, present at Burkersdorf (20-21 July). A detachment was part of the defence of Schweidnitz.

IR23 Baden-Baden

Formed in 1673 and disbanded in 1809. The regiment was re-raised in 1814 in Lombardy.

Lapels & cuffs	1740 Dark blue
Turnbacks	White with blue trefoil turnback badge
Buttons	Yellow
Shoulder straps	White
Pom-Pom	None

Garrison: Slovenia (1756).

IR23 Baden-Baden
(Brauer)

Inhaber
1672 *Ferdinand Ludwig Frhr. Wopping*
1674 *Hermann Markgraf Baden-Baden*
1676 *Ludwig Wilhelm Markgraf Baden-Baden*
1707 *Georg Ludwig Markgraf von Baden-Baden*
1761 *August Georg Simpert Markgraf Baden-Baden*
1771 *Joseph Heinrich Frhr. von Reid*

Commanders
1748 *Philipp Frhr. von Müffling*
1757 *Franz Dimpfel*
1758 *Alois Graf Harrach*
1764 *Peter Frhr. von Mac-Elligot*

Campaigns
War of Austrian Succession: In 1741, at Mollwitz. In 1742 with the Main Army at the siege of Prague. In 1743-44, in Bavaria at the

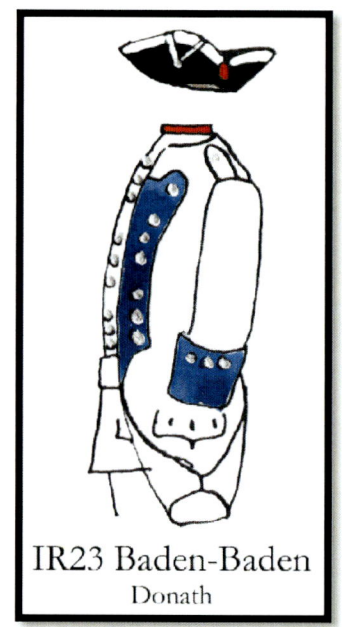

IR23 Baden-Baden
Donath

sieges of Straubing and Ingolstadt. In 1745, in Bohemia at Hohenfriedberg and Soor.

Seven Years War In 1757, present at Kolin (18 June), Breslau (22 Nov) and Leuthen (5 Dec). In 1758, part of Corps Durlach. In 1759 it fought at Kunersdorf (12 Aug) where it suffered heavy losses. In 1760, the regiment fought at Landshut, Liegnitz and the storm of Glatz. In 1761, two battalions participated in the storm of Schweidnitz. In 1762, a battalion was distinguished at Burkersdorf and a detachment was present at the defence of Schweidnitz.

IR24 Starhemberg

IR24 Starhemberg
(Brauer)

Raised in 1632 and was the third oldest infantry regiment in the Austrian army. In 1918, IR24 Ritter von Kummer.

Lapels & cuffs	1741 Dark blue
Turnbacks	White with dark blue turnback tab
Buttons	Yellow
Shoulder straps	Dark blue
Pom-Pom	None

Garrison
1756 Lombardy (*Como, Mantua, San Martino*); 1763 Pavia.

Inhaber
1632 *Philipp Graf Mannsfeld* [d. 1657]
1657 *Lucas Frhr. von Spieck*
1665 *Jakob Graf Leslie*
1675 *Heinrich Franz Fürst Mannsfeld-Fondi*
1702 *Jakob Ernst von Ghelen*
1703 *Graf Max Adam Starhemberg* [d. 1741]
1741 *Emanuel Michael Graf Starhemberg* [d. 1771]
1771 *Johann Peter Frhr. von Preiss* [d. 1797]

Commander
1756 *Sylvester Ferdinand von Alemann* (killed at Kolin (18 June 1757))
1757 *Guido Graf Starhemberg*
1763 *Peter Freiherr von Creutz*

Campaign

[Thürheim (1880) I: 149-150]

War of Austrian Succession: In 1742, at Chotusitz (17 May) then the siege of Prague. In 1744, a Bn was present at the siege of Freiburg. In 1745, the regiment was at Trautenau before transferring to Italy. In 1746 it was at Piacenza and Rottofreddo then the expedition to Provence. In 1747 it was present at the siege of Genoa.

Seven Years War In 1757, fought at Reichenberg, a Bn at Prague (6 May) and 2 Bns at Kolin (18 June). In 1758 it actively participated in the Domstadtl ambush and the battle of Hochkirch. In 1760, fought at Landshut (23 June), storm of Glatz (26 July) and reduced to a single battalion due to heavy losses after Liegnitz (15 Aug). A detachment was present at the defence of Schweidnitz.

IR25 Piccolomini

The Regiment was raised in 1672. In 1918, IR25 Edler von Pokorny.

Lapels & cuffs	1740 Red, 1743 Blue, 1751 Red
Turnbacks	White
Buttons	Yellow
Shoulder straps	Red
Pom-Pom	None

Garrison:
1753 *Brünn*; 1756 *Moravia*; 1763 *Linz*

IR25 Piccolomini
(Brauer)

Inhaber
1672 *Johann Carl Graf Serenyi* [d. 1691]
1691 *Franz Christof Frhr. von Amenzaga* [d. 1693]
1693 *Scipio Graf Bagni* [d. 1721]
1721 *Philipp Frhr. Langlet* [d. 1727]
1727 *Marquis Mathew de Luciny* [d. 1729]
1731 *Carl Franz Frhr. von Wachtendonk* [d. 1741]
1741 *Octavio Fürst Piccolomini d'Aragona* [d. 1757]
1757 *Franz Ludwig Graf Thürheim* [d. 1782]
1783 *Ludwig Graf Brechainville* [d. 1799]

Commander
1752 *Marchese Vittelleschi*
1758 *Franz Wocher*

Campaigns [Thürheim (1880) I: 158]
War of Austrian Succession: In 1743, fought at Campo Santo (8 Feb). In 1744 it participated in the expedition to Naples. In 1746, the regiment was at Piacenza (16 June) and Genoa (1 Sept).

Seven Years War In 1757, fought at Kolin (18 June), one Bn at the siege of Schweidnitz, Breslau (22 Nov) where 3 Bns were distinguished and at Leuthen where a whole battalion and a grenadier company was captured on 9 Dec. In 1758, lost 7 officers and 312 men captured at the surrender of Schweidnitz (16 Apr), distinguished at Hochkirch (14 Oct).

In 1759, the grenadiers were at Frauenwald (4 Mar), Kulmbach and Bamberg (14-16 May), Trachtenberg (5 Sept) and Meissen (21 Sept). In 1760, the regiment was part of Lacy's raid on Berlin and at Torgau (3 Nov). In 1761 it campaigned in Saxony. In 1762, the regiment fought at Freiberg (15 Oct). A detachment was present at the capitulation of Schweidnitz (9Oct).

IR26 Puebla

IR26 Puebla
(Brauer)

Formed in 1717. A good combat record. [Duffy (2008) 432] Lost to France in 1809 and regained in 1815. In 1918, IR26 Schreider.

Lapels & cuffs	1743 Red
Stock	Red
Turnbacks	White with red tab (Brauer) or red turnbacks (Albertini).
Buttons	Yellow
Shoulder straps	Red
Pom-Pom	White

Garrison:
Transylvania (1756).

Inhaber
1717 *Friedrich Wilhelm Markgraf von Brandenburg-*
    Anspach [d. 1723]
1724 *Heinrich Frhr. Müffling* [d. 1737]
1737 *Nikolaus Franz Graf Grünne* [d. 1751]
1751 *Anton Graf Puebla, Conde de Portugallo*
    [d. 1776]
1776 *Franz Carl Frhr. von Reise* [d. 1786]

Commanders
1752 *Carl Frhr. von Würzburg*
1758 *Ferdinand Graf Grünne*
1762 *Franz Xavier Graf Harrach*
1771 *Franz Frhr. von D'Armont*

Campaign [Thürheim (1880) I: 166]
War of Austrian Succession: In 1741, at Mollwitz (10 Apr). In 1742, the regiment fought at Chotusitz (17 May) and siege of Prague. In 1744 it campaigned in Rhine and Bohemia. In 1745, the regiment was at Habelschwert. At Hohenfriedberg (4 June), the Bayreuth Dragoons rode down the regiment and it lost 23 officers and it later participated at the battle of Trautenau. In 1746 it was in Italy. In 1747 it participated in the siege of Genoa.

Seven Years War In 1757, present at Kolin (18 June), Schweidnitz, Breslau (22 Nov), Leuthen (5 Dec). In 1758, distinguished at Hochkirch (14 Oct), Dommitzch, distinguished at Dresden where it captured a Prussian battery and at Burkersdorf. The regiment took part in the disastrous first counterattack at Torgau (3 Oct) where it lost 900 men and all it flags. In 1762, a detachment participated in the defence of Schweidnitz.

IR27 Baden-Durlach

IR27 Baden-Durlach
(Brauer)

Raised by the patent of Emperor Leopold I dated 3 February 1682. In 1918, IR27 Albert König der Belgier [King Albert of Belgium].

Lapels & cuffs	1740 Light blue
Turnbacks	Light blue
Buttons	White
Shoulder straps	Light blue
Pom-Pom	None

Garrison
1754 *Pisek*; 1756 in *Lombardy* with the Garrison Bn in *Hungary* and in 1763 Gent.

Inhaber
1682 *Octavio Graf Nigrelli*
1703 *Johann H. Frhr. von Zum-Jungen* [d. 1732]
1732 *Max Prinz Hessen-Kassel* [d. 1763]
1753 *Christof Prinz von Baden-Durlach* [d. 1789]
1791 *Leopold Graf Strasoldo* [d. 1809]

Commanders
1753 *Ferdinand von Chukelsky* (Killed at Prague)
1757 *Carl Freiherr von Bülow*
1757 *Rudolph Felix Freiherr von Stein*

Campaign [Thürheim (1880) I: 171]

War of Austrian Succession: In 1742, at Chotusitz then the siege of Prague. In 1744, campaigned on the Rhine and in Bohemia. In 1745, at Hohenfriedberg (4 June) and Trautenau (30 Apr).

Seven Years War In 1756, fought at Lobositz (1 Oct). In 1757, Prague (6 May), Schweidnitz, Breslau (22 Nov) and at Leuthen (5 Dec) it suffered total losses of 30 officers and 900 men of which many were captured. A detachment was captured when Dresden surrendered on 19 Dec.

In 1758, the re-constituted regiment fought at Hochkirch (14 Oct). In 1759 it was present at Maxen (20 Nov). In 1760, defence of Dresden and at Torgau (3 Nov). In 1761 it participated in the storm of Schweidnitz and at the battle of Leutmannsdorf. In 1762, one battalion was distinguished at Burkersdorf and another in the defence of Schweidnitz.

IR28 Wied-Runkel

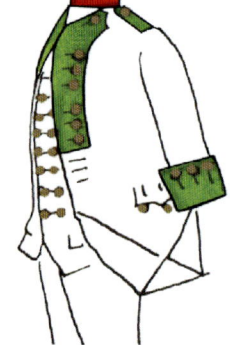

IR28 Wied-Runkel
(Brauer)

It was raised in 1698. In 1915, IR28 Viktor Emmanuel III König von Italien when it was disbanded.

Lapels & cuffs	1740 Medium green
Turnbacks	White
Buttons	Yellow
Shoulder straps	Medium green
Pom-Pom	Medium green with red centre

Garrison
1754 *Antwerp*; 1763 *Nikolsburg* [*Mikulov*]

Inhaber
1698 *Franz Sebastian Graf Thürheim* [d. 1726]
1713 *Friedrich Ludwig von der Lanken* [d. 1716]
1716 *Leopold Philipp Dueg von Arenberg* [d. 1754]
1754 *Leopold Frhr. Scherzer* [d. 1754]

1754 *Friedrich Georg Graf Weid-Runkel* [d. 1779]
1779 *Wilhelm Graf Wartensleben* [d. 1798]

Commander
1755 *Sigmund Freiherr von Burmann*
1759 *Sigmund Freiherr von Gemmingen auf Hornberg und Teschklingen*

Campaign [Thürheim (1880) I: 181]
War of Austrian Succession: In 1743, at Dettingen. In 1745 it was part of Traun's army on the Main. In 1746, the regiment fought at Rocoux. In 1747 it was at Lawfeld and in 1748 participated in the siege of Maastricht.

Seven Years War In 1757, distinguished with heavy losses at Prague (6 May), at Breslau (22 Nov) and captured at the surrender of the city (19 Dec). Raised again in 1758, a Bn was at the siege of Neisse and the regiment fought at Hochkirch (14 Oct). In 1759 it was distinguished at Maxen (20 Nov). In 1760 it suffered heavy losses including 24 officers at Torgau (3 Nov). In 1761 it was in Saxony. In 1762, a battalion was captured at Freiberg (15 Oct).

IR29 Alt-Wolfenbüttel

IR29 Alt-Wolfenbüttel
(Brauer)

Raised in 1709 from five companies of IR11 Hasslinger and the disbanded Wirich-Daun IR. [Thürheim (1880) I: 187] Should not be confused with the Loudon Green Grenadiers when Loudon became its Inhaber.

Hat	Tricorn with white scalloped lace
Pom-Pom	None
Lapels & cuffs	1740 Blue
Shoulder strap	Blue
Turnbacks	White with white turnback tab edged blue
Buttons	Yellow

~ 93 ~

Austrian Seven Years War Infantry

Garrison
1755 *Brüx*; 1763 *Tschaslau* in central *Bohemia*

Inhaber
1704 *Johann Adam Graf De Wend*
1709 *Ferdinand Albert Herzog von Braunschweig-Wolfenbüttel-Bevern*
1736 *Carl Herzog von Braunschweig-Wolfenbüttel*
1760 *Gideon Ernst Graf von Loudon* [d. 1790]
1791 *Olivier Remigius Graf Wallis* [d. 1799]

Commander
1752 *Friedrich Freiherr von Müffling*
1758 *Johann Marchese Botta d'Adorno*
1761 *Patrick Olivier Graf Wallis*

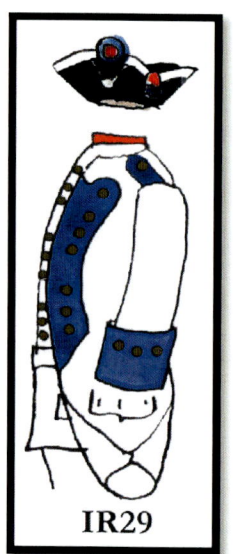

IR29

Campaigns [Thürheim (1880) I: 188]
War of Austrian Succession: In 1742, at the siege of Prague. In 1743, the regiment was in Bavaria. In 1745 it was part of Traun's Army on the Main before transferring to Italy.

Seven Years War In 1756, present at Lobositz (1 Oct). In 1757, the regiment was at Reichenberg (21 Apr), Prague (6 May), at Breslau (22 Nov) in the attack on the redoubts of Schmiedefeld and Leuthen (5 Dec) where it suffered heavy losses.

In 1758 it fought at Gundersdorf and Domstadtl (28-30 June) where it played a prominent role capturing 2 guns and at Hochkirch (14 Oct). A detachment was captured at the capitulation of Schweidnitz (16 Apr). In 1759, present at Meissen (2-3 Dec).

In 1760, at Landeshut (23 June), Liegnitz (15 Aug). In 1761, a Bn was at the storm of Schweidnitz (1 Oct). In 1762 it was present at Burkersdorf (21 July) and Leutmannsdorf. A detachment was lost of Schweidnitz.

IR30 – Netherlands IR
IR31-34 – Hungarian IR

IR35 Waldeck

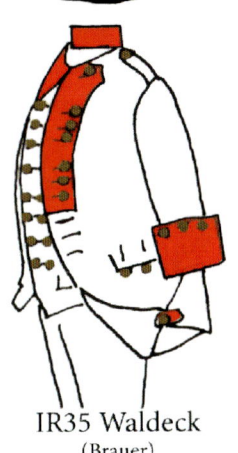

IR35 Waldeck
(Brauer)

The regiment was raised in 1682.

Lapels & cuffs	1743 Red
Turnbacks	White with red tab edged white.
Buttons	Yellow
Shoulder strap	White
Pom-Pom	None

Garrison:
Vienna (1755); *Prague* (1763)

Inhaber
1682 *Georg Friedrich Herzog von Württemberg-Stuttgard* [d. 1685]
1685 *Ulysses Marchese de Spinola* [d. 1686]
1688 *Guidobald Graf Starhemberg* [see IR13]
1688 *Carl Ludwig Archinto Conte de Tayna*
1693 *Johann Martin Geschwind Frhr. von Pöckstein*
1721 *Johann Daniel Graf Fürstenbusch* [d. 1738]
1739 *Carl August Fürst Waldeck* [d. 1763]
1763 *Johann Sigmund Graf Maguire* [d. 1767]
1767 *Ludwig IX, Landgraf von Hessen-Darmstadt*

Commander
1756 *Philipp Wilhelm Freiherr von Biela*
1759 *Anton Freiherr von Formentini*
    (Killed at Liegnitz)
1760 *Josias Bellizari*
1763 *Christian Graf Erbach*

Campaigns [Thürheim (1880) I: 232-3]
War of Austrian Succession: In 1742, part of the winter expedition in Upper Austrian and Bavaria then at Chotusitz and siege of Prague. In 1743, the regiment fought in Bavaria. In 1744 it was in Bohemia. In 1745, a Bn was at Habelschwert and Trautenau. The regiment was at Kesseldorf. In 1746 it was at Rocoux. In 1747 it was at Lawfeld. In 1748, at Rosendael.

Seven Years War In 1756, fought at Lobositz (1 Oct). In 1757, Prague (6 May), Breslau (22 Nov) and Leuthen (5 Dec) where it received very heavy losses. In 1758, the reformed regiment fought at Hochkirch (14 Oct). In 1759, at Kunersdorf (12 Aug). In 1760, Landeshut and Liegnitz. In 1761, a Bn was present at Loudon's storm of Schweidnitz. In 1762, at Leitmannsdorf, Burkersdorf (21 July) and a detachment was present at the siege of Schweidnitz.

IR36 Browne

IR36 Browne
(Brauer)

Raised in 1630 and the second oldest infantry regiment in the Austrian Army. Disbanded in 1915 when it was known as IR36 Reichsgraf Browne.

Lapels & cuffs	1738 Blue
Turnbacks	White with blue tab
Buttons	White
Shoulder straps	Blue
Pom-Pom	White with red centre

Garrison: 1752 *Laibach* [*Ljubljana*] in *Slovenia*; 1756 *Carniola* (*Slovenia*); Prague (1763)

Inhaber
1683 *Jakob Graf Leslie* [d. 1692]
1692 *Philipp Erasmus Fürst zu Liechtenstein*
1704 *Max Ludwig Graf Regal* [d. 1717]
1718 *Franz Paul Graf Wallis* [d. 1737]
1737 *Max Ulysses Graf Browne de Camus* [d. 1757]
1757 *Joseph Graf Browne* [d. 1759]
1759 *Johannes Freiherr von Tillier* [d. 1761]
1761 *Franz Ulrich Graf Kinsky* [d. 1792]
1792 Vacant

Commander
1756 Joseph Graf Browne de Camus
1758 Johann Freiherr von Koch
1763 Wenzel Graf Herberstein

Campaign [Thürheim (1880) I: 240-1]
War of Austrian Succession: In 1741, at Mollwitz (16 Apr), a Bn & grenadiers in the siege of Brieg Fortress that surrendered on 4 May. In 1742, the regiment was at Sahay and the siege of Prague.

In 1744, I-II Bns & grenadiers were on the Rhine and in Bohemia. The III Bn as garrison of Freiburg fortress. In 1745, at Hohenfriedberg (4 June) and Trautenau (30 Sept). In 1746, at Rocoux (11 Oct). In 1747, at Lawfeld (2 July). In 1748, a Bn was at the siege of Maastricht.

Seven Years War In 1756, fought at Lobositz (1 Oct). In 1757, the regiment was at Prague (6 May), Schweidnitz, Breslau (22 Nov), and Leuthen (5 Dec) with heavy losses. In 1758, the regiment was distinguished at Hochkirch (14 Oct) and Maxen. In 1760, at Kunzendorf (17 Sept) and distinguished at Torgau (3 Nov). In 1762, present at Burkersdorf (20-21 July).

IR37 and **IR39** –Hungarian IR.
IR38 –Netherlands IR.

IR40 Jung (Karl) Colloredo

The regiment was raised in 1733. On 9 July 1761, *FM Daun* reported that the regiment was in a poor state being made up of mainly new recruits. [Duffy (2008) 435]

Lapels & cuffs	1740 Blue, 1743 Red 1748 Dark blue
Turnbacks	White with dark blue badge
Buttons	Yellow
Shoulder straps	White
Pom-Pom	White with light blue centre

Garrison
1752 *Mons*; 1763 *Loeben*

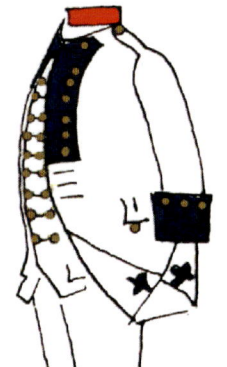

IR40 Jung-Colloredo
(Brauer)

Inhaber
1733 *Wolfgang Sigmund Frhr. von Damnitz*
1754 *Carl Borromaus Graf Colloredo-Waldsee*
1786 *Josef Graf Mitrowsky* [d. 1808]

Commander
1754 *Franz Fürst Sulkowski*
1758 *Carl Freiherr von Stein*
1763 *Friedrich Freiherr Haller von Hallerstein*

Campaigns [Thürheim (1880) I: 268-9]
War of Austrian Succession: In 1742, siege of Freiburg. In 1745, the regiment was at Trautenau (30 Sept) where it was shattered by the Prussian CR9 Bornstadt Cuirassier Regiment.

Seven Years War In 1756, most distinguished at Lobositz under Franz Moritz Lacy. In 1757 it fought at Prague (6 May), Moys (7 Sept), a detachment with Hadik's raid on Berlin. In 1758 it was assigned to the *Reichsarmee*. In 1759 it fought at Pretzch and Maxen (20 Nov). In 1760 it was distinguished at Torgau (3 Nov). In 1761 it was with the main Army. In 1762, the regiment fought at Freiberg.

IR41 Bayreuth

Raised in 1701 by Markgraf of Brandenburg-Bayreuth. It suffered the fourth highest infantry desertion of 1,125 men. [Duffy (2000) 446]

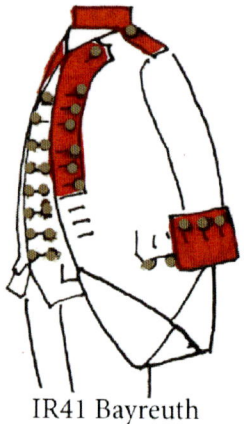

IR41 Bayreuth
(Brauer)

Lapels & cuffs	1740 Light blue
	1743 Red
Turnbacks	White
Buttons	Yellow
Shoulder straps	Red
Pom-Pom	Light blue with red centre

Garrison
1749 and 1763 *Luxemburg*

Inhaber
1701 *Christian Markgraf von Brandenburg-Bayreuth*
1704 *Georg Wilhelm Prinz Brandenburg-Bayreuth*
1727 *Wilhelm Ernst Prinz Brandenburg-Bayreuth*
1734 *Friedrich Markgraf von Brandenburg-Bayreuth*
1763 *Thomas Graf Plunquet* [d. 1770]
1770 *Josef Wenzel Fürst zu Fürstenberg-Stuhlingen*

Commander
1755 *Franz Felix*
1758 *Carl Freiherr von Kavanagh*
1763 *Heinrich Graf O'Donnell*

Campaigns [Thürheim (1880) I: 276]
War of Austrian Succession: In 1742, part of the winter expedition to Upper Austria and Bavaria. In 1743 it blockaded Braunau. In 1744, a Bn was at the siege of Freiburg. In 1745 it fought at Trautenau (30 Sept) before transferring to the Netherlands. In 1746, at Rocoux (4 Oct). In 1747 it was present at Lawfeld. In 1748, the regiment participated in the siege of Maastricht.

Seven Years War In 1757, fought at Prague (6 May), at Moys where it received heavy losses and at the siege of Schweidnitz. In 1758, a Bn was at the siege of Neisse. In 1760, the regiment fought at Kunersdorf and was captured at Torgau (3 Nov) by the Prussian Bayreuth Dragoons. In 1761, the regiment was re-raised by taking its III (garrison) battalion from Luxembourg. In 1762 it was present at Burkersdorf (20-21 July) and a detachment was at the defence of Schweidnitz.

IR42 Gaisruck

IR42 Gaisruck
(Brauer)

Raised on 21 February 1674 by Bishop Johann Hartmann von Würzburg and Bamberg for Emperor Leopold I. The regiment entered Austrian service in 1685. According to *FM Daun*, this regiment was made up mainly of recruits. It had a good record. [Duffy (2008) 435]

Lapels & cuffs	1740 Blue, 1743 Red 1757 Blue
Turnbacks	White with blue tab
Buttons	Yellow
Shoulder straps	Blue
Pom-Pom	Yellow with white centre

Garrison
1754 *Leipnik* [*Lipník nad Bečvou*] with Garrison Bn in *Erfurt* (1756); 1763 *Eger*

Inhaber
1683 *Hans Carl Thüngen*
1694 *Leopold Frhr. Von Thavonat* [d. 1694]
1694 *Wenzel Graf Guttenstein*
1706 *Franz Josef Frhr. von Wetzel* [d. 1720]
1720 *Philipp Ludwig Frhr. von Bettendorf* [d. 1733]
1734 *Alexander Graf O'Nelly* [d. 1743]
1743 *Franz Sigmund Graf Gaisruck* [d. 1769]
1769 *Reinhardt Frhr. von Gemmingen auf Hornberg und Treschklingen* [d. 1775]

Commander
1755 *Jacob Freiherr von Brinken*
1758 *Joseph Ittner* (killed on 3 Nov 1760 at Torgau)
1760 *Eustachius von Wieder*

Campaigns [Thürheim (1880) I: 284]
War of Austrian Succession: In 1743, at Dettingen (27 June). In 1744, I-II Bn was at the siege of Antwerp and Dendermonde. III Bn and Grenadiers fought at Kronweissenburg (6 July). In 1746, a Bn at Rocoux (11 Oct). In 1747, at Lawfeld (2 July).

Seven Years War In 1757, very distinguished at Kolin (18 June), Breslau (22 Nov) and Leuthen (5 Dec 1757) with heavy losses. In 1758, the regiment was distinguished at Hochkirch (14 Oct). In 1760 it was distinguished at the defence of Dresden, Torgau (3 Nov) where it received the second highest regimental losses. In 1762 it fought Burkersdorf (20-21 July).

IR43 Platz

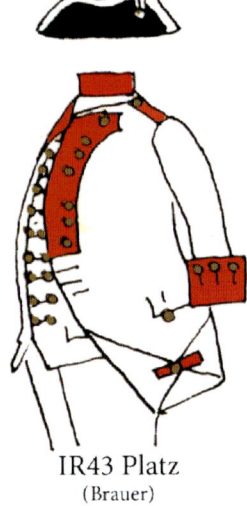

IR43 Platz
(Brauer)

The regiment was raised in 1715. It suffered the second highest desertion of 1656 men exceeded by IR14 Salm. In 1762, *Obrist Carl Vernada* attributed this heavy desertion rate to laborious outpost duty and absorbing large numbers of foreigners and Prussian deserters. [Duffy (2000) 446 and Duffy (2008) 436] Disbanded in 1809.

Lapels & cuffs	1740 Blue 1743 Red
Turnbacks	White with red tab.
Buttons	Yellow
Shoulder straps	Red
Pom-Pom	None

Garrison
1748 *Luxemburg*; 1763 *Lodi*

Inhaber
1723 *Erasmus Graf Stahemberg*
1730 *Johann Adrian von Lochstädt*
1732 *Bartholomäus Valparalso, Marchese D'Andia*
1734 *Matthias Heinrich Frhr. von Wuschletitz*
1737 *Johann Anton Graf Platz*
1768 *Ludwig Graf Buttler*

Commander
1748 *Carl Freiherr von Guldenhof*
1757 *Johannes Freiherr von Hussey*
1761 *Carl Graf Verneda*

IR43 Platz

Campaigns
War of Austrian Succession: In 1741-42, one Bn in Bavaria and the other was in Transylvania. In 1743-4 it was in Corps Batthyányi. In 1745, the regiment fought at Soor and Trautenau. In 1747, the regiment fought at Lawfeld.

Seven Years War In 1757, two Bns and the grenadiers were in Bohemia and at Kolin (18 June) where it suffered heavy losses. The grenadiers were at Moys (7 Sept). In 1758 it was present at the siege of Neisse. In 1759, at Krakau [Cracow] (23 Nov). In 1760, the regiment was in Corps Loudon, where it was distinguished at Landeshut (23 June) and Liegnitz (15 Aug). One Bn was stationed at Königgrätz. In 1761, one Bn took part in the storming of Schweidnitz. In 1762, the regiment was with the Army in Silesia. One Bn and a grenadier coy under *Captain Carl Frhr. von Sterndahl* was besieged in Schweidnitz.

IR44 – Italian IR

IR45 Heinrich Daun

IR45 Heinrich Daun
(Brauer)

An excellent record recruited from Bohemia, Upper and Lower Austria just like IR47 Harrach. [Duffy (2008) 436] Lost to France in 1809.

Lapels & cuffs	1740 Red
Turnbacks	White with red tab.
Buttons	Yellow
Shoulder straps	Red
Pom-Pom	Yellow with red centre

Garrison:
Transylvania (1756).

Inhaber
1682 *Joachim Sigmund Graf Trautmansdorff*
1711 *Heinrich Graf Daun*
1761 *Wilhelm Frhr. von O'Kelly*
1767 *Friedrich Frhr. von Bülow*

Commanders
1740 *Joseph Kager von Stampach*
1746 *Frhr. von Chevereuil*
1750 *Rudolf Carl Graf Gaisruck*
1758 *Zorn von Blowsheim*
1759 *Leopold von Frankendorf*
1771 *Ellis Schwarz Elder von Scharzsculen*

Campaigns

Seven Years War In 1757, present at Breslau (22 Nov) and Leuthen. In 1758, the regiment fought at Hochkirch. In 1760 it participated in Lacy's raid on Berlin. Distinguished in the counterattack at Torgau (3 Nov). In 1762, the regiment was distinguished again at Teplitz (2 Aug).

IR46 Maguire

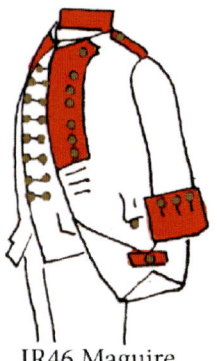

IR46 Maguire
(Brauer)

It was originally raised in 1745 as the *Tiroler Land- and Feld-Regiment* from the *Tiroler Land-Bataillon* that had been formed in 1703. Recruiting within the Tyrol was not very easy with only 20% from that area according to the returns for 24 May 1759. High proportion of recruits in 1761 and suffered from heavy desertion in 1762. [Duffy (2008) 436] Disbanded in 1809.

Lapels & cuffs	1740 Red
Turnbacks	White with red tab
Buttons	Yellow
Shoulder strap	Red
Pom-Pom	Green

Garrison
Innsbruck in Tyrol (1745 and 1763).

Inhaber
1745 *Spauer*,
1748 *O'Gilvy*,
1751 *Sincère*,
1752 *Johann Sigmund Graf Maguire*
1764 *Migazzi*

Commander
1755 *Anton Freiherr von Kottwitz*
1760 *Aeneus Graf Caprara*

Seven Years War
In 1757 it fought at Prague (6 May), Moys (7 Sept), Schweidnitz, Breslau (22 Nov) and Leuthen. In 1760, participated in the defence of Dresden and then covered the retreat after Torgau.

IR47 Harrach

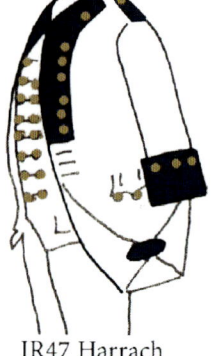

IR47 Harrach
(Brauer)

The regiment was raised in 1682 raised in Silesia. A reliable regiment recruited in Bohemia, Upper and Lower Austria. [Duffy (2008) 436]

Lapels & cuffs	1740 Blue, 1743 Red, 1757 Blue
Stock	Red
Turnbacks	White with blue tab
Buttons	Yellow
Shoulder strap	Blue
Pom-Pom	Yellow

Garrison
Villach in *Carinthia* (*Slovenia*) in 1750; *Marburg* (1763)

Inhaber
1682 *Georg Frhr. von Wallis*
1689 *Franz Helfried Graf Jörger de Tollet*
1691 *Notger Wilhelm Graf Ottingen-Baldern*
1694 *Lorenz Graf Solari* [d. 1704]
1704 *Joseph Philipp Graf Harrach zu Rohrau*
1764 *Margrave of Brandenburg-Bayreuth*

Commander
1753 *Karl Graf Engelhaussen*
1757 *Ferdinand Freiherr von Baumbach*
1760 *Paul Graf Seriman*

Campaigns [Thürheim (1880) I: 308-9]
War of Austrian Succession: In 1741m at Mollwitz (10 Apr). In 1742, at Chotusitz (17 May). In 1744 it campaigned on the Rhine and Bohemia. One Bn was at the siege of Freiburg. In 1745, the regiment fought at Hohenfriedberg (4 June) and Trautenau (30 September).

Seven Years War Fought at Lobositz (1 Oct 1756), distinguished at Prague (6 May 1757), Moys, Kolin (18 June 1757), Breslau (22 Nov 1757), Leuthen, Hochkirch (14 Oct 1758) and Bamberg. In 1760, part of the *Reichsarmee* and was distinguished with heavy losses at Torgau (3 Nov 1760). One battalion was at the storm of Schweidnitz in 1761. The regiment fought at Reichenbach.

IR48 – Italian IR

IR49 Angern

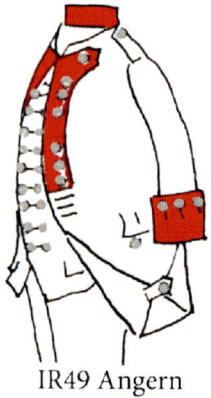

IR49 Angern
(Brauer)

Raised in 1715 by the Margrave of Baden-Durlach for Imperial Service and in 1724 became part of the Austrian Army.

Lapels & cuffs	1740 Red
Turnbacks	White with white tab
Buttons	White
Shoulder strap	White
Pom-Pom	None

Garrison
Wels in the *Archduchy of Austria* (1754); *Carlsberg* (1763)

Inhaber
1715 *Markgraf Carl von Baden-Durlach* [d. 1738]
1724 *Otto Graf Walsegg* [d. 1743]
1743 *Johann Leopold Frhr. von Bärnklau* [d. 1746]
1747 *Carl Gustav Freiherr von Kheyl* [d. 1758]
1758 *Ludwig Frhr. von Angern*
1767 *Carl Graf Pellegrini* [d. 1796]

Commanders
1751 *Jakob Graf Molza*
1762 *Christian Eichholz*

Campaigns [Thürheim (1880) I: 325]
War of Austrian Succession: In 1742-5, campaigned in Bavaria and along the Rhine. In 1746, transferred to Italy where it fought at Piacenza, Rottofreddo, siege of Genoa and the invasion of Provence. In 1747 took part in the siege of Genoa.

Seven Years War In 1756, fought at Lobositz (1 Oct). In 1757 it was distinguished at Prague (6 May), Breslau (22 Nov) where its *Inhaber* Graf Kheul was killed and Leuthen (5 Dec). In 1758 it was part of the ambushes at Gundersdorf and Domstadtl, Olmütz (28 May-2 July) and Hochkirch (14 Oct). In 1759, at Pretzch, Maxen (20 Nov), Meissen. In 1760, at Landeshut (23 June), distinguished at Liegnitz (15 Aug). In 1761 it participated in Loudon's storm of Schweidnitz. In 1762, the regiment was at Burkersdorf (20-21 July).

IR49 Angern

IR50 Harsch

IR50 Harsch
(Brauer)

Raised in 1629 and was the oldest infantry regiment in the Austrian Army. Considered the model for uniform and drill for the rest of the army. [Duffy (2008) 437] Lost in 1809 to the Duchy of Warsaw. [Wrede II: 254]

Lapels & cuffs	1740 Red with white buttonholes loops.
Turnbacks	Red
Buttons	Yellow
Shoulder strap	Red
Pom-Pom	None

Garrison
1749 *Eger*; 1756 in *Bohemia*; 1763 *Vienna*.

Inhaber
1691 *Leopold Graf Herberstein*
1740 *Casimir Heinrich Graf Wurmbrand-Stuppach*
1749 *Ferdinand Philipp Graf Harsch*
1766 *Andreas Fürst Poniatowski*

Commander
1754 *Nicolaus Freiherr von Weichs*
1758 *Andreas Graf Poniatowski*
1760 *Richard Chevalier d'Alton*

Campaigns [Wrede II: 254]
War of Austrian Succession: In 1742, part of the garrison of Prague. In 1743 it was in Corps Batthyany. In 1744, the I-II Bn was on the Rhine while the III Bn was besieged in Prague. In 1745, one Bn was at Hohenfriedberg and Trautenau and two Bns were at Kesseldorf. In 1746, transferred to the Netherlands and fought at Rocoux. In 1747 it fought at Lawfeld.

Seven Years War In 1756, fought at Lobositz (1 Oct) and one Bn in Passberg Fortress. In 1757, at Prague (6 May), Breslau (22 Nov). In 1758, at Hochkirch (14 Oct). In 1759 it was with the main army at Maxen (20 Nov). In 1760 it was distinguished at Torgau (3 Nov) and one Bn present at the defence of Dresden. In 1762 it was in Silesia at Pretzschendorf.

IR51-IR53 – Hungarian IR

IR54 Sincère

Raised in 1620 by Adam Wilhelm Schellhardt in the *Reich* and joined Austrian service in 1661.

Lapels & cuffs	1740 Red
Turnbacks	White
Buttons	Yellow
Shoulder strap	Red
Pom-Pom	Yellow

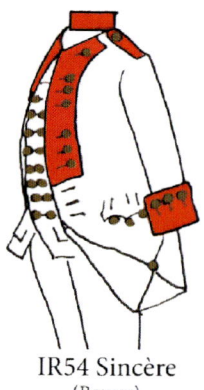

IR54 Sincère
(Brauer)

Garrison:
1754 *Znain*; 1763 *Pilsen*

Inhaber
1620 *Adam Wilhelm Schellhardt*
1627 *Johann Frhr. von Aldringer* [d. 1634]
1634 *Johann Franz Frhr. Barwitz von Fernamont*
1649 *Otto Christoph Graf Sparre*
1669 *Ernst Rüdiger Graf Starhemberg* [d. 1701]
1701 *Georg Friedrich Frhr. von Kreichbaum*
1710 *Bertrand Frhr. von Wachtendonk* [d. 1720]
1720 *Lothar Graf Königsegg-Rothenfels* [d. 1751]
1751 *Claudius Frhr. von Sincère* [d. 1769]
1769 *Carl Graf Callenberg* [d. 1800]

Commander
1754 *Christoph Freiherr von Bibow*
1758 *Jakob Graf Nugent*
1760 *Johann Graf Annoni*
1760 *Ferdinand Graf Kokorzowa*

Campaigns [Thürheim (1880) I: 367]
War of Austrian Succession: In 1742-3 in Bavaria. In 1744 it was in Bohemia. In 1745, the regiment was at Hohenfriedberg (4 June) and Trautenau (30 Sept) before transferring to the Netherlands. In 1746, at Rocoux (11 Oct). In 1747, at Lawfeld (2 July).

Seven Years War In 1757, fought at Reichenberg, Prague and a detachment participated in Hadik's raid on Berlin. In 1759 it was present at Maxen. In 1760, suffered the sixth highest losses at Torgau (3 Nov). It was still unfit for action in 1761 stationed in Saxony. The regiment participated in the battles of Burkersdorf and Reichenbach. A detachment distinguished itself during the defence of Schweidnitz.

IR55 – Netherlands IR

IR56 Mercy

IR56 Mercy
(Brauer)

In 1684, formed 10 companies with a total of 1500 men in Breslau. Also known as Merci-Argenteau.

Lapels & cuffs	1741 Dark blue
Turnbacks	White with dark blue tab
Buttons	Yellow
Shoulder strap	Blue
Pom-Pom	Blue

Garrison
1748 *Milan* and *Lodi*; 1763 *Peterwardein* [*Petrovaradin*]

Inhaber
1684 *Paul Anton Frhr. von Houchin* [d. 1699]
1690 *Philipp Wirch Graf von Daun* [d. 1771]
1741 *Antoine Graf Merci-Argenteau* [d. 1767]
1767 *Jakob Graf Nugent* [d. 1784]

Commander
1750 *Johann Jakob Graf Herberstein*
1758 *Leopold Freiherr von Stain*
1763 *Joseph Freiherr von Dreschel*

Campaigns [Thürheim (1880) I: 382-3]

War of Austrian Succession: In 1741, at Mollwitz (10 Apr). In 1742, the regiment was at Sahay (25 May) and siege of Prague. In 1743 it was in Bavaria. In 1744, the regiment was in Bohemia. In 1745 it was at Pfaffenhofen (15 Apr). In 1746, in Italy at siege of Genoa and in December part of the invasion of Provence.

Seven Years War In 1757, fought at Reichenberg (21 Apr), I-II Bn & grenadiers at Prague (6 May), III Bn at Kolin (18 June), Moys (7 Sept), storm of Schweidnitz (11 Nov), Breslau (22 Nov) and Leuthen (5 Dec) where it stood outside the village before it ran away. In 1758 it was present at the siege of Neisse and Hochkirch (I-III Bn). In 1759 it was with the main army. In 1760, the regiment was distinguished at Torgau (3 Nov) where it received heavy losses. In 1761, one battalion was present at the Loudon's storm of Schweidnitz. In 1762 it was at Leutmannsdorf and Burkersdorf (20-21 July). The whole regiment was at Reichenbach. A detachment of 200 men was at the defence of Schweidnitz.

IR57 Andlau

IR57 Andlau
(Brauer)

The regiment was raised on 9 December 1688.

	1741
Lapels & cuffs	Red
Turnbacks	White
Buttons	Yellow
Shoulder strap	White edged red
Pom-Pom	None

Garrison
1756 *Cremona*; 1757 *Milan*; 1763 *Klagenfurt*

Inhaber
1688 *Albrecht III von Sachsen-Coburg* [d. 1699]
1699 *Carl Sebastian Frhr. von Kratze* [d. 1704]
1704 *Johann Damian von Sickingen*
1713 *Johann Hannibal Frhr. zu Wallenstein*]
1715 *George Graf Browne* [d. 1729]
1731 *Patrik Frhr. von Oneullau* [d. 1734]
1734 *Sigmund Adam Frhr. von Thüngen* [d. 1745]
1745 *Joseph Freiherr von Andlau* [d. 1767]
1769 *Graf Joseph Colloredo-Waldsee* [d. 1818]

Commanders
1756 *Franz Chevalier de Perelli*
1757 *Otto Heinrich von Rath*

Campaigns [Thürheim (1880) I: 393-4]
War of Austrian Succession: In 1741, at Mollwitz (10 Apr). In 1742, the regiment fought at Chotusitz (17 May) and siege of Prague. In 1743 it was in Bavaria. In 1744 it was present at the siege of Olmütz then Silesia. In 1745 it was at Hohenfriedberg (4 June) where it lost 789 men. The III Bn was at Jägersdorf and the storm of Kosel. In 1746 it was in Italy at Piacenza, siege of Gavi and on 5 December *Obrist Frhr. Buttler* was murdered during the revolt in Genoa. In 1747, the regiment was at the siege of Genoa.

Seven Years War In 1757, I Bn & the grenadiers were at Prague (6 May), a detachment at Moys (7 Sept), Breslau (22 Nov), Leuthen (5 Dec). In 1758, Hochkirch (14 Oct). In 1759 it was captured at Sebastiansberg (15 April). The III Bn joined the main army from Italy and the reconstituted regiment fought in 1760 at Landshut (23 June), Liegnitz (15 Aug). In 1762 it was at Burkersdorf (20-21 July). A detachment of 208 men under *Major Graf Berchtold* was part of the defence of Schweidnitz.

IR58 – Formed in 1756 and was transferred from French service in 1763.

IR59 Leopold Daun

The regiment was raised on 30 January 1682 in Upper and Lower Austria by patent. Suffered above average losses in action and deserters. [Duffy (2008) 438]

Lapels & cuffs	1741 Red
Turnbacks	White with red tab
Buttons	Yellow
Shoulder strap	Red
Pom-Pom	White

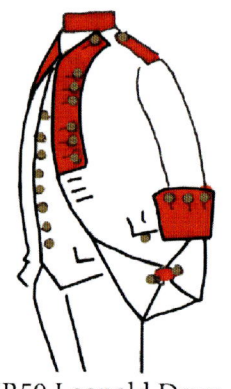

IR59 Leopold Daun
(Brauer)

Garrison:
1755 *Vienna*; 1763 *Vienna*

Inhaber
1682 *Melchior Leopold Frhr. van der Bück*
  [d. 1693]
1693 *Ludwig Ferdinand Conte Marsigli* [d. 1730]
1704 *Anton Aegydius Frhr. Jorger von Tollet*
  [d. 1716]
1716 *Ottokar Graf Starhemberg*
1731 *Franz Wenzel Graf Wallis*
1740 *Margrave Leopold Joseph Daun, Fürst von Thiano*
1766 *Franz Graf Daun, Fürst von Thiano*
  [d. 1771]

Commander
1749 *Johann Wolf*
1757 *Carl Graf Pellegrini*
1759 *Franz Graf Daun*

Campaigns [Thürheim (1880) I: 412-3]
War of Austrian Succession: In 1741, at Neisse (22 May). In 1742, the regiment was at Chotusitz (17 May) and the siege of Prague. In 1743, at Simbach (9 May). In 1744 it was at Lautenberg (3 July). In 1745 it was at the siege of Amberg, a Bn at Habelschwert (14 Feb), at Hohenfriedberg lost 9 officers and 380 men and Soor (30 Sept). In 1746 it was in Italy and participated in the invasion of Provence. In 1747 it blockaded Genoa and was at Bisagno (13-14 June).

Seven Years War In 1757, fought at Reichenberg (21 Apr), Kolin (18 June) and Gabel. One battalion participated in Hadik's raid on Berlin and the other at the storming of Schweidnitz. I-III Bns were present at Breslau (22 Nov) and Leuthen (5 Dec). In 1758, at Hochkirch (15 Oct). In 1759, at Maxen (20 Nov). In 1760 it was part of Lacy's expedition to Berlin and at Torgau (3 Nov). In 1761 it was in Saxony. In 1762, the regiment was at Burkersdorf (20-21 July). It was distinguished in the defence of Schweidnitz.

Italian Infantry

In summer of 1756, the two national-Italian regiments stationed in Italy had fusilier companies of only 3 officers and only 113 men due to lack of recruits. This gave battalion strength of 18 officers and 678 men.

IR44 Clerici

The regiment was raised in 1744 by Antonio Marquis Clerici at his own cost. It had a dashing reputation from the outset. Interestingly, this regiment in 1859, proved the most loyal of the Milanese regiments with many re-engaged by the Austrians after Milan was lost. [Duffy (2008) 436]

IR44 Clerici
(Brauer)

Lapels & cuffs	Red
Turnbacks	White with red turnback badge
Buttons	Yellow
Shoulder strap	Red
Pom-Pom	None

Garrison:
1756 *Hungary* and *Banat*.

Inhaber
1744 *Anton Georg Marquis Clerici* [d. 1768]
1769 *Rudolf Carl Graf Gaisrück* [d. 1778]

Commander
1745 *Ascano Graf Cocogna*
1752 *Franz Frhr. von Valentini*
1758 *Francesco de Feretti*
1771 *Antonio Lombardi*

Campaigns [Thürheim (1880) I: 294-5]
War of Austrian Succession: In 1744 it was at Coni (30 Sept). In 1745 it was stationed in Bassignana, Piedmont, Italy. In 1746-47 it was stationed in Mantua.

Seven Years War In 1757, fought at Schweidnitz, Breslau (22 Nov), Leuthen (5 Dec). In 1758 it was at Hochkirch (14 Oct) where it received the heaviest losses of any regiment during its unsuccessful attacks upon the churchyard. Its brutal commander, *Obrist Valentini* was mortally wounded. In 1759, the regiment was surprised at Hoyerswerda (29 Sept 1759). Fought at Pretzch (29 Oct) and Maxen (20 Nov). In 1761-62, the regiment suffered heavy desertion.

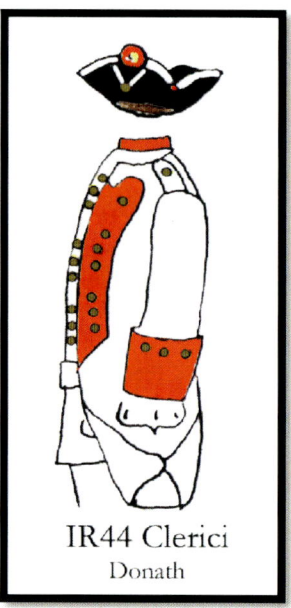

IR44 Clerici
Donath

IR48 Luzan

IR48 Luzan
(Brauer)

Italian national regiment recruited in Austrian Lombardy, Görz [Gorizia] and Gradisca. During the Seven Years War it suffered the sixth highest desertion at 1078 men with a large number of raw recruits 1761-62. [Duffy (2008) 436-7] Disbanded in 1795 after France had taken Lombardy.

Lapels & cuffs	Grass Green
Turnbacks	White
Buttons	Yellow
Shoulder strap	Grass Green
Pom-Pom	None

Garrison:
Banat (1721-36), *Hermannstadt* (1739), *Peterwardein* (1746), *Esseg* (1748), *Temesvar* (1750), *Essegg* (1753), *Temesvár* (1755) and *Cremona* (1763).

Inhaber [Wrede II: 222]
1721 *Anton Graf Alcaudete, Marchese di Portugalo*
1734 Johann Jakob *Vasquez de Pinas*
1755 *Emanuel Graf Luzan*
1765 *Joseph Heinrich Frhr. Ried*

Commanders
1722 *Bartgolomäus Valparaiso, Marchese d'Andia*
1727 *Graf Scotti*
1739 *Obrist Bulvarini*
1744 *Emanuel Graf Luzan*
1748 *Anton Marchese Velasco*
1754 *Heinrich Frhr. von Uracca*
1757 *Guido von Bagno*
1758 *Carl Marchese Gaggi*
1770 *Christoph Graf Migazzi zu Wall-Sonnenthurm*

Campaigns
War of Austrian Succession: In 1743, I-II Bn and Grenadiers were with the army in Bavaria and III Bn was in Italy. In 1744 it participated in the invasion of Naples.

Seven Years War In 1757, I-II Bn and Grenadiers were in Bohemia where it was present at Schweidnitz, Breslau (22 Nov 1757) and Leuthen. In 1758, at Hochkirch (14 Oct). In 1759, the regiment was with the Main Army. In 1760, one Bn participated in the defence of Dresden (1760). In 1761 it was with the main army. In 1762, the regiment was in Saxony fighting at Döbeln and Pretzschendorf.

Netherlands Infantry

Immediately following the French defeat at Ramillies in 1706, many from Belgium loyal to Philip V of Bourbon went over to Spain. Others sickened by the greed and taxation of Louis XIV in the Low Countries to support his grandson's forces, formed seven infantry [Sart, Claude de Ligne, Los Rios, Hartog, Maldeghem, Lannoy and Pancarlier], two dragoon [Ligne and Holstein-Norburg] and one heavy cavalry regiments [Westerloo] in the national army of Charles of Habsburg in opposition to Philip V of Spain.

The Treaty of Utrecht (1713) that ended the War of Spanish Succession ceded the Spanish Netherlands to Austria. The principle goal of Habsburg rulers was to exchange the Austrian Netherlands for Bavaria that would consolidate the Habsburg possessions in southern Germany. In 1725, the Netherlands National Regiments were incorporated into the Austrian army in the Low Countries.

By the 1757 Treaty of Versailles, Austria agreed to the creation of an independent state in the Southern Netherlands ruled by Duke Philip of Parma and garrisoned by French troops in exchange for French help in recovering Silesia. The four Walloon infantry battalions attached to the French army in 1757 were from IR9, 30, 38, and 58. These took to the field with only 5 companies each of 2 officers and 112 men plus a single grenadier company of 90 grenadiers. This agreement was revoked by the Third Treaty of Versailles just a year later.

In 1788, the Austrian Netherlands rebelled against Austria but Austrian power was restored by the end of 1790. In 1794, the entire region was overrun by France and became an integral part of French troops. Austria confirmed the loss of its territories by the Treaty of Campo Formio (1797).

The Walloon Infantry Regiments had 3 battalions of 4 companies each throughout most of the Seven Years War. During the course of the war, their garrison battalions were disbanded due to insufficient replacements. It is interesting that the Walloon Infantry suffered among the lowest desertion rates of the infantry.

IR9 Los Rios

This Walloon regiment first served in the Dutch service at Oudenaarde (1708) and Malplaquet (1709). In May 1725, transferred into Austrian service and recruited in the Netherlands and Liege. During the Seven Years War, it suffered the lowest infantry desertion rate of only 224 men [Duffy (2000) 446]

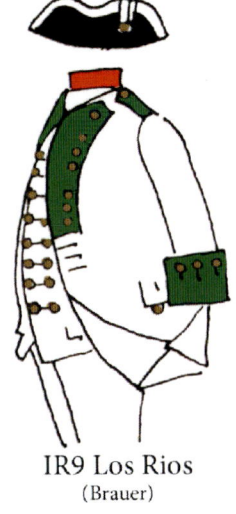

IR9 Los Rios
(Brauer)

Lapels & cuffs	Apple green
Turnbacks	White
Buttons	Yellow
Shoulder strap	Apple green
Pom-Pom	None

Garrison
1748-56 *Brussels* and *Bruges*; 1763 *Mons*.

Inhaber
1725 *Francesco Gutierrez, Marquis Los Rios*
1775 *Carl Graf Clerfait* [d. 1798]

Commanders
1756 *Franz Marquis Los Rios de Gutierrez*
1757 *Joseph Murray de Melgum*
1761 *Franz Fürst Gavre d'Aiseau*

Campaigns [Thürheim (1880) I: 43-44]
War of Austrian Succession: In 1743, at Dettingen (27 June). In 1744 it was part of *Arenberg Corps*. In 1745, the regiment was in *Traun's Army*. In 1746, campaigned along the Main Valley at Rocoux (11 Oct) and Lawfeld (2 July 1747).

IR9 Los Rios

Seven Years War In 1757, the III (garrison) Bn was part of the Austrian Contingent sent to the assistance the French for the invasion of Hanover. It occupied Wesel before participating in the blockade of Guelders and was present at Hastenbeck (1757). In 1758, the III Bn was recalled to reinforce the Austrian army in Bohemia. The I-II Bns fought at Prague where it received heavy losses during the counterattack. In 1757 it performed well at Kolin (18 June), Moys (7 Sept), Breslau (22 Nov) and Leuthen (5 Dec). In 1758 it was at Hochkirch.

Musketeer of IR9 Los Rios c1757

In 1759, after Kunersdorf (12 Aug) reduced to only one Bn for the rest of the war due to the cumulative losses and problems of obtaining recruits from the Netherlands.

Fought at Czenstochowa (1759), Landshut, Liegnitz (1760), Reichenbach (16 Aug 1762) and the defence of Schweidnitz (8 Aug-9 Oct 1762).

IR30 Sachsen-Gotha

IR30 Sachsen-Gotha
(Bauer)

The regiment was raised on 1 May 1725 from the Netherlands National Regiments of Pancarlier, Lannoy and Maldeghem. [Thürheim (1880) I: 194] During the Seven Years War it suffered the lowest desertion rate of only 268 men [Duffy (2000) 446].

Lapels & cuffs	1740 Blue
Turnbacks	White
Buttons	Yellow
Shoulder strap	White with red stripes
Pom-Pom	Red

Garrison
1749 *Ostend* and *Bruges*; 1763 *Luxemburg*.

Inhaber
1725 *Johann Anton Prie-Turinetti, Marquis de Pancarlier* [d. 1753]
1753 *Wilhelm Prinz von Sachsen-Gotha* [d. 1771]
1771 *Prince Charles Joseph de Ligne* [d. 1814]

Commander
1752 *Franz Baxeras*
1758 *Joseph von Navarro*
1762 *Peter von Langlois*

Campaigns [Thürheim (1880) I: 194-5]
War of Austrian Succession: In 1742, in the Netherlands. In 1743, at Dettingen (27 June). In 1744 it garrisoned the Netherlands. In 1745, the regiment was at the siege of Dendermonde and Ostend. In 1747 it occupied Luxembourg castle.

Seven Years War In 1757, a Bn took part in Domstasle's contingent with the French Army at Hastenbeck (26 July). Another Bn was at Kolin, Moys (7 Sept), Breslau (22 Nov) and Leuthen. In 1759, at Hochkirch (14 Oct). In 1760, a Bn and the Grenadiers were at the siege of Dresden then at Strehlen (24 Aug), Torgau (27 Sept) and Wittenberg (2 Oct). In 1761, the grenadiers were distinguished at Loudon's storm of Schweidnitz. In 1762, the grenadiers lost 2 officers and 200 men when the magazine exploded which caused the capitulation of Schweidnitz.

IR38 de Ligne

IR38 de Ligne
(Brauer)

The regiment was raised in 1725 from the Netherlands national Regiment. Disbanded in 1809.

Lapels & cuffs	Light red
Turnbacks	White
Buttons	White
Shoulder strap	Light Red
Pom-Pom	None

Garrison
1733-35 *Luxembourg*; 1754 *Bruges*; 1763 *Brussels*

Inhaber
1725 *Claude Lamoral Fürst de Ligne*
1766 *Carl Merode Marquis d'Ayne*

Commander
1725 *Leves Graf de Chanclos*
1730 *Jakob Graf Rumigny-Peyssant*
1748 *Herzog D'Ursel*
1752 *Max Graf Bournonville*
1760 *Carl Prinz de Ligne*
1764 *Nikolaus Graf D'Arberg*

Campaigns [Wrede II: 237]
War of Austrian Succession: In 1743, the I Bn was present at Dettingen. In 1744-5 it was stationed in Luxembourg. In 1746, one Bn and the grenadiers were at the siege of Mons. In 1747, I-II Bn was at Lawfeld.

Seven Years War
In 1756, I Bn and the grenadiers were in Bohemia. In 1757, one Bn was in Dombasle's contingent at Hastenbeck. In 1757, the rest of the regiment fought at Kolin (18 June) and Moys near Görlitz (7 Sept). In 1758, transferred to the Reichsarmee and was distinguished at Hochkirch (14 Oct). In 1759, Pretzch, Maxen (20 Nov). The III Bn was in Luxembourg. In 1760 it participated in Lacy's raid on Berlin. In 1761 it was with the main army. In 1762 it fought at Burkersdorf (20-21 July) and a detachment under *Obrist-Lt Hörger* in Schweidnitz.

IR55 D'Arberg

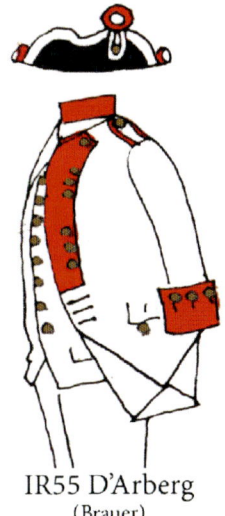

IR55 D'Arberg
(Brauer)

The regiment was raised in 9 May 1742 by *Obrist Graf d'Arberg* from the 1st Netherlands National Regiment. In 1747-48 it absorbed the Heister and Jung-Arenberg Regiments. In 1769 it received the regimental number 55. Disbanded in 1809.

Lapels & cuffs	1743 Red
	1767 Light blue & white buttons.
Turnbacks	White
Buttons	Yellow
Shoulder strap	Red
Pom-Pom	Red

Garrisons
1748 *Netherlands*, 1753 *Bruges*, 1764 *Gent*.

Inhaber
1746 *Carl Anton Graf d'Arberg*
1768 *Joseph Graf Murray de Melgum*

Commander
1742 *Carl Graf D'Arberg*
1745 *Carl Herzog D'Ursel*
1748 *Gustav Prinz Stollberg-Geldern*
1755 *Graf Clarincini*
1757 *Philipp Graf Merode*
1759 *Hyppolit Chevalier Orlandini*
1760 *Carl Graf Vinchant de Gontreuil*
1769 *Nikolaus Graf D'Arberg*

War Austrian Succession: In 1743, fought at Dettingen. In 1744 it was in the Netherlands. In 1745 it was at the siege of Nieuport.

Seven Years War I-II Bns arrived in Bohemia from the Netherlands in 1757 and fought at Prague, Moys, Breslau and Leuthen. III Bn was in *Corps Dombasle* at Hastenbeck. In 1759 it was with the main army in Saxony, fighting at Landeshut, Liegnitz, Adelsbach and Burkersdorf.

German Infantry Uniforms

Uniform details differ according to sources. The most reliable source for uniforms was Albertini (1762) and this has been followed where possible.

German Fusilier Uniforms

HEADGEAR: Black tricorn laced white and black cockade on the left. Only IR3, IR21, IR26, IR28, IR36 and IR54 had scalloped. The sprig of green leaves was normally worn on campaign as the field sign.

FORAGE CAP: Simple cloth forage cap made from old coats was worn for manual work.

HAIR: Unpowdered queue at the rear and rolls at the temple. Moustaches were worn by the rank and file.

POM-POM: Some regiments had pom-poms. At the rear corners were bobs that often followed the facing colour according to Albertini (1762).

No pom-poms:
IR4, IR8-IR9, IR11, IR13-IR14, IR16, IR18, IR23-IR27, IR29, IR35, IR38, IR43-IR44, IR48-IR50 and IR57.

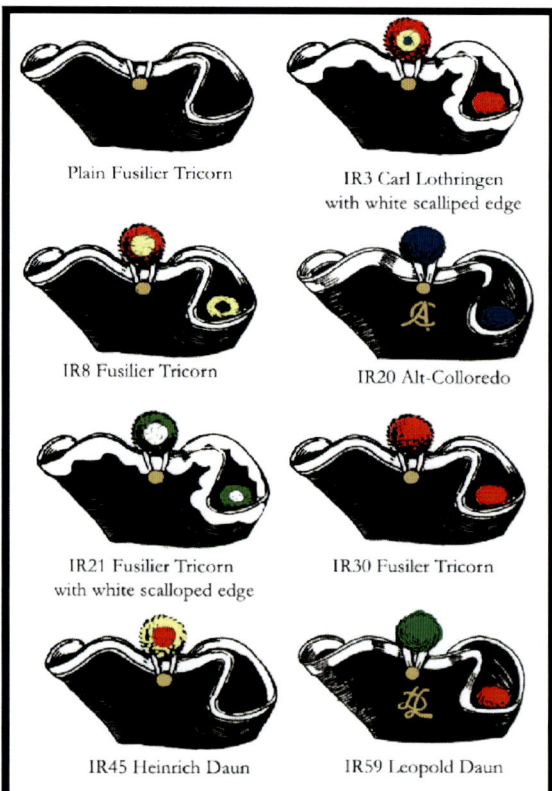

Black: *IR55*
Blue and white: *IR56*
Blue-white-blue: *IR12*
Blue-yellow-blue: *IR10*
Dark blue: *IR20*
Green: *IR46, IR59*
Green-white-red: *IR28*
Green-yellow-white: *IR41*
Green and white: *IR21*
Red: *IR30*
Mixed red-black-yellow: *IR1*
Red-white-red-white: *IR15*
Red and yellow: *IR7, IR36*
Red-yellow-blue: *IR3*
White and blue: *IR40*
Yellow: *IR47, IR54*
Yellow and blue: *IR42*
Yellow and red: *IR45*
Yellow-red-white: *IR22*
Yellow-red-yellow: *IR17*

Austrian Seven Years War Infantry

STOCK: A red or a black fabric stock. For parades the regimental commanders agreed before on the colour of the neck-stocks.

COAT: White woollen collarless coat with lapels and large square cuffs in the facing colour. The lapels had nine buttons arranged in three groups of three. The horizontal pockets and cuffs had three buttons.

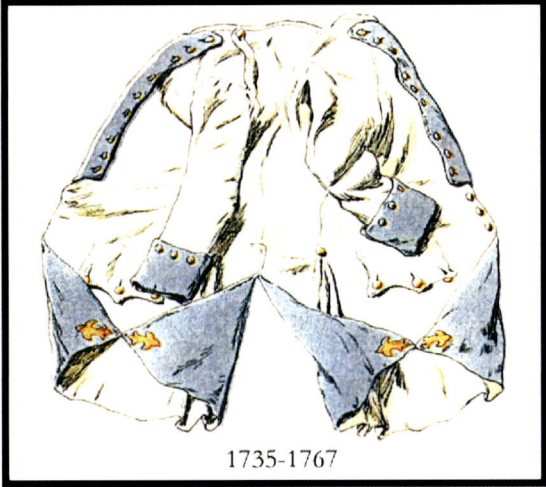
1735-1767

SHOULDER STRAP: The shoulder strap was on the left shoulder only. There is great variation in the colour and design of these according to the literature. [Pengel (1982) 40-44]. The shoulder straps consisted of the following [According to Donath (1970) and Albertini (1762).]

    Blue with white border: *IR23*
    Blue with wavy white border: *IR21*
    Blue with white border and central wavy stripe: *IR42*
    Red with white border: *IR25*
    Red with red and white border: IR15, IR17
    Rose pink: IR38
    White: *IR4, IR7-IR9, IR11, IR13, IR22-IR24, IR26, IR35, IR40-IR41, IR44-IR45* and *IR48-IR49*.
    White with black-red-white border: *IR30*
    White with blue border and central wavy line: *IR42*
    White with light blue border and central wavy line: *IR36*
    White with green border and wavy stripe: *IR28*
    White with red border: *IR3, IR26, IR55, IR57*.
    White with red zigzag border: *IR54*
    Yellow with red border: *IR3*
    Facing colour: *IR10, IR14, IR16, IR18, IR20, IR27, IR29, IR43, IR46-47, IR50, IR56* and *IR57*.

TURNBACKS: Many regiments retained coloured turnbacks of the facing colour at the start of the Seven Years War but by 1762 all except three regiments had white turnbacks.

In 1762, the following regiments still had coloured turnbacks.
    Red turnbacks and no turnback badge: IR26 and IR50.
    Light blue turnbacks and no turnback badge: IR27.

TURNBACK TAB: Many of the German Infantry regiments had a distinctive turnback tab. However there is a great deal of conflict between sources. [Pengel (1982) 46-47] White turnbacks and no turnback badge: *IR4, IR8-IR14, IR28, IR30, IR41, IR44, IR48, IR55, and IR56.*

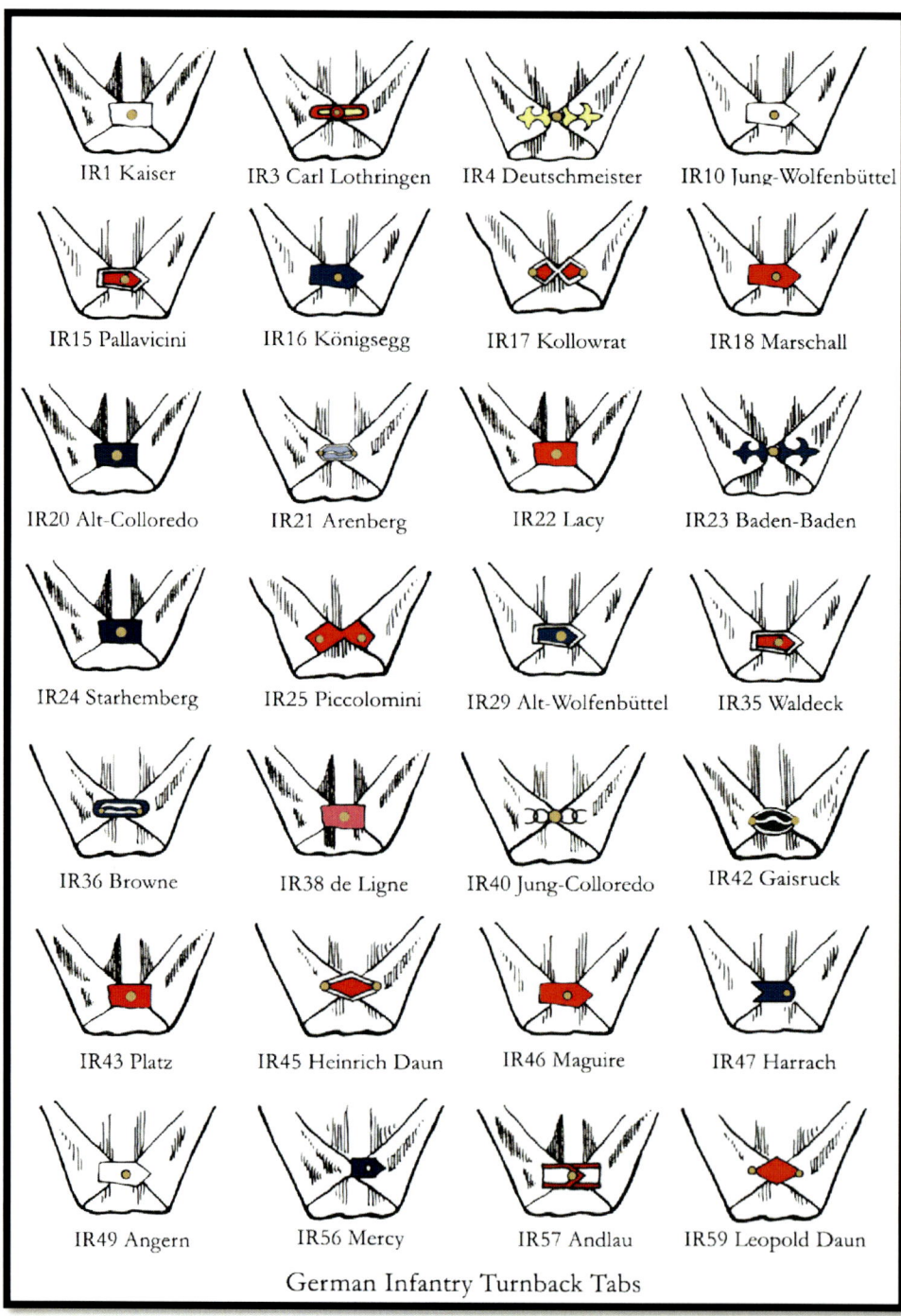

German Infantry Turnback Tabs

WAISTCOAT: White long skirted waistcoat with buttons either in a single or double row. Before 1760 the waistcoat was often in the regimental facing colour. In 1760, the regulations were more rigorously enforced and these became all white. According to Pengel (1982b: 24).

> 28 regiments with double row of yellow buttons [*IR1, IR4, IR9, IR12-IR18, IR20, IR21, IR23, IR24, IR25, IR30, IR35, IR40-IR48, IR54, IR56, and IR57*].
> 3 regiments with single row of yellow buttons [*IR3, IR26* and *IR55*]
> 1 regiment with double row of white buttons [*IR11*]
> 2 regiments with single row of white buttons [*IR27* and *IR38*]

LEGWEAR: White breeches with black gaiter for winter and white gaiters for summer and parades.

FOOTWEAR: Black leather shoes with strap buckle.

EQUIPMENT: White leather belt over the left shoulder carrying a black cartridge box with a small brass plate carrying the initials "MT" was worn on the right hip. A white waist-belt carrying the bayonet was worn under the coat. A narrow white belt was worn over the right shoulder for the calfskin knapsack. The drum or egg shaped canteen had a brown leather strap.

SIDEARMS: The M1745 musket for fusiliers with bayonet until they were replaced by the M1754 musket.

Fusilier NCOs

HEADWEAR: Sergeants [*Feldwebel* and *Führer*] had gold or silver hat lace. Corporals had white or yellow hat lace to their black tricorns.

UNIFORM: As Fusiliers.

POLEARMS: Until 1759, sergeants carried the halberd and corporals the half pike.

SIDEARMS: Sergeants had a wooden cane suspended from a coat button and grenadier sabre. Corporals only had a grenadier sabre.

Fusilier Officers

HEADWEAR Tricorn laced gold or silver hat lace depending upon button colour.

STOCK: White cloth neck stock.

COAT: Similar cut to the other ranks but with finer cloth and no turnbacks. No shoulder strap.

SASH: Yellow and black woollen sash for lieutenants. Yellow and black silk sash were worn by majors and above.

SWAGGER STICKS: Carried by officers to identify their ranks.
   Lieutenant had a bamboo stick without knob
   Captain long rush stick with a bone knob
   Major long rush stick with a silver knob and a small silver chain
   Lieutenant-colonel long rush stick with a larger silver knob without chain
   Colonel long rush stick with a golden knob

POLEARMS: Up to 1759, partisans were carried by officers.

SIDEARMS: Fusilier officers carried straight bladed swords.

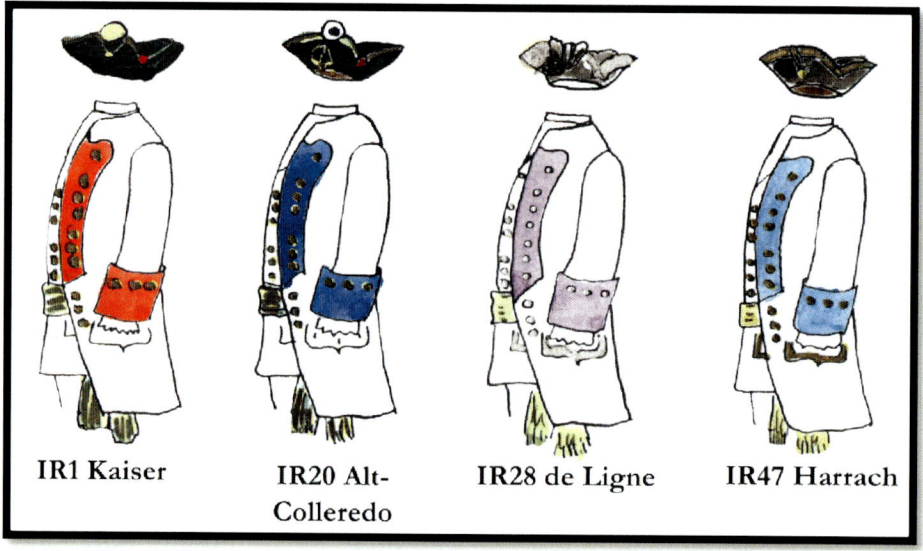

Fusilier Officers
[After Donath (1970) and Pengel (1982)]

Musicians

Up to 1760, the 1755 regulations that stipulated that musicians would wear white coats with swallow nest in facing colour bordered with lace in button colour was generally ignored. Table 8 gives some known examples where the regimental facing colour was used for the coat colour with white lapels, and turnbacks. The swallow nest often had lace in the silver or gold button colour. After 1760, the 1755 regulations were strictly enforced.

Musicians did not carry a musket or cartridge box. The brass drum was decorated with black flames at the bottom and with a black double headed eagle on a yellow field. The rims were decorated with red and white diagonal stripes. The bandolier was white.

Drum used by Infantry and Dragoons

Table 7: Pre-1760 facing colours for German Infantry musicians.
[Pengel (1982b) 53-54 and Donath (1970)]

Coat	Facings	Infantry Regiment
Black coat	White	IR14
Blue coat	White	IR4, IR16, IR24, IR30, IR36, IR40, IR56
Green coat	White	IR9, IR28, IR48
Red coat	White	IR3, IR8, IR15, IR22, IR26, IR41, IR43, IR44, IR55, IR57
Rose-pink	White	IR38
White coat	Blue	IR21, IR27, IR47, IR56

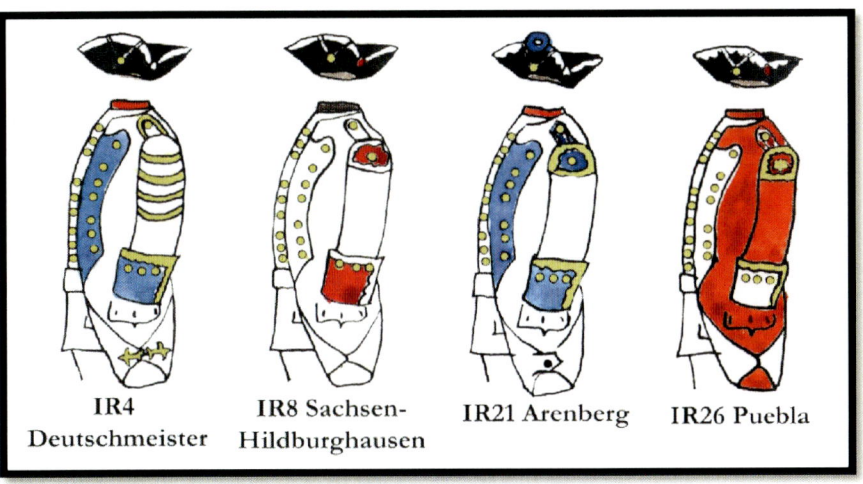

German Infantry Drummers of IR4-IR26
[After Donath, (1970) and Pengel (1982)]

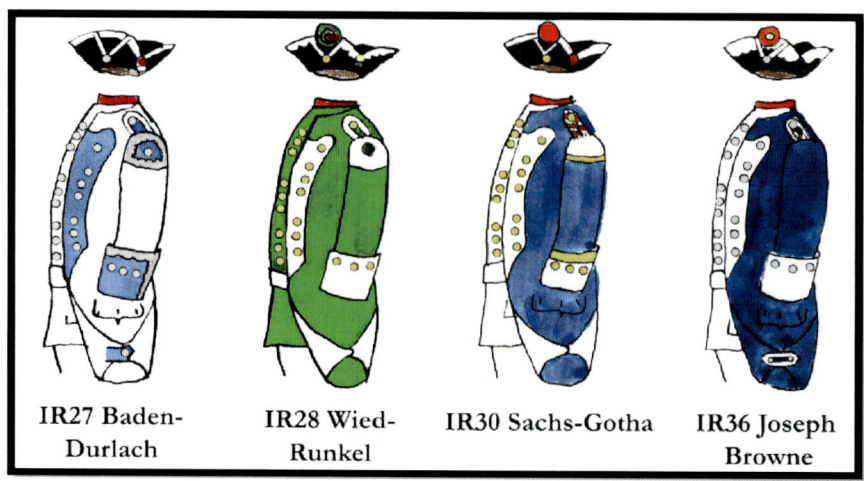

German Infantry Drummers of IR27-IR36

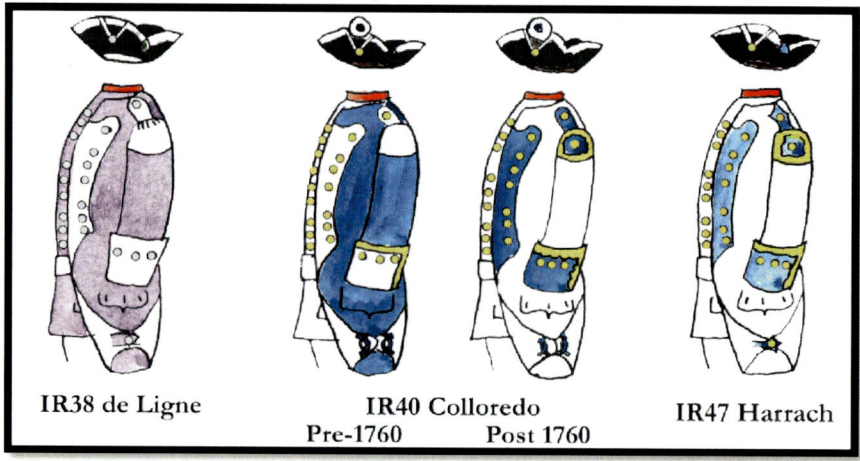

German Infantry Drummers of IR38-IR47

German Infantry Drummers of IR50-IR56
[After Donath, (1970) and Pengel (1982)]

Chapter 6
Hungarian Infantry

Hungarian Infantry c1762

IR2 Erzherzog Karl

The regiment was raised in Western Hungary and Transylvania in 1741. An excellent regiment with a remarkable officer corps including the commentator *Jacob Cogniazzo* and *Lieutenant Waldhütter* who was an unlikely hero of Schweidnitz (8 Aug - 9 Oct 1762). [Duffy (2008) 429]

IR2 Erzherzog Karl
(Brauer)

Cuffs	Medium blue
Turnbacks	Medium blue
Piping	Yellow
Coat lace	Yellow
Barrel sash	Yellow and dark blue
Shoulder strap	One white
Pom-Pom	Yellow
Grenadier cap	Yellow bad with yellow piping
Tassel	Yellow

Garrison
1752 *Olmütz* in *Moravia*; 1763 *Netherlands*

Inhaber
1741 *Ladislaus Frhr. Ujvaryi* [d. 1749]
1749 *Erzherzog Karl Joseph* [d. 1761]
1762 *Erzherzog Ferdinand* [d. 24 Dec 1806]

Commander
1752 *Joseph Freiherr von Siskovics*
1757 *Joseph Freiherr von Kokenyesdy de Vettes* [killed at Breslau (22 Nov 1757)]
1757 *Ignaz Szallaghi*
1760 *Joseph Freiherr Orosz von Csicser*

Campaigns [Thürheim (1880) I: 6-7]
War of Austrian Succession: In 1743, at the siege of Ingolstadt. In 1744 it was present at the battle of Prague. In 1746 it transferred to the Netherlands and fought at Rocoux (11 Oct) and Lawfeld (2 July).

Seven Years War Distinguished at Kolin (18 June 1757) under *Obrist Graf*

Albertina (1762)

Siskowitz, Meuselwitz (8 Oct), siege of Schweidnitz, Breslau (22 Nov 1757), Leuthen (5 Dec 1757). In 1758 it was present at Domstadtl and Hochkirch. In 1760, suffered the heaviest losses at Torgau (3 Nov) resulting from its numerous counterattacks. The regiment was reformed in Bohemia before participating in the storming of Schweidnitz 1761). In 1762, a detachment was part of its defence before fighting at Burkersdorf.

IR19 Pálffy

The regiment was formed in 1734 at the cost of the first *Inhaber*.

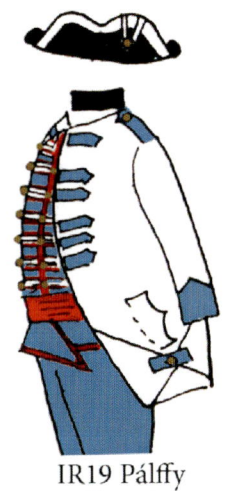

IR19 Pálffy
(Brauer)

Lapels & cuffs	Medium blue
Stock	Black
Turnbacks	White
Buttons	Yellow
Shoulder strap	Medium blue
Pom-Pom	None
Barrel sash	Yellow and dark blue
Grenadier cap	Medium blue bag with white piping
Tassel	White

Garrison
1756 *Lombardy* with Garrison Bn in *Hungary*.

Inhaber
1734 *Leopold Graf Pálffy ab Erdöd* [d. 1773]
1773 *Richard Graf d'Alton*

Commanders [Wrede I: 249]
1736 *Leopold Frhr. von Andrassy*
1739 *Jakob Frhr. von Preysach*
1752 *Joseph Ziggan von Cserma*
1758 *Wolfgang Frhr. von Faber du Faur*
1767 *Leopold Schuller de Raad*

Campaigns [Thürheim (1880) I: 6-7]
War of Austrian Succession: In 1742, participated in the Winter Expedition in Upper Austria and Bavaria before transferring to Bohemia to fight at Chotusitz (17 May) and at the siege of Prague. In 1743 it was in

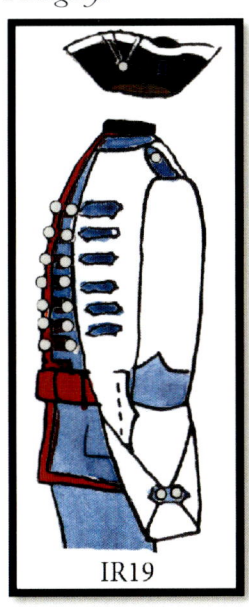

IR19

Bavaria. In 1746 it was in Italy fighting at Rottofreddo and the siege of Genoa. III Bn was part of the invasion of Provence. In 1747, the regiment was at the siege of Genoa.

Seven Years War In 1757, fought at Hirschfeld, Prague (6 May), Moys (7 Sept), distinguished at the siege of Schweidnitz, Breslau (22 Nov) and Leuthen (5 Dec). In 1758, at Hochkirch (14 Oct). In 1759 at Kunersdorf (12 Aug) and Troppau (18 Nov). In 1760 at Landshut and Liegnitz (15 Aug). In 1761, present at the storm of Schweidnitz and suffered heavy losses at Torgau.

IR31 Haller

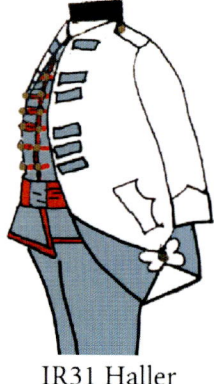

IR31 Haller
(Brauer)

The regiment was raised on 1 November 1741 in Transylvania with strength of 1500 men in two battalions. [Thürheim (1880) I: 201]

Lapels & cuffs	Light blue
Stock	Black
Turnbacks	White
Buttons	Yellow
Shoulder straps	Light blue
Pom-Pom	None
Barrel sash	Yellow and dark blue
Grenadier cap	Medium blue bag with white piping
Tassel	White

Garrison
1756 Moravia with Garrison Bn in Hungary.

Inhaber
1741 *Samuel Frhr. Haller von Hallerstein* [d. 1777]
1777 *Anton Graf Esterhazy de Galantha*

Commanders
1754 Franz Deseö
1758 Johann Graf Rhedey
1760 Sigmund von Kerekes
1769 Joseph Georg Browne.

Campaign [Thürheim (1880) I: 201-2]
War of Austrian Succession: In 1742, campaigned in Bohemia and was present at the siege of Prague. In 1744, in Bohemia. In 1745, transferred to

the Netherlands being presnt at Rocoux (1746), Lawfeld (1747) and the siege of Maastrict (1748).

Seven Years War In 1757, the grenadiers showed great bravery at Reichenberg (21 Apr). The regiment was distinguished at Kolin (18 June) losing 689 dead and *Obrist Deszö, Major Kerekes*, 27 Officers and 906 men wounded. Present at Gabel, Zittau (5 Sept) and Moys (7 Sept). A detachment was part of the defence of Schweidnitz, Breslau (22 Nov). The regiment fought at Breslau and Leuthen (5 Dec). In 1758, participated in the ambush at Gundersdorf and Domstadtl, fought at Hochkirch (14 Oct) where it stormed a redoubt and lost 500 men, and at Maxen (20 Nov 1759). In 1760, part of the expedition to Berlin and fought at Torgau (3 Nov). In 1762, the Regiment was at Burkersdorf (21 July) and a detachment at the defence of Schweidnitz.

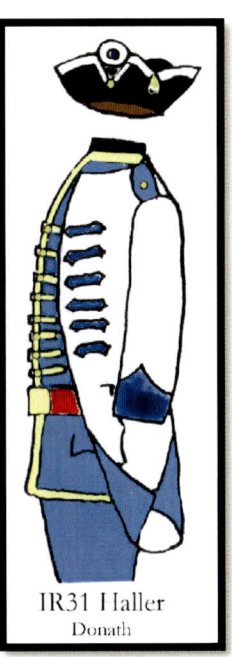

IR31 Haller
Donath

Hungarian Fusilier
c1760

IR32 Forgách

IR32 Forgách
(Brauer)

Raised in 1741 in Hungary.

Lapels & cuffs	Medium blue
Waistcoat	Medium blue with red lace
Turnbacks	Medium blue with white diamond badge
Buttons	Yellow
Shoulder straps	Medium blue
Pom-Pom	None
Barrel sash	Red and medium blue
Grenadier cap	Medium blue bag with yellow piping
Tassel	Yellow

Garrison
Lombardy with Garrison Bn in *Hungary* (1756).

Inhaber
1741 *Ignaz Graf Forgách de Ghymies*
1773 *Samuel Graf Gyulai* [d. 1802]

Commanders
1754 *Friedrich Frhr. von Altkirchen*
1768 *Anton Graf Grisoni*

Alberina (1762)

Campaigns [Thürheim (1880) I: 209]
War of Austrian Succession: In 1743, at the siege of Ingolstadt. In 1744, at Lautenberg (4 July) and Weissenberg (5 July). In 1745 it was on the Main before transferring to Italy. In 1746 it was at Piacenza, the siege of Genoa and participated in the invasion of Provence. In 1747, at Exilles it captured the French *General Chevalier Belle Isle*.

Seven Years War In 1757, present at Prague (7 July), Moys (7 Sept), a battalion surrendered at Schweidnitz, Breslau (22 Nov) and Leuthen (5 Dec). In 1758, the regiment fought at Hochkirch and Maxen. It suffered heavy losses at Torgau and Liegnitz (15 Aug 1760). In 1761, one battalion was distinguished at Loudon's storm of Schweidnitz (1 Oct). In 1762, at Fischerberg (16 Aug).

IR33 Nicolaus Esterhazy

IR33 Nicolaus Esterhazy (Brauer)

The regiment was raised in 1741. A hard fighting regiment. [Duffy (2008) 434]

Lapels & cuffs	Dark blue
Waistcoat	Dark blue with yellow lace
Turnbacks	Dark blue
Buttons	Yellow
Shoulder straps	Dark blue
Pom-Pom	Yellow with white centre
Barrel sash	Yellow and dark blue
Grenadier cap	Dark blue bag with white piping
Tassel	White

Garrison:
In Bohemia with Garrison Bn in Hungary (1756).

Inhaber
1741 *Johann Adam Frhr. von Andrassy* [d. 1753]
1753 *Nicolaus Joseph Graf Esterhazy de Galantha* [d. 1790]
1791 *Anton Graf Sztaray* [d. 1808]

Commander
1756 *Johann von Gueber*
1757 *Carl Frhr. von Amadei*
1761 *Johann Joseph Khevenhüller-Metsch*

Campaign
[Thürheim (1880) I: 215-6]
War of Austrian Succession: In 1742-3, campaigned in Bavaria before transferring to Italy for the invasion of Naples (1744). In 1746, the regiment fought at Rottofreddo and present at the siege of Genoa. One Bn was part of the expedition to Provence.

Albertina (1762)

Seven Years War In 1756, at Lobositz (1 Oct). In 1757, at Prague (6 May), Schweidnitz, Breslau (22 Nov) and at Leuthen (5 Dec) lost heavily with many taken prisoner. In 1758, distinguished at Hochkirch where it had the second highest regimental losses. Present at the defence of Dresden. In 1761, the regiment was at Loudon's storm of Schweidnitz and at the battle of Dommitzch. In 1762 it was with the *Reichsarmee* in Saxony. One Bn was distinguished at Teplitz.

IR34 Batthyány

IR34 Batthyány
(Brauer)

The regiment was raised on 13 November 1733 with 2300 men from Pest and Debreczin at the Inhaber's expense. [Thürheim (1880) I: 223]

Lapels & cuffs	Dark blue
Waistcoat	Dark blue with yellow lace
Turnbacks	Dark blue
Buttons	Yellow
Shoulder straps	Dark blue
Pom-Pom	Yellow with black centre
Barrel sash	Yellow
Grenadier cap	Dark blue bag with white piping
Tassel	White

Garrison
From 1748-56 in Lombardy with Garrison Bn in Hungary.

Inhaber
1734 *Ladislaus Frhr. von Kökenyesdi de Vettes* [d. 1754]
1756 *Adam Wenzel Graf Batthyány (Batthyányi)* [d. 1787]
1780 *Anton Fürst Esterhazy de Galantha* [d. 1794]

Campaigns [Thürheim (1880) I: 224]
War of Austrian Succession: In 1742, part of the winter expedition to Upper Austria and Bavaria. Fought at Czaslau (17 May) where it was attacked by two Prussian regiments losing 7 officers and 491 men. It participated in the siege of Prague.

In 1743 it was at the siege of Straubing and Ingolstadt. In 1744 it campaigned in Bohemia. In 1745, at Hohenfriedberg (4 June) and

Trautenau (30 Sept). In 1746, in Italy at Piacenza (16 June), Rottofreddo and occupied Genoa. In 1748 it was at the siege of Genoa.

Seven Years War In 1757, one Bn and the grenadiers were present at Reichenberg, Moys (7 Sept), Breslau (22 Nov), Leuthen (5 Dec). In 1758 it was at Hochkirch (14 Oct) where it suffered heavy casualties of 400 men while capturing 4 guns and 4 flags. In 1759, Czenstochowa (21 Nov). In 1760 it was at Landeshut (23 June), storm of Glatz (26 July) and Liegnitz (15 Aug) where it received heavy casualties of 928 men. In 1761 it participated in Loudon's storm of Schweidnitz. In 1762, the regiment was at Reichenbach (16 Aug).

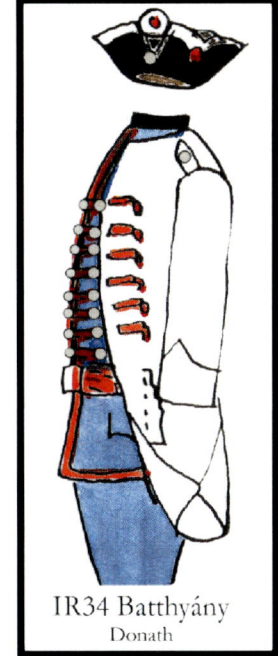

IR34 Batthyány
Donath

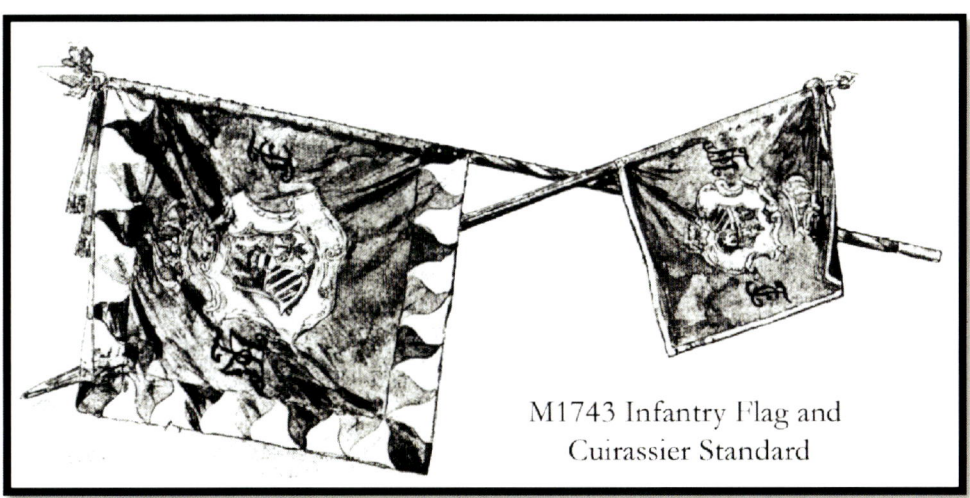

M1743 Infantry Flag and Cuirassier Standard

IR37 Joseph Esterházy

IR37 Joseph Esterházy
(Brauer)

Raised in 1741

Lapels & cuffs	Red
Waistcoat	Red with green lace
Turnbacks	Red with white turnback tab edged red
Buttons	Yellow
Shoulder straps	White edged red
Pom-Pom	Yellow with red centre
Barrel sash	White and green
Grenadier cap	Red bag with yellow trim
Tassel	Yellow

Garrison:
Bohemia with Garrison Bn in Hungary.

Inhaber
1741 *Thomas von Szirmay* [d. 1743]
1744 *Joseph Graf Esterhazy de Galantha* [d. 1762]
1762 *Joseph Graf Siskovics* [d. 1783]
1784 *Josef Nikolaus Frhr. De Vins* [d. 1798]

Commanders
1752 *Ladislaus von Szent-Ivany*
1756 *Franz Anton Graf Karolyi*
1759 *Joseph von Weiss*
1760 *Nikolaus Lumaga*
1768 *Carl Frhr. von Haugwitz*

Campaign
[Thürheim (1880) I: 248-9]
War of Austrian Succession: In 1742, at the siege of Prague. In 1743 it was part of the blockade of Eger and then the siege of Ingolstadt. In 1744 it fought at Lautenberg.

In 1745, a Bn with Trenk's Pandours at the storming of Kosel in Silesia

Albertina (1762)

before the regiment transferred to Italy. In 1746, the regiment was at siege of Genoa and the invasion of Provence. In 1747 it was at siege of Genoa.

Seven Years War Present at Lobositz (1 Oct 1756) and part of Browne's relief expedition to relieve the Saxons surrounded at Pirna. Fought at Prague (6 May 1757), Breslau (22 Nov 1757), Leuthen (5 Dec 1757), Gundersdorf and Domstadtl. The regiment ran away at Hochkirch (14 Oct 1758). Present at Maxen, Meissen (2-3 Dec 1759), Landeshut and covered the retreat from Liegnitz (15 Aug 1760).

IR37 Joseph Esterhazy
[After Herbert Knötel]

IR39 John Pálffy

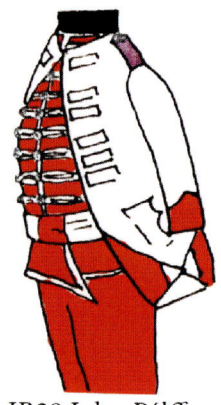

IR39 John Pálffy
(Brauer)

The regiment was raised by *John Pálffy ab Erdöd* in 1756 in Hungary. An impressive campaign record. [Duffy (2008) 435]

Lapels & cuffs	Red
Waistcoat	Red with white lace
Turnbacks	Red
Buttons	White
Shoulder straps	Lilac
Pom-Pom	None
Barrel sash	Red and white
Grenadier cap	Red bag with white piping
Tassel	White

Garrison in *Hungary* (1756).

Inhaber
1756 *Johann Leopold Pálffy ab Erdöd*
1758 *Jacob Frhr. von Preysach* [d. 1787]
1787 *Thomas Graf Nádasdy* [d. 1800]

Commanders
1756 The *Inhaber*
1758 *Joseph Frhr. Formentini*
1760 *Johann von Komka*
1768 *Gabriel Anton Frhr. Splényi von Miháldy*

Campaigns
[Thürheim (1880) I: 258-9]
Seven Years War In 1757, present at Prague (6 May), Moys (7 Sept), Schweidnitz (11 Nov), Breslau (22 Nov) and Leuthen (5 Dec).

Albertina (1762)

In 1758 it was in Moravia at the defence of Olmütz (28 May-2 July), siege of Neisse, Troppau and Hochkirch. In 1759 it participated in numerous actions in Bohemia and Saxony. In 1760 it was distinguished at Landeshut (23 June), Loudon's storm of Glatz (26 July), then Liegnitz (15 Aug). In 1762 it fought at Burkersdorf (20-21 July). A detachment was present at the defence of Schweidnitz.

IR51 Gyulai

IR51 Gyulai
(Brauer)

In 1702, *Adam Frhr. von Baboczay* raised 2,000 men and this regiment was the oldest Hungarian Infantry Regiment. Also known as the Transylvanian National Regiment [*Siebenbürgisches National-Regiment*]

Coat lace	Red
Cuffs	Blue
Turnbacks	Blue
Buttons	Yellow
Shoulder straps	Blue
Pom-Pom	Yellow with black centre
Barrel sash	Red and blue
Grenadier cap	Dark blue bag with yellow piping
Tassel	Yellow

Garrison
Lombardy with Garrison Bn in *Transylvania* (1756).

Inhaber
1702 *Adam Frhr. von Baboczay* [d. 1707]
1707 *Franz Graf Gyulai* [d. 1729]
1729 *Franz Graf Pálffy von Erdöd* [d. 1734]
1735 *Stephan Graf Gyulai* [d. 1759]
1759 *Franz Graf Gyulai* [d. 1788]
1788 *Gabriel Frhr. Splényi von Miháldy* [d. 1818]

Commanders
1752 *Thomas Graf Kálnoky*
1757 *Adolph von Gernert*
1760 *Samuel Graf Gyulai*
1767 *Joseph Frhr. Orosz von Csicser*

Campaigns [Thürheim (1880) I: 338]
War of Austrian Succession: In Dec 1741, in Italy with Khevenhüller Corps. In 1742 it was part of the winter expedition to Upper Austria and Bavaria. In 1744 it campaigned on the Rhine and in Bohemia. In 1745 it was at Habelschwert, Hohenfriedberg and Trautenau before transferring to Italy. In 1746 it was part of the siege of Genoa and

Albertina (1762)

the invasion of Provence. In 1747 it participated in the siege of Genoa.

Seven Years War In 1757, present at Reichenberg (21 April), Prague (6 May). A detachment was present in Lacy's raid on Berlin. Fought at Moys (30 June), Pretzch. In 1759, Maxen (20 Nov) and Torgau. In 1761 it participated in Loudon's storm of Schweidnitz. In 1762, its outstanding performance decided the battle of Teplitz in the Austrian favour.

IR52 Bethlen

IR52 Bethlen
(Brauer)

Formed in 1741. One of the best Hungarian regiments but difficult to handle. [Duffy (2008) 437]

Lapels	White
Cuffs	Medium blue
Turnbacks	White
Buttons	Yellow
Shoulder strap	None
Pom-Pom	Yellow with black centre
Barrel sash	Red and yellow
Grenadier cap	Medium blue bag with white piping
Tassel	White

Garrison: in *Friaul* [*Friuli*] in north-eastern Italy with Garrison Bn in *Hungary*.

Inhaber
1741 *Wolfgang Graf Bethlen* [d. 1763]
1763 *Franz Anton Graf Károly* [d. 1791]
1791 *Erzherzog Anton Victor*

Commanders
1741 *Wolfgang Graf Bethlen*
1745 *Joseph Graf Nádasdy*
1749 *Gabriel Frhr. von Balassa*
1752 *Franz von Reinhardt*
1758 *Joseph Maximilian Frhr. von Tillier*
1771 *Paul Orosz de Balasfalva.*

Campaigns [Thürheim (1880) I: 345-6]
War of Austrian Succession: In 1742, siege of Prague. In 1743 it blockaded Eger. In 1744 it was in Bohemia. In 1745 it was at Kesseldorf before transferring to the Netherlands. In 1746, at Rocoux

IR52 Bethlen
Donath

(11 Oct). In 1747, at Lawfeld (2 July).

Seven Years War In 1757, present at Prague (6 May), Schweidnitz, distinguished at Breslau (22 Nov), and Leuthen (5 Dec). In 1758, Hochkirch (14 Oct). In 1759 it was part of Corps Loudon at Kunersdorf (12 Aug). In 1760, Liegnitz (15 Aug) and Torgau (3 Nov). In 1762 it was distinguished at Adelsbach (6 July), Leutmannsdorf (21 July) and a detachment in the defence of Schweidnitz.

Panduren-Corps (1741-1756)

On 27 February 1741, Major Franz Frhr. von der Trenk raised *Panduran-Corps* in Slavonia. On 17 March 1745 it was renamed the *Trenck Panduren Regiment* with 20 coys and 2 grenadier coys. In 1748 it was reduced to a single battalion and renamed the *Slavonisches Panduren Bn*.

Inhaber *Panduren-Corps (Regiment)*
1741 *Franz Frhr. von der Trenk* [d. 1749]

Commander *Panduren-Corps (-Regiment)*
1741 *Franz Frhr. von der Trenck*
1747 ad interim *Obrist-Lt D'Olne* then *Major Graf Madrenas*

Commander *Slavonisches Panduren-Bn*
1748 *Christian von Mainstein*
1750 *Adam von Buday*
1753 *Joseph Carl Frhr. von Simbschen*

Campaigns of the Panduran-Corps

War of Austrian Succession: In 1741, the Pandour Corps was in Silesia. Near Neisse captured 34 wagons and 300 horses before transferring to Khevenhüller Corps. In 1742, part of the winter expedition to upper Austria and Bavaria. In 1743 it campaigned on the Rhine. In 1744, at Lautenberg (4 July) and attack on Kolin (14 Nov). In 1745, in Silesia at Radaun (11 Feb), Habelschwert (14 Feb), Loslau (29 Mar), Ratibor (20 Apr), the storm of Cosel (26 May) and Trautenau (30 Sept). In 1746, at Rocoux (1746). In 1747, a Bn was present at Lawfeld (2 July) before transferring to Italy.

IR53 Simbschen (17

This on 8 September 1756, the *Slavonisches Panduren-Bn* became a regular infantry battalion and by early 1757 it had been augmented to 16 Füsilier and 2 Grenadier Coys. It was recruited mainly in Croatia and Slavonia so not strictly a Hungarian regiment. In 1769 it received infantry number 53.

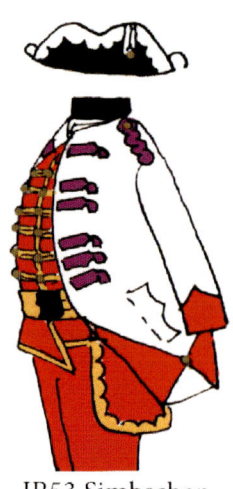

IR53 Simbschen (Brauer)

Cuffs & turnbacks	Red
Piping & buttons	Yellow (*Brauer*) or white (*Donath*)
Coat lace	Lilac (Brauer)
Barrel sash	Yellow and black
Shoulder strap	Lilac
Pom-Pom	None
Grenadier cap	Red bag with white piping
Tassel	White

Garrison:
Peterwardein (1749), *Philipsburg* (1750), *Freiberg* in *Moravia* (1751), *Fulnek* (1755), *Troppau* (1756 and 1763).

Inhaber
1756 *Joseph Carl Frhr. von Simbschen* [d. 1763]
1763 *Levin Philipp Frhr. von Beck* [d. 1768]
1768 *Johann Leopold Graf Pálffy von Erdöd* [d. 1791]

Commander
1756 *Joseph Carl Frhr. von Simbschen*
1758 *Robert Freiherr von Amelungen*
1764 *Lorenz Frhr. von Rasp*

Campaigns [Thürheim (1880) I: 352]
Seven Years War In 1756, in Silesia at Reinerz (4 Nov). In 1757, the regiment was present at the storming of Gabel (14-15 July), Moys (7 Sept), Schweidnitz, Breslau (22 Nov). In 1758 it was distinguished in the defence of Olmütz. In 1760, at Landeshut (23 June), distinguished at Liegnitz (15 Aug) and Leutmannsdorf.

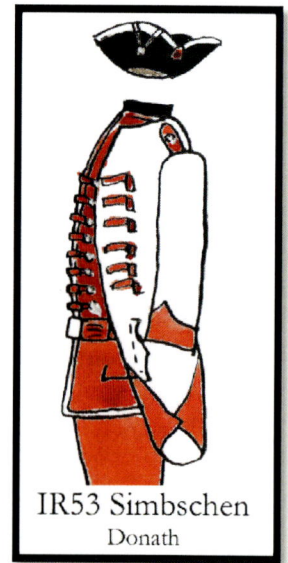

IR53 Simbschen Donath

Hungarian Fusilier Uniform

HEADGEAR: Black tricorn laced white and black cockade on the left. At the rear corners were bobs that often followed the facing colour. Some regiments had pom-poms. The sprig of green leaves was normally worn on campaign as the field sign. Simple cloth forage cap made from old coats was worn for manual work.

HAIR: Unpowdered queue at the rear, braids at the temple and moustaches for the rank and file.

STOCK: A red and a black fabric stock. For parades the regimental commanders agreed before on the colour of the neck-stocks.

COAT: White woollen collarless coat without lapels. The large square cuffs, turnbacks and button lace [Litzen] were in the facing colour. The shoulder strap was on the left shoulder only. The buttons were arranged one, two and three from the top of the coat, each had lace in the facing colour.

WAISTCOAT: Long skirted single or double breasted Hussar style waistcoat in the facing colour.

LEGWEAR: Breeches with Hungarian knots. Short black "Hungarian" boots instead of gaiters.

SASH: A barrel sash.

EQUIPMENT: White leather belt over the left shoulder carrying a black cartridge box with a small brass plate carrying the initials "MT" was worn on the right hip. A white waist belt carrying the bayonet and sabre was worn under the coat. A narrow white belt for the calfskin knapsack was worn over the right shoulder. The drum or egg shaped canteen had a brown leather strap.

SIDEARMS: The M1745 musket for fusiliers with bayonet until they were replaced by the M1754 musket. Black bayonet scabbard and grenadier sabre.

Hungarian Fusilier NCO Uniform

HEADWEAR: Sergeants had gold hat lace and corporals had white hat lace to their black tricorns.

UNIFORM: As Fusiliers.

SIDEARMS: Sergeants carried a halberd (or half pike) until 1759, a wooden cane suspended from a coat button and grenadier sabre. Corporals had silver hat lace, a halberd until 1759 and a grenadier sabre.

Hungarian Infantry Officers
[After Donath (1970) and Pengel (1982)]

Hungarian Fusilier Officer Uniform

HEADWEAR Tricorn laced gold or silver hat lace depending upon button colour.

STOCK: White cloth neck stock.

COAT: Similar cut to the other ranks but with finer cloth and no turnbacks. No shoulder strap.

SASH: Yellow and black silk sash.

FOOTWEAR: Short Hungarian boots in black leather.

SWAGGER STICKS: As German Fusiliers.

Chapter 7
Grenadiers

From 1757, the grenadiers were normally formed into battalions of 4 to 8 companies. These in turn were usually concentrated into the elite "Grenadier Corps." That varied throughout the campaign. Grenadiers deployed in 3 ranks. The grenadier company was divided into 4 platoons [pelotons]. When the grenadiers were present with their regiment, the artillery piece was placed within the 6 paces interval separating the battalion and the flanking grenadiers.

Table 8: Grenadier Company organisation in 1748
[3 officers, 6 NCOs, 4 Musicians 1 Pioneer, and 99 Grenadiers]

	Austrian Rank	Notes
Officers (3 officers)		
1	Hauptmann / Capitän-Lieutenant	Captain /Captain-Lieutenant (2nd Captain) [Kapitan in modern German]
1	Lieutenant / Oberlieutenant (from 1759)	1st Lieutenant [Oberleutnant in modern German]
1	Fähnrich / Unterlieutenant (from 1759)	Ensign/2nd Lieutenants [Unterleutnant in modern German]
NCOs (6 NCOs)		
1	Feldwäbel	Company Sergeant-major [Feldwebel in modern German]
4	Corporal	Corporal [Korporal in modern German]
1	Fourier	Company clerk (civilian)
Men (97 men)		
83	Grenadiere	Grenadier
2	Zimmerleute	Pioneer/Sapper
1	Fourierschützen	Officer's servants (batmen)
2	Tambour	Drummers
2	Pfeifer	Fifers
1	Fourier	Civilian clerk

Grenadier Uniform

HEADWEAR: Conical black or dark brown bearskin and a hanging bag in facing colour piped with button colour. Some had the metal plate or grenade badge in brass or white metal depending on button colour was introduced.

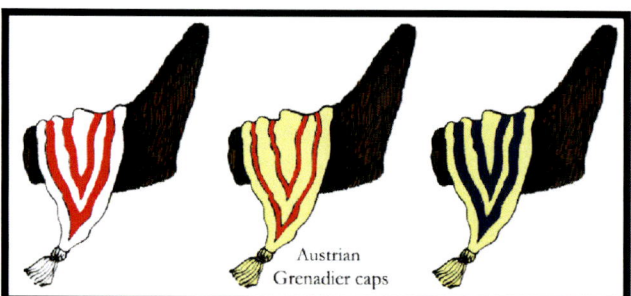
Austrian Grenadier caps

HAIR: Unpowdered queue at the rear and no rolls at the temple because these would not fit under the cap. Moustaches were worn by the rank and file.

UNIFORM: As parent regiment.

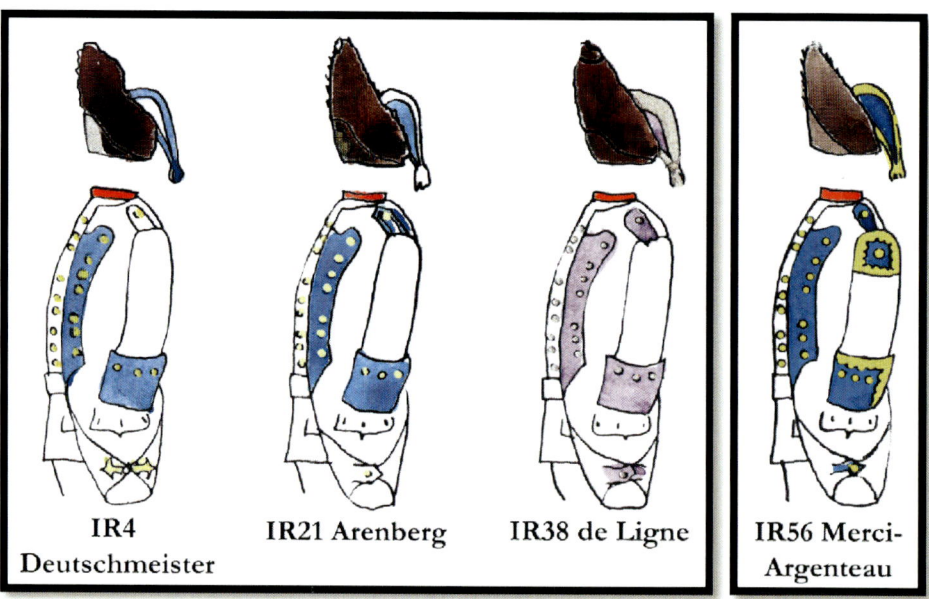

IR4 Deutschmeister   IR21 Arenberg   IR38 de Ligne   IR56 Merci-Argenteau

Grenadiers and Grenadier Drummer (far left)
[After Donath (1970) and Pengel (1982)]

EQUIPMENT: Grenadiers carried a small black cartridge box at the front and a brass match case on the front of the cartridge belt. This was a relic from the time when they carried hand grenades. Otherwise the uniform was as for Fusiliers.

SIDEARMS: Model 1754 musket for grenadiers. Grenadiers carried a sabre and bayonet.

Grenadier NCOs

HEADWEAR: Conical black or dark brown bearskin and a hanging bag in facing colour battens in gold or silver lace for sergeants and yellow or white lace according to the button colour.

UNIFORM: As Fusiliers.

SIDEARMS: Carried muskets, a wooden cane suspended from a coat button and a grenadier sabre. Corporals had silver hat lace, a musket and a grenadier sabre.

Grenadier Officers

HAIR: Unpowdered queue at the rear and no rolls at the temple because these would not fit under the cap. Officers were normally clean shaven.

COAT: Similar cut to the other ranks but with finer cloth and no turnbacks. No shoulder strap.

SIDEARMS: Silver mounted black wooden canes, straight bladed sword and often a musket instead of the Partizan.

Chatper 8
Infantry Weapons

Austria had widely separated firearms factories located in *Vienna, Wiener-Neustadt, Hainfeld* and *Steyr* in Upper Austria, and *Carlsbad* [*Karlovy Vary*], *Pressnitz* [*Přísečnice*] and *Weipert* [*Vejprty*] in Bohemia. In 1656, the state owned arms factory at *Wiener-Neustadt* just 50km south of Vienna was established with 100 armourers and gunsmiths from Liege and the Spanish Netherlands. This produced about 2,000 muskets per year. With the introduction of the flintlock musket, production in Steyr declined from 1700. In the 1720s, Anton Penzendener took over the arms factories in Steyr as well as controlled the production facilities in and around Vienna including Hainfeld after obtaining a guaranteed order from the government. [Hochedlinger (2003) 128-9]

On 12 May 1757 it was decreed that all gunsmiths and swordsmiths in the Hereditary Lands would work only for the Imperial Army for the duration of the war and their weapons would be delivered to the Vienna Arsenal in return for payment.

Muskets

In 1702, the regulations stated that the infantry were armed with flintlock muskets and that the old matchlock muskets would be handed in and scraped or modified. It was not until spring 1722 that a standardised musket was introduced with a socket bayonet. [Hochedlinger (2003) 127]

At the beginning of 1758, the Austrians had a reserve of 45,000 muskets mostly in poor condition. The Austrians were faced with another shortfall at the end of 1762 when they were threatened by a Turkish invasion. The largest contractor was *Anton Penzeneter* who had factories in Vienna, Steyr and Hainfeld that could produce 20,000 muskets per year.

Further muskets were obtained from Malines in the Austrian Netherlands, the Bishopric of Liege and from north-west Europe, in particular Thuringia. On 10 January 1758, *Major Franz de Piza* of the Wied IR who had been wounded at Moys on 7 September 1757 arrived in Brussels with the task to obtain 10,000 firearms and 6,000kg of gunpowder. [Duffy (2000) 320]

The stock of the musket was stained black or brown for fusiliers and polished walnut for grenadiers. The sling and lock covers were white. Austrian muskets suffered from wooden ramrods and the poor quality of coarse musket powder that was reluctant to ignite compared to the

Prussian musket powder. In 1745, iron ramrods were introduced. [Duffy (2000) 247]

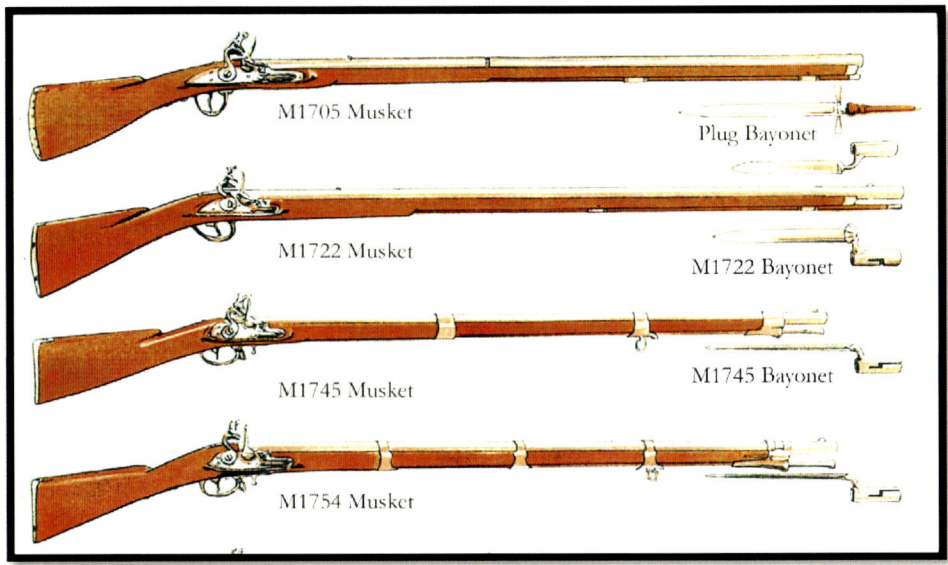

Austrian muskets 1705-1769
[After Ottenfeld (1895)] – Courtesy of Ken Trotman publishing]

M1722 *Ordinäre Flinte* [Musket]
This was the first standardised flintlock musket used by the Austrian Army and was based upon the musket produced by Suhl in Thuringia that had been supplied during the Spanish War of Succession. [Hochedlinger (2003) 127] It had a curved lock plate and the barrel secured by pins. The bayonet was a triangular pointed knife. The wooden ramrod was found to be a disadvantage in the Silesian War when the Prussians had replaced theirs with iron. From 1744, the wooden ramrod was replaced with iron.

M1745 Musket
This musket had a curved lock plate and the barrel was secured with steel bands instead of pins through the stock as in the previous pattern muskets. An iron ramrod was issued for the first time. The knife bayonet was retained.

M1748 Musket
The lock plate was now flat rather than curved and the bayonet was replaced by a triangular-section bayonet that had far superior penetrating power.

M1754 *Commissflinte* [Musket]

The musket was designed by a committee presided over by *General-Artillerie-Director Prince Liechtenstein* and incorporated the design features from the designs of *Johann Schmeid* and *Anton Penzeneter*. It had four bands that secured the barrel to the stock with a barrel of high grade iron bored in a single controlled operation. The trigger guard and butt plate was of iron rather than brass as in Prussian weapons. In October 1755, all infantry regiments in Bohemia were equipped with this new musket except KR1 Kaiser that had captured French muskets with their own pattern bayonet. [Duffy (2000) 246-7]

Table 9: Infantry small-arms.
[Ottenfeld (1898 rp 2003) II: 850-3]

	Calibre	Length	Weight	Rifling
Muskets				
M1722 Musket	18.3mm	157cm	4.8kg	None
M1744 Musket	18.3mm	151cm	5.0kg	None
M1745 Musket	18.3mm	150cm	4.86kg	None
M1748 Musket	18.3mm	150cm	5.0kg	None
M1754 Musket	18.3mm	151cm	4.9kg	None
Rifles				
M1759 Penzeneter Jäger Rifle	14.8mm	112cm	3kg	6 grooves
M1769 Jäger Rifle	14.5mm	105½cm	4.2kg	7 grooves
Grenade Pistol				
M1761 Grenade Pistol	74mm	32½cm	1.60kg	None

M1759 Penzeneter Rifle

The first Austrian Jäger was armed with forester rifles. These were replaced in 1759 by the M1759 Penzeneter Jäger Rifle of 14.8mm had a 79cm barrel and six rifle groves.

Infantry Swords

Grenadiers and Hungarian infantry carried swords. German Fusiliers did not receive swords until 1765.

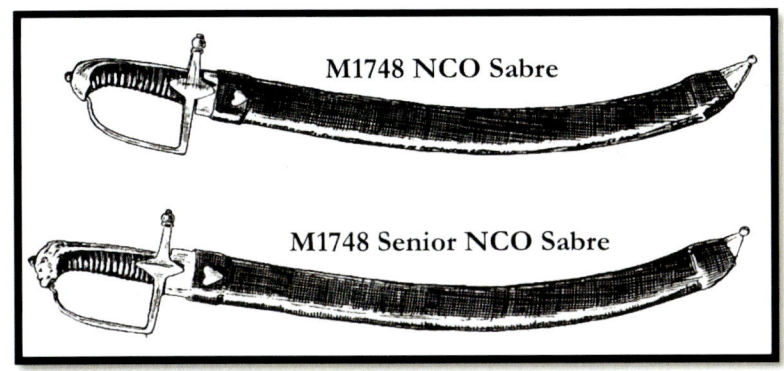

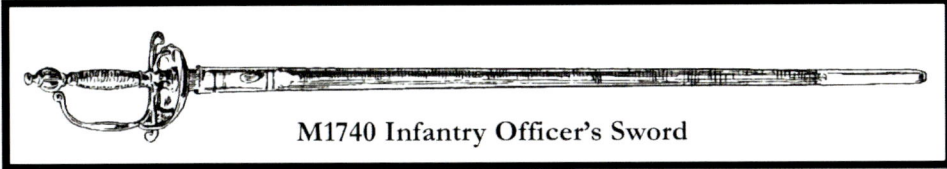

Table 10: Infantry sabres

The scabbards were constructed of wood and leather except the M1705 Grenadier Sabre had a leather scabbard.
[Ottenfeld (1898 rp 2003) II: 827]

	Bland length (cm)	Blade width (mm)	Weight (kg)
Grenadier Sabre			
M1705 Grenadier Sabre	75cm	40mm	1.3kg
M1748 Sabre for Senior NCOs	70cm	42mm	1.6kg
M1748 Sabre for NCOs	66cm	42mm	1.5kg
M1765 Grenadier Sabre	58cm	40mm	0.8kg
Hungarian Infantry Sabre			
M1748 Hungarian NCO sabre	66cm	42mm	1.5kg
M1748 Hungarian sabre	66cm	42mm	1.1kg
Light Infantry Sabre			
M1754 Jäger sabre	53cm	45mm	1.0kg
M1748 Büchsenmeister-Hirschfänger	58cm	40mm	0.9kg

Polearms

Polearms were in use until about 1759 to denote rank of Officers and NCOs.

NCOs who wore the same uniform as the ordinary soldier were equipped with a polearm and a stick. The latter was used to denote their rank and to beat their inferiors. The *Kurzgewehr* [half pike] was used by company NCOs until 1759 when they were exchanged for muskets. [Duffy (2000) 229]

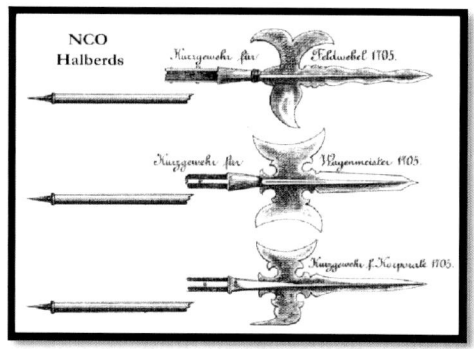

The partisans (or spontoons) had engraved heads and fringed depending upon rank. By 1759, officers were only armed with swords.

Spingstock des Fähnrich [ensign half-pike] was used by the *Fähnrich* [Ensign / 2nd Lieutenant] from 1748 when the colour [*Fahnen*] was permanently carried by the *Fuhrer* [a senior NCO].

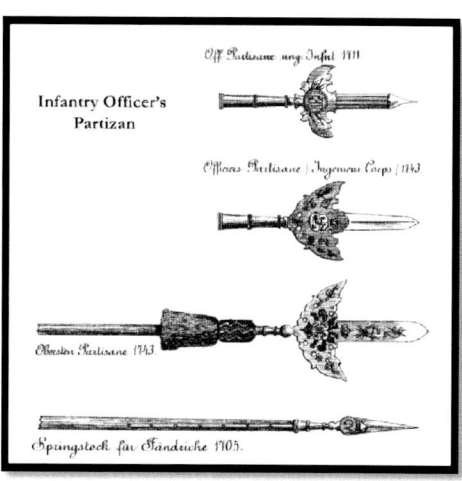

Couse der Hartschiere [Glaive] was a ceremonial pike with a flat engraved blade. By Maria Theresa's reign, the blade had been reduced to 56cm.

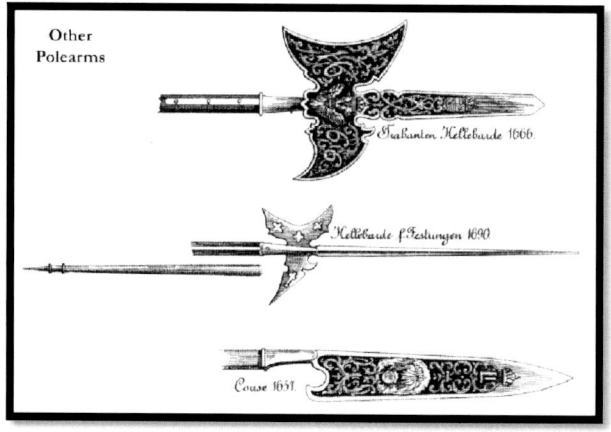

The *Copia* was a 3-6m long light lance used by Hussars.

The *Pikenierpike* was the standard issue long pike for pikemen.

Table 11: NCO and Officer pole-weapons.
[Ottenfeld (1898 rp 2003) II: 835]

	Blade length (cm)	Hilt length (cm)	Total length (cm)	Weight (kg)
NCO Halberds				
M1705 NCO halberd [Feldwebel Kurzgewehr]	45cm	155cm	200cm	2.2kg
M1705 Corporal halberd [Kurzgewehr]	45cm	155cm	200cm	2.0kg
Officer's Pole-arms				
M1705 Ensign spontoon [Springstock des Fähnrich]	15cm	190cm	205cm	1.0kg
M1711 Officer partisan [Partizan]	30cm	160cm	190cm	1.4kg
Ceremonial Pole-arms				
M1711 Hayduk guard axe [Leibhajdukenbeil]	24cm	120cm	144cm	1.6cm
M1666 Trebant halbard [Trebanten-Hellebarde]	60cm	190cm	250cm	3.0kg
M1690 Fortress halberd [Festungshellebarde]	100cm	160cm	260cm	2.2kg
M1740 Glaive [Couse der Hartschiere]	56cm	140cm	196cm	2.5kg
Obsolete Pole-arms				
Boarding axe [Enterbeil]	12cm	45cm	57cm	0.9kg
Half-pike [Enterpike]	29cm	200cm	229cm	1.6kg
Pike [Pikenierpike]	10cm	5-600cm	610cm	2.8kg

Chapter 9
Infantry Colours

Each regiment had one white *Leibfahne* (Colonel's colour) and three yellow *Ordinairefahne* (battalion colours) of painted silk. The flagpoles had a golden finial and were decorated with black and yellow spirals of cloth. The streamers were gold or silver depending upon the regimental button colour. In peacetime, each of the four battalions of had one colour with the I Bn carrying the Leibfahne. In 1756, the two 6 company field battalions carried two colours. The I Bn had the Leibfahne and one Ordinairefahne. The II Bn had two Ordinairefahne. The colours were carried by NCOs known as "Fuhrers."

Leibfahne

The **Leibfahne** was carried by the first battalion. The M1745 Leibfahne had a white field bordered with alternating white-yellow outer wavy triangles pointing inwards, and alternating red-black inner wavy triangles pointing outwards. The flag measured 180cm by 140cm. [Pengel (1982b) 66-69]

> **REVERSE** (left): The black Imperial double-eagle has a silver sword in his right hand and a golden orb in his left hand. The "*Lothringen-Toscanian*" arms on a halved shield and surmounted by a gold crown. The left has a red diagonal with three flying eagles in white on a yellow field. The right has five red circles and a blue circle with three white lilies. The initials of the "CF" [*Franciscus Corregans*] on the left wing and "IM" [*Imperator = Emperor*] on the right.

> **OBVERSE** (right): The Immaculate Mother of God in a white dress on a pale blue or white cloud, crushing a snake under her foot and surrounded by golden rays of light. Her cloak was royal blue with red lining. Emperor Ferdinand III declared her as the patroness of the army.

Regimentsfahne

The **M1745** *Regimentsfahne* had a yellow field with a border of alternating white and yellow outer waved triangles pointing inwards, red and black inner waved triangles pointing outwards. The flag measured 180cm by 140cm. [Pengel (1982b) 66-69]

> **REVERSE** (left): The black Imperial double headed eagle did not have a sword or orb. On the outstretched wings, there is an "M" (left) and "T" (right) standing for "Maria Theresa." On the chest of the eagle was the coat of arms of Hungary and Bohemia. The first quarter had four horizontal white lines on red field. The second quarter had a white cross of Lorraine surmounted by a golden crown on a red field. The right half had an upright lion with a crown on its head.
>
> **OBVERSE** (right): The black Imperial double-eagle had a silver sword in his right hand and a golden orb in his left hand. The "*Lothringen-Toscanian*" [Lorraine-Tuscan] arms on a halved shield were surmounted by a gold crown. The left has a red diagonal with three flying eagles in white on a yellow field. The right has five red circles and a blue circle with three white lilies. The initials of the "CF" [*Franciscus Corregans*] on the left wing and "IM" [*Imperator = Emperor*] on the right.

Chapter 10
Grenz Regiments

In 1538, Emperor Ferdinand I established the Militärgrenze along the Austro-Ottoman border that gave sanctuary and permanent settlement to the displaced Serbs escaping from Turkish rule. This chain of fortified villages, blockhouses and watch towers were garrisoned by settled military colonists. This placed them under Austrian military administration in exchange for freedom of religion and tax exemption in return for military service in the Austrian army. This also gave them license to raid and pillage Turkish settlements across the border.

The three Serb captaincies of *Koprivnica* in northern Croatia, Kreutz [*Križevci*] in central Croatia and *Ivanic* near Zagreb eventually formed the *Warasdin* [*Varaždin*] Command.

On 12 September 1683, a relieving force under Polish King Jan III Sobieski (1627-96) surprised and defeated the Turkish army at Kahlenberg near Vienna so ending the second Siege of Vienna. The victory at Zenta (11 Sept 1697) by Prince Eugene of Savoy marked the turning point in the Austrian struggle against the Turks. Following the Treaty of Karlowitz (26 Jan 1699), the Karlstadt [*Karlovac*], Warasdin [*Varaždin*], and Banat Grenz Commands were created. In 1702, the Slavonian border was established along the Save, Theiss and Maros Rivers, which were largely incorporated into Hungary in 1747.

General Adolf Buccow and, following his death in 1764, *András Reichsgraf Hadik von Futak* established the Transylvanian border, consisting of the Székely (1764) and Wallachian borders (1766). By 1770-87, the cordon sanitaire was complete and a system of permanent cantonments was installed.

Grenz Commands
- Karlstädt [Karlovac] Command (Croatian), 1699
- Warasdin [Varaždin] Command (Serbian), 1699
- Banat Command, 1699
- Slavonian Command, 1702
- Székely Command, 1764
- Wallachian Command, 1766

St. Georger.   Brooder.   Ottachaner.   Oguliner.
               Szluiner.   Creutzer.   Liccaner.

Grenz Infantry c1762

Grenz-Infantry-Regiment

A new administration presided over the Grenz and replaced the tribal structure in 1744, Prince Joseph Saxe-Hildburghausen reorganised the Grenz into regiments according to their districts.

- Karlstädt (1746) – *Likaner, Ottochaner, Oguliner* and *Szluiner* Grenz Infantry Regiments from Croat Roman Catholics.
- Warasdin (1745) – *Creutzer* and *St. Georg* Grenz Regiments from Croat Roman Catholics.
- Slavonian (1747) – *Broder, Grasdiscaner* and *Peterwardeiner* Grenz Infantry Regiments were formed from Greek Orthodox and Serbians. The *Czarkisten* Battalion was also from this area.
- Banal (1750) – *1ˢᵗ* and *2ⁿᵈ Banal* Grenz Infantry Regiments.

Further regiments were formed
- Transylvania [Siebenbürgen]
  - *1ˢᵗ & 2ⁿᵈ Székely* Grenz Infantry Regiments were formed in 1764 from Hungarians
  - *1ˢᵗ & 2ⁿᵈ Wallach* [1766] Grenz Infantry Regiments were formed from Greek Orthodox Wallachian in 1766.
- Banat of Temesvár (formed 1765-6)
  - *Deutsch-Banater* Grenz Infantry Regiment formed from German colonists in 1765. It was also known as *Tremescar Ansiedlungs Regiment* [Tremescar Colony Regiment]. In 1769, became IR71.
  - Renamed *Illyrisches-Banater* in 1766 and in 1769 became IR72. In 1775 amalgamated with the *Walakische* GIR to become IR72 *Walachisch-Illyrisches* Grenz Infantry Regiment

In 1748, Grenz-Infantry Regiments were re-organized into 16 fusilier companies, 2 grenadier and 2 rifle companies that formed two field battalions and a depot battalion. The company strength was 100 men. Each field battalion also had a squadron of 130 Grenz hussars attached. In times of war, the grenadier companies were detached from their parent regiments to serve in the Imperial Grenadier Corps.

Regimentsstab (regimental staff)
1ˢᵗ Battalion
    Bataillonsstab (battalion staff)
    1. *Grenadier* Company
    1.-6 *Füsilier* Companies
    1. *Schützen* Company (Rifle Company)

2nd Battalion
> *Bataillonsstab* (battalion staff)
> 2. *Grenadier* Company
> 7.-12. *Füsilier* Companies
> 2. *Schützen* Company (Rifle Company)

3rd Battalion (Depot)
> *Bataillonsstab* (battalion staff)
> 13.-16. Füsilier Companies

The "*Kleine Krieg*" [Small or Petty War] was an important part of the Seven Years War. The Austrians had an inherent advantage over the Prussians in the availability call upon large forces of skilled light infantry- the *Grenz-Infanterie* (Border Infantry), generally referred to as Croats, from the Military Border.

At Kolin (18 June 1757), Prussian infantry were unnerved by the unusual sound of 1-pdr battalion guns employed by the Austrian Grenz opposing them.

Grenzer c1760

The Grenz through their constant practice against the Turks were among the most experienced soldiers of the Austrian army. They fought primarily in open order, taking advantage of difficult terrain which favoured skirmishes. They played an important part in raids against enemy supply lines and outposts.

Croatian General Command – Karlstädt District

The *Karlstädt* [*Carlstadt*] Command was largely Croat in nationality and Roman Catholic. Ceded to France in 1809 and provided Napoleon's Croatian Léger.

GIR1 Likaner Grenz Infantry Regiment

The regiment was raised in 1746 around *Lika* and *Korbavja* in the south-east of the *Carlstadt General Command* with its staff stationed in Gospic. Also spelt *Liccaner* [now *Lica*]. In 1769, IR60 Carlstädter Likaner.

Inhaber
1746 *Graf Guicciardi*:
1754 *Benvenuto Graf Pestazzi*

Commander
1753 *Franz Friedrich von Vela*;
1758 *Max Pelican*

Campaigns
Seven Years War
In 1757, at Prague (6 May), Moys (7 Sept). In 1759 at Kunersdorf (12 Aug). In 1760 at Landeshut (23 June), storm of Glatz (26 July) and Liegnitz (15 Aug). In 1761, distinguished in the Loudon's storm of Schweidnitz. In 1762 in Saxony and the defence of Schweidnitz

Headwear	Black felt peak-less shako with dark blue with red centre tuft.
Coat	Red with green cuffs
Lace	Yellow
Shoulder strap	None
Waistcoat	Green with yellow lace
Barrel sash	Red and Green
Breeches	Red piped yellow

GIR2 Ottochaner Grenz Infantry Regiment

The regiment was raised in 1746 in the southern mountainous region of *Carlstadt General Command* with staff Otocac. Also spelt *Ottocaner* [now *Otocac*]. In 1769, IR61 Carlstädter Ottochaner

Inhaber
1746 *Graf Herbenstein*

Commander
1753 *Joseph Dietrich von Adelsfels*
1762 *Peter Vukassovich*

Campaigns
Seven Years War
In 1757, at Prague. In 1758 it captured a Prussian Bn at Liebau in Bohemia. In 1759, a detachment was distinguished at Kunersdorf and Meissen (2-3 Dec). In 1760, at Landeshut (23 June), the storm of Glatz (26 July) and Liegnitz. In 1761. one Bn was at Loudon's storm of Schweidnitz. In 1762, with the *Reichsarmee*.

Headwear	Black peak-less shako with dark blue with red centre tuft.
Coat	Red with light blue cuffs
Lace	Yellow
Shoulder strap	None
Waistcoat	Light blue with yellow lace
Barrel sash	Red and blue
Breeches	Red piped yellow breeches.

GIR3 Oguliner Grenz Infantry Regiment

The regiment was raised in 1746 in the Oguliner [now *Ogulin*] district of the *Carlstadt General Command*. In 1769, IR62 Carlstädter Oguliner.

Inhaber
1746 *von Dillis*

Commanders
1746 *Von Adelsfels*
1762 *Peter Vukassovich*

Campaigns
Seven Years War
In 1756, at Lobositz (1 Oct). In 1757, at Prague (6 May) and some were lost at Breslau. In 1759, at Kunersdorf (12 Aug) and Meissen (2-3 Dec). In 1760, one Bn was at Landeshut (23 June), the storm of Glatz (26 July) and Liegnitz (15 Aug). It suffered heavy losses at Troppau. In 1762, one Bn was involved in the defence of Schweidnitz.

Headwear	Black felt peak-less shako without tuft.
Coat	Dark blue with light blue cuffs and yellow lace
Waistcoat	Dark blue with yellow lace
Barrel sash	Red and yellow
Breeches	Red piped yellow

GIR4 Szluiner Grenz Infantry Regiment

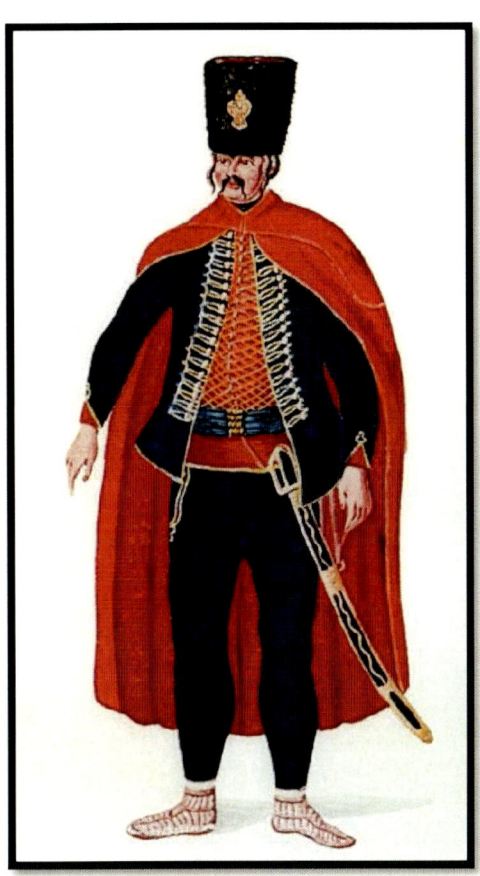

Raised in 1746 in the north east of *Carlstadt General Command*. In 1769, IR63 Carlstädter Szluiner.

Inhaber
1746 Graf Petazzi

Commanders
1746 von Kleefeld
1758 Peter Vukassovich
1761 Johann Kallinic
1762 Frhr. von Lezzeny

Campaigns
Seven Years War
In 1757, small detachments were involved in numerous small actions in Silesia and Bohemia. It fought at Kaltenberg. In 1759, the regiment was part of Hadik's raid on Berlin, at Maxen, Meissen and other small actions in Saxony. In 1760, once again in Saxony. Also presnt at Dresden, Torgau, and Strehla. In 1762, Wartenleben's Bn was distinguished at Pretzschendorf..

Headwear	Black felt peak-less shako with brass plate
Coat	Medium blue with red cuffs
Waistcoat	Red with yellow lace
Breeches	Medium blue piped yellow
Shoulder strap	None
Barrel sash	Blue and yellow

Croatian General Command – Warasdin District
GIR5 Kreutz Grenz Infantry Regiment

Raised in 1749 from the west of *Warasdin Military Command*.

Commander
1749 *Michael Frhr Mikassinovich Schlangenfeld.*

Campaigns
Seven Years War
In 1757, one Bn was at Prague (6 May) and another was at Kolin (18 June). The whole regiment surrendered at Breslau. In 1758-59, the regiment was reconstituted as detachments in Saxony. It was present at Meissen (2-3 Dec 1759). In 1760, *Major Eder's* Bn participated in Lacy's raid on Berlin, at Landeshut (23 June), Sebastiansberg, Leutmannsdorf and Peilau. In 1762 it was distinguished at Adelsbach, Burkersdorf and Reichenbach.

Headwear	Black felt peak-less shako with yellow tuft.
Coat	White with light green cuffs
Coat lace	Light green
Shoulder strap	Green
Waistcoat	Light green with white lace
Barrel sash	White and yellow
Breeches	White with no piping

GIR6 St. George Grenz Infantry Regiment

Raised in 1749 in the east of the *Warasdin Military District*. In 1769, IR65 Warasdiner St. George.

Commander
1749 *Joseph Brentano-Cimarolli*
1758 *Franz Frhr. Reise*

Campaigns
Seven Years War
In 1756 it was stationed in Bohemia. In 1757 it was present at Prague (6 May), Moys and one Bn was lost at the surrender of Breslau. In 1758 it operated in Bohemia and Saxony. In 1759, at Maxen (20 Nov) and Meissen (2-3 Dec). In 1760, part of Lacy's raid on Berlin, at Landeshut (23 June) and Stolpen. In 1761, part of *Loudon's* storm of Schweidnitz. In 1762, at Adelsbach (6 July), Burkersdorf (20 July) and Reichenbach.

Headwear	Black felt peak-less shako with no tuft.
Coat	White with dark green cuffs and dark green lace
Shoulder strap	Dark green
Waistcoat	Dark green with white lace
Barrel sash	White and yellow
Breeches	White with no piping

Slavonian District
GIR7. Broder Grenz Infantry Regiment

Recruited along the lower Sau (Sava) River in the *Slovonian General Command* in 1747. In 1769, IR Slavonisch Broder.

Inhaber
1747 *Antoine Graf Mercy d'Argenteau.*

Commander
1747 *Michael Prodanovich von Ussicka.*
1761 *Friedrich Graf Dönhoff*

Campaigns
Seven Years War
In 1756, one Bn was distinguished at Brandeis. In 1757, at Kolin (18 June), Moys (7 Sept) and one Bn lost at the surrender of Breslau. In 1760, at Landeshut (23 June) and the 2nd Bn was at Torgau (3 Nov).

Headwear	Black felt peak-less shako with yellow and light blue centre to the tuft.
Coat	Dark brown with yellow cuffs
Shoulder strap	Yellow
Waistcoat	Dark brown with yellow lace
Barrel sash	Yellow and dark brown
Breeches	Dark blue with yellow piping

GIR8. Grasdiscaner Grenz Infantry Regiment

Raised in 1747 in the *Slavonian General Command*. In 1769, IR67 Slavonisch Gradiscaner.

Inhaber
1747 *Frederic Daniel Frhr. von Saint Andre*

Commanders
1747 *Joseph Frhr. von Reid.*
1758 *Hieronymus Liubibratich von Trebinya*

Campaigns
Seven Years War
Fought at Kolin (18 June 1757). Distinguished at Passberg (1759) and Loudon's storm of Schweidnitz (1761).

Headwear	Black felt peak-less shako with
Coat	Dark blue with white round cuffs
Shoulder strap	White
Waistcoat	Dark blue with white lace
Barrel sash	White and yellow
Breeches	Medium blue with white piping

Grenzer c1760

GIR9. Peterwardeiner Grenz Infantry Regiment

Raised in 1747

Inhaber
1747 *Christian Frhr. von Helfreich*
1757 *Friedrich Frhr. von Lietzen*
1762 *Christian Frhr. Wulffen*

Commander
1747 *Franz Joseph Eberstädt*
1758 *Carl Graf Lanjus von Wellenburg*

Campaigns
Seven Years War
In 1757 it was distinguished at the storm of Schweidnitz. In early Summer 1758, the regiment operated around Olmütz. In 1759, one Bn was at Kunersdorf and another at Maxen (20 Nov). The regiment was present at Landeshut (23 June 1760) and Loudon's storm of Schweidnitz. In 1762, distinguished at Saubsdorf in Silesia.

Headwear	Black felt peak-less shako with no tuft.
Coat	Dark brown
Coat lace	None
Cuffs	Yellow
Waistcoat	Light blue
Waistcoat lace	Red
Breeches	Light blue with red piping
Shoulder strap	Red
Barrel sash	Red and yellow

Banal District

Ceded to France in 1809 and provided Napoleon's Croatian Léger.

GIR10. 1st Banal Grenz Infantry Regiment

Raised in 1750 by *Franz Leopold Graf Nádasdy* in his capacity as Ban of Croatia from the south-western part of the *Banal Military Command*. In 1769, IR69 1st Banal Regiment.

Inhaber
1750 *Franz Leopold Graf Nádasdy*

Commanders
1750 *Johann Frhr. von Zedtwitz*
1762 *Friedrich Göhlichich*

Campaigns
Seven Years War
In 1757, at Prague (6 May), Kolin (18 June), Moys (7 Sept) and the storm of Schweidnitz. In 1758, at the siege of Neisse and at Gruenberg. In 1759, at Meissen (2-3 Dec 1759). The regiment was heavily engaged in Saxony. In 1761-2, in Saxony and Silesia.

Headwear	Black felt peak-less shako with white and black centre to the tuft.
Coat	Dark blue
Coat lace	Yellow
Cuffs	Yellow
Waistcoat	Dark blue
Waistcoat lace	Yellow
Breeches	Red with yellow piping
Shoulder strap	None
Barrel sash	Dark blue and red

GIR11. 2nd Banal Grenz Infantry Regiment

Raised in 1750 by *Franz Leopold Graf Nádasdy* in his capacity as Ban of Croatia from the south-western part of the *Banal Military Command*. In 1769, IR69 2nd Banal Regiment.

Inhaber
1750 *Franz Leopold Graf Nádasdy*

Commanders
1750 *Christoph Frhr. von Orssich*
1761 *Peter Graf Sermage.*

Campaigns
Seven Years War
In 1756, at Lobositz (1 Oct). In 1757, at Prague, and Kolin (18 June). In 1758-59 it was participated in Welmina (Reschni-Auje), Nollendorf and Gottleuba. In 1759, at Meissen, Buchau and Strehla. In 1760 it was heavily enagaged in Saxony and fought at Torgau (3 Nov). In 1761-2 it was involved in numerous small enagements.

Headwear	Black felt peak-less shako with no tuft.
Coat	Blue
Coat lace	Red and yellow
Cuffs	Red
Waistcoat	Red
Waistcoat lace	Yellow
Breeches	Red with yellow piping
Shoulder strap	None
Barrel sash	Red and black

Tschaikist Bn
The Tschaikist battalion was raised in 1740 as a naval river protection force operating along the river borders of Slavonia and Syrmia against smuggling and the spread of the bubonic plague. In 1763 it was redeployed to Titl between the Danube and Theiss Rivers. In 1764, the battalion establishment was increased from two to four companies. The Tschaikist battalion operated small oared and sail gunboats [Imperial *Freikriegsschiffe*] armed with one heavy and several smaller guns. Tschaika gunboats (Slavic for "lapwing") were similar in construction to the Nassadist flat-bottomed gunboats built in Hungary. *Komárom* [*Komorn*] Fortress in Hungary became the key strongpoint, naval shipyard and repair facility. It was renamed the Titler Grenz-bataillon in 1769.

Grenz Uniform
The Grenz-Regiments initially wore a variety of regional costume or folk dress that was replaced by Hussar type military uniforms after 1750.

HEADWEAR: Brimless shakos

TUNIC: Karlstädt (Croat) and Banal Grenz-Regiments wore hussar-style coats with pointed cuffs. Warasdin (Serb) and Slavonian Grenz-Regiments were distinguished by round cuffs.

GREATCOATS: Red cloaks

LEGWEAR: Tight-fitting Hungarian breeches,

FOOTWEAR: short Hungarian boots or laced Opanka sandals.

SIDEARMS: Infantry muskets and cavalry sabres.

In 1767, the Grenz adopted the *Casket* and the single breasted

Chapter 11
Jäger Corps and Freikorps

Deutsches Feld-Jäger Korps

Raised in 1756 from 50 game keepers [Jäger] volunteered by the nobility. Worked closely with the Pioneers and at the immediate call of the General Staff. Increased to 2 coys in 1758 and 10 coys in 1762. This very successful unit paid the price of the close association with Lacy who fell out of favour with Kaunitz. It suffered a low desertion of only 374 men and only 24 men killed in action. Disbanded in 1763. [Duffy (2008) 439]

Headwear	Black leather helmet with upright front.
Coat	Light blue grey [pike grey] with green collar and cuffs.
Waistcoat	Light blue grey [pike grey]
Turnbacks	Light green
Buttons	White
Shoulder strap	None

Jäger Casket c1762

Commander
1757 *Captain Richard Christian*
1760 *Major Carl Enzenberg*

Campaigns
Seven Years War
Distinguished in the defence of Dresden (1760), Nieder-Arnsdorf and Torgau.

German Freikorps

The Freikorps unlike the Prussians was not widely used by the Austrians due to large number of inexpensive light troops from the Grenz.

Green-Loudon Freikorps

In 1757, *Oberst Gideon Ernst Freiherr von Loudon* led light troops with great effect against the Prussians in Bohemia. Loudon had first considered setting up grenadier units to support the Croats in the autumn of 1757 when he was actively engaged in small war operations, and he noted that the Croats' general inability to fight in formed bodies was a great disadvantage, as it prevented the successful conclusion of numerous promising situations.

In April 1758, *Loudon* formed a force of grenadiers that was officially called *Freiwilligen-bataillon Loudon*. Unofficially they became known as the *Loudon-Grenadiere* or *Grün Loudon*. These were raised mostly from foreigners and Prussian deserters.

The letter of *GFWM Loudon* dated 11 May 1758 is interesting as he mentions in passing that he had already once before attempted to set up a corps of 1,500 grenadiers from the Croats without success. He also stated that he chose green instead of white uniforms because this would relieve the regular task of cleaning them.

The Staff [11 men] consisted of:
    1 *Obrist-Lt*, 2 *Obristwachtmeister*, 1 *Regimentsquartiermeister*, 1 *Auditor*, 1 *Caplan*, 1 *Regiments Feldscheer*, 1 *Proviantmeister*, 1 *Wagenmeister*, 1 *Bataillon Feldscheer*, 1 *Profos cum suis*

The battalion had six companies of 154 men.
    1 *Hauptmann*, 1 *Ober-Lt*, 2 *Unter-Lts*, 2 *Feldwäbel*, 1 *Fourier*, 1 *Feldscheer*, 6 *Corporals*, 3 *Tambours*, 1 *Pfeiffer*, 12 *Gefreiten*, 2 *Fourierschützen*, 2 *Zimmerleute*, 120 men.

In early March 1759, *Loudon* in his *Pro-Memoria* [Memorandum] to *Empress Maria-Theresa,* he requested permission to form a second battalion and describes the use of the battalions in detail, together with sources of manpower etc. The report dated 13 March 1759 of FM *Graf Harrach* (President of the *Hofkriegsrat*) and *Graf Neipperg* (Vice-President of the *Hofkriegsrat*) to the *Queen-Empress* supported the establishment of a second battalion. On 16 March 1759, *Loudon* was directed by *Graf Harrach* to set up the second battalion.

Green Loudon Freikorps c1760

Pom-Pom	None
Coat	Light green coat and waistcoat
Lapels & cuffs	Red
Turnbacks	Light Green
Buttons	Yellow
Shoulder strap	Light green
Legwear	Light green with black gaiters and shoes.

Commander
1758 *Major Richard Chevalier d`Alton*
1763 Disbanded

Campaigns
Seven Years War
These fought throughout their existence under Loudon. In 1758, they were distinguished at Arnsdorf. In 1759 it fought well at Kunersdorf. In 1760 they were distinguished at Landeshut and were then involved in covering the retreat after Liegnitz. In 1761, they participated it manoeuvred in Silesia, and in 1762, they took part in the defence of the redoubts at Leutmannsdorf. It was disbanded in 1763.

Von Böck Freikorps

von Böck Freikorps
c1760

FML Beck in Silesia raised a battalion in 1759. Better disciplined than *Loudon's Green Grenadiers*. Disbanded in 1763. Also known as the *Voluntaires Silesiens* or *Voluntaires Beck*. During the Seven Years War, the battalion lost to desertion 871 men and 253 killed. [Duffy (2008) 439]

Coat	Dark green with light green waistcoat
Lapels & cuffs	Buff or straw yellow
Turnbacks	Light green
Buttons	White
Shoulder strap	None
Legwear	White breeches and black gaiters.
Sidearms	Grenadier sabre

Commander
1759 *Major Rochus Montagutti*

Campaigns
Seven Years War
Fought in numerous small actions. Then in *Corps Beck* at Reichenberg.

Deutsches Frei-Jäger-Korps Otto

It was raised in 1759 by *Lieutenant* [later *Major*] *Michael Otto* in his native Saxony. It had 1 company of Jäger and a 100 strong detachment of Chevauleger and hussars. This was the nearest Austrian equivalence to a Prussian Freikorps.

Deutsches Jäger Korps Otto c1760

Commander
1759-63 *Michael Ludwig Otto*

Headwear	Tricorn hat with white edge
Coat	Green long tailed coat with black cuffs and lapels. Yellow buttons
Waistcoat	Green double breasted waistcoat
Legwear	Green, white or yellow breeches and black gaiters. Chevauleger wore heavy cavalry boots.
Sidearms	The Jäger were armed with rifles

Campaigns [Wrede (1901) III: 912]
Seven Years War
Seven Years War Engaged in many actions as part of the Reichsarmee in Saxony and Thuringia involved mainly in the Kleine Krieg. In 1760 it suffered many casualties.

Company de Lacy
Formed by Lacy in 1758.

Inhaber
1758 *Lacy*
1763 Disbanded

Headwear	Casket with brass front plate bearing a black doubled headed eagle and black tipped red plume.
Lapels & cuffs	Yellow with white Litzen
Turnbacks	White with yellow tab
Buttons	White
Shoulder strap	Yellow

Netherland Freikorps

Freikorps Bethüne
Raised 1757 with 3 coys; increased in 1762 to 8 foot coys (950 men) and 7 horse coys (450 men). The infantry wore tricorn hats, white or pale straw-yellow coats with red facings, white waistcoat, breeches and gaiters.
Inhaber
1757 *Obrist-Lt Jacques de Bethüne*;
1760 *Obrist-Lt Frhr. Drais*

Freikorps Le Bon
Raised 1762 with 3 foot coys (560 men) and 1 squadron each of hussars and Jäger zu Pferde (230 mounted men).

Freikorps Kühlwein
Raised 1762 with 7 foot coys (1,000 men) and 2 hussar sqns (220 men).

Korps Wurmser
Raised 1762 with 1 Bn (about 800 men) and 1 hussar regiment (about 850 men).

Chapter 12
Engineers

The French and the Dutch were the leading experts in fortress construction during the second half of the 17th century. *Sebastian Vauban*, chief engineer to Louis XIV, created a professional engineer corps with a comprehensive education and pay structure. He produced an almost complete chain of fortress to secure the borders of France. In comparison, the Habsburg fortresses at this time were created by architects and draftsmen. Engineers were poorly respected within the Austrian Army despite their important contribution to the war and were treated very badly by noble born field officers. Despite all the influence and power of Liechtenstein, he had not been able to win over the nobles to the artillery and there was little prospect for the engineer.

> *An aristocrat with an income of 30-40,000 florins will be unwilling to consign his son to a corps where courage and hard work are your own reward.* [Armfeld, 20]

Gribeauval, Jean Baptiste Vacquette de (1715-89) transferred into Austrian service in 1758 with the rank of *Obrist* (Mar 1758) then *GFWM* (1 Nov 1758), *Marechal de Camp* in the French Army (17 July 1762), *FML* (22 Oct 1762 in his absence). [See Chapter 12]

Harsch, Ferdinand Philipp Graf (1704-92) was appointed Deputy-Director of Engineers (1 Feb 1760) upon the death of *Deputy-Director Bohn*. *Inhaber* of IR50.

Engineer Corps

Engineering Academies were finally set up by *Prince Eugene* in 1718 in Laimgrube near Vienna, another in Brussels and Prague. The first principle of the Academy near Vienna was the Italian born *Leander Anguissola* (1653-1720) who was the Vienna city engineer. The deputy-director from 1733 was the court mathematician *Giovanni Giacomo Marinomi* (1676-1755). Between 1718 and 1743, more than 300 pupils attended the Academy. The *Savoyische Ritterakademie* [Savoy Noble Academy] was opened in 1749 and gave increasing attention to science and engineering. After the death *Marinoni* in 1755, his Engineering Academy was merged with the Savoy Noble Academy to create a new state-run school of engineering in 1756. In 1760 it was fully militarised under the corps of engineers. The best pupils entered the corps of engineers with the others joining the infantry and cavalry. [Hochedlinger (2003) 124 and 306-7]

Engineer to 1761

In 1732, two Engineer Brigades were founded in the Austrian Netherlands in Brussels and Mecheln each with only 30 officers. On 6 February 1747, *Maria Theresa* agreed to a proposal of the council of war to form engineer corps consisting of four brigades (German, Hungarian, italian and the Dutch). *Prince Charles of Lorraine*, Governor General of the Netherlands, was appointed the Director General of Engineers. *Paul Ferdinand Bohn* became his Deputy Director. Each brigade consisted of an Obrist and some engineers. From 20 July 1747, engineer officers were now equal to those in the field army. They were responsible for the inspection of fortresses and defensive works and drew up plans for new arrangements. Officers were also assigned to field armies to organise the construction of field works. In 1758, only 30 engineer officers out of 98 were capable of active service.

During the War of Austrian Succession, the campaigns were in areas devoid of many fortresses. Following the loss of Silesia, it became important to protect Bohemia. The critical gateways were east of Prague along the Elbe towards Silesia. In the 1750s, Olmütz in Moravia was considerably reinforced and successfully withstood a Prussian siege in 1758. [Hochedlinger (2003) 308]

This situation changed at the beginning of the Seven Years War when the theatre of operation shifted to Prussian Silesia and Saxony. The Austrian Army had no suitable officer that could have lead the siege of Schweidnitz which had been blockaded in September. In consequence, *Maria Theresa* decided to entrust the *Brigadier Riverson* sent by the French king with this job. This humiliated the Austrian engineer corps.

In 1758 sent Louis XV sent *Jean Baptiste Gribeauval* to the Austrians and was promoted to *GFWM* [brigadier-general]. He undertook radical steps to improve the Austrian engineer corps. In 1759, *Obrist Bohn* died and was succeeded by *GFWM Ferdinand Philipp Harsch*.

1761 Engineer Corps Uniform

Major 1761 — Lieutenant 1761

HEADWEAR: Tricorn with thin gold border.
STOCK: Black cloth neck stock.
COAT: Light blue long tailed coat with carmine red small collar, cuffs and lapels. Gold aiguillette was worn on the right shoulder on parade.
WAISTCOAT: Light blue waistcoat with 12 buttons, gold buttonholes and border.
LEGWEAR: Carmine red breaches were worn on parade. Leather or white cloth breeches were worn in the field.

In January 1760, *Unterlieutenant Nicolas-Joseph Cugnot* (1725-1804) of the Austrian engineer corps who later designed the steam driven artillery transporter,[1] wrote a letter of resignation to the *Hofkriegsrat* [Austrian War Ministry] that claimed the Austrian engineer corps was spoilt by favouritism. [Duffy (2000) 189-90] On 20 January 1760, *Gribeauval* and *Prince Charles of Lorraine* [Director of Engineering from 1758] were tasked to investigate these claims.

Gribeauval's report dated 2 February informed the *Hofkriegsrat* that the faction riven engineer corps had overlooked merit in promotions, was little regarded by the rest of the army and the engineers were poorly trained. He proposed that the aged officers be purged and that Austria should set up a Corps of Sappers to provide a skilled labour force for the engineers as well as draughtsmen and cartographers.

> *"I [Gribeauval] do not know what system has been followed ... But I can assert that a number of officers, even among those how have reached high rank, are devoid of the aptitudes needed for the profession and have never been equal to meeting their responsibilities. In junior officers who have ideas and abilities that*

---

[1] **Nicolas-Joseph Cugnot** (1725-1804) was a 2nd Lt in the Austrian Engineer Corps who resigned in 1760 and had started thinking of steam locomotion in the 1750s. In 1765, *Gribeauval* and *Duc de Choiseul* supported his experiments and in March 1770 the first working model of a steam driven artillery tractor was demonstrated. The full scale prototype was ready in June 1771 but both *Duc de Choiseul* and *Gribeauval* were not in office so no further funds were available. [Duffy (2000) 189-191]

fit them for a successful career in the high reaches of their profession, but they nearly all complain of having been passed over repeatedly for promotion, and a number of them – including some of the best – up to 12 or 15 times. They say that it is because of favouritism.

The [Austrian] Engineer Corps is filled with factions, intrigues and cabals without end, but little evidence of enthusiasm, and not at all ambition. Most of them have shunned effort on the excuse that their goodwill has been abused – and here they are not entirely wrong. However, by dint of making promises (which we are admittedly not sure we can keep), and by pricking their vanity, we have begun to bring them into a better way of thinking."

[Engineers] are treated in a way that is harsh and even indecent. A number of generals know only how to convey their orders in terms of threats, holding out the prospect of confinement in chains as if they were criminals. When an officer, no matter how junior, is dispatched on some mission, he invariably takes a couple of engineers with him to see to the hard and uncongenial parts of the task; they load the blame on them if it anything goes wrong, but take the credit if turns out well. Just look at the state of the engineers to the middle of any campaign – you will see that most of them have lost their horses and money, and that they are worn out by exhaustion and maltreatment.

The soldiers and even their officers ... just wish to exist until nightfall or the end of their duty overtakes them. New troops arrive, and with them a new crop of difficulties. The remedy must be to raise companies of sappers that will be distributed along the works to support the efforts of the soldiers and they can carry out demonstrations for the benefit of the officers of the engineer corps, which at the moment has neither the structure nor the training for this kind of warfare.

The engineers should employ four or five auxiliary draftsmen... A further body of civilian cartographers could be attached to the General Staff to produce maps of terrain and campsites... As this will be their sole occupation, they will soon acquire the necessary accuracy and facility – something that is impossible for an officer who can attend to such work for only a little while before he has to pass on. They will not be coming under fire, and will therefore have no right to military honours, which will put a limit to the cost and to any inconvenient pretensions on their part. They will be given rank equivalent to junior officers and be respected in their work by the soldiers and the local peasants. We have 80 such people in France [the Ingénieurs Géographes] divided into 1st and 2nd class."

[*Gribeauval* (2 Feb 1760), Dresden]

It is interesting to note that many of his observations could be made of most armies including Britain, France, Prussia and Russia. This report was sent to the newly appointed General Pro-Director of Engineering, *GFWM*

Harsch who had been in office for only a few days. The proposals received his full support and in his report added that the education of engineers should be modelled on that of France.

On 27 February 1760, *Maria Theresa* decided that the Gumpendorf School was to be put under the complete control of *Deputy-Director of Engineers, GFWM Harsch*. [SS (2011) 264]

On 7 March, *Prince Charles of Lorraine* replied defensively against the accusations of *Gribeauval* on the poor state of Austrian Engineering on his directorship. He defended the late *Deputy-Director Paul Ferdinand Bohn* by writing:

> "*A Deputy-Director* [of Engineering] *is not like a regimental commander, who has the opportunity to become acquainted with every officer detail. He must rely on reports….. All advancement of this kind* [ignoring seniority] *engenders resentment even among senior officers, for this part of human nature to have an inflated and unrealistic opinion of oneself.*"
> [*Charles of Lorraine* to *Maria Theresa* (7 Mar 1760) from Duffy (2000) 295]

The latter was a pointed reference to *Gribeauval's* intervention in a couple of promotions. Despite this, he broadly supported the positive recommendations of both reports but requested that *Gribeauval* name the individuals at fault. [Duffy (2000) 293] Both agreed that *Unterlieutenant Cugnot* should be permitted to resign. [Duffy (2000) 190]

Miner Corps

In 1716, *Prince Eugene v. Savoy* formed the first permanent Miner Company for siege work against the Turks. Under *Maria Theresa*, two Miner companies attached to the artillery had 119 officers and men. Every company was commanded by a major and a captain with 3-4 sergeants. The demands on the men were very high and they should come from a mining background with robust health. The officers had to master mathematical knowledge, above all that which dealt with the mining and fortress construction.

It should not be forgotten the achievement of the Miners in the defence of the Schweidnitz Fortress between the 4 August and 9 October 1762. The commander of the Miner-Detachments was *Captain Joseph Pabliczek*. By a series of mines and countermines, he waged a desperate fight under the glacis of the fortress. The fortress surrendered only after the explosion of a powder magazine.

Sapper Corps

In the 2 February report by *GFWM Jean Baptiste de Gribeauval* recommended the need for companies of sappers based on his first-hand experience of the inadequate field fortifications set up in the defence of Dresden in the winter of 1759-60. On 16 February 1760, Gribeauval submitted his proposals to the *Hofkriegsrat*. On 23 March, the *Hofkriegsrat* informed the infantry regimental commanders that a *Sappers Corps* of three companies was being set up. They were expected to send a draft of 4 men who were healthy, strong and of at least 174cm. One of these men was to be literate and suitable for promotion to NCO. By 20 April, the strength had growb to 186 men with another 60 on their way. They were stationed in Dresden under *Major Johann Bechardt* where they remedied the failings of the field defences. [Ottenfeld (1895) I: 169-70] According to Duffy (2000: 298), the Corps of Sappers was the most important contribution by *Gribeauval* to Austrian engineering service.

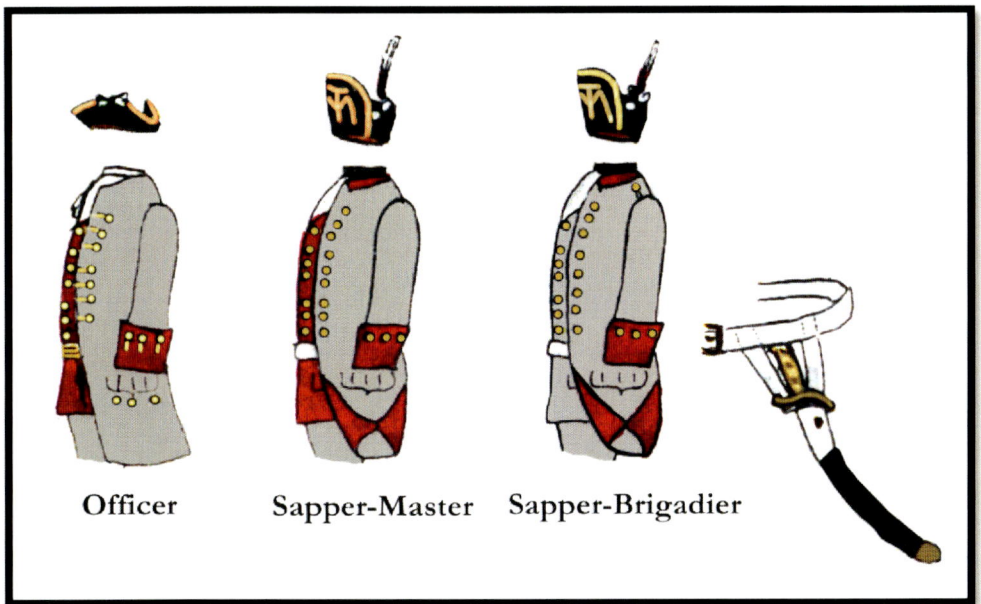

Officer   Sapper-Master   Sapper-Brigadier

Commander
1760-63 *Major Johann v. Bechard*

The Sapper Corps had originally of 3 companies each split into six brigades of 12 men plus 4 volunteers.

> **Staff** – *Hauptmann* [Captain], *Oberlieutenant* [1st Lieutenant], *Unterlieutenant* [2nd Lieutenant]
> **NCOs** – 3 *Sappeurmeister* [sapper master], 6 *Brigadiers* [NCOs]

Men – 32 *Obersappeur* [senior sappers], 36 *Untersappeur* [junior sappers], 36 *Gemeine* [men], 1 drummer.

Equipment – 50 picks and shovels, 10 long coils of ropes, 6 large picks, 4 great saws, 14 large cauldrons, and 42 flasks.

Sapper, 1762

Uniform
HEADWEAR: Black casket with brass border and "MT" cipher, white over red feather.
STOCK: Black cloth neck stock.
COAT: Cornflower blue long-tailed coat with poppy red collar and cuffs.
DISTINCTIONS: Black tricorn with gold edge and black leather cavalry boots.
LEGWEAR: Cornflower blue breeches, black gaiters and black shoes.
ARMOUR: In sieges, Sappers wore leather clothing, cuirass and a steel helmet.
EQUIPMENT: The Sapper had a carbine with a long bayonet, a short robust sabre as well as a cartridge pocket with 45 cartridges.

The newly raised *Sappers Corps* established their reputation during the storming of Glatz on the 26 July. *Captain Jakob Enghel* of the Sappers was awarded the Military Order of Maria Theresa [2] and their commander, *Major Bechardt* was promoted to *Obrist-Lieutenant* [Lieutenant Colonel] when he had the honour given to him by *FZM Loudon* to take the 33 captured colours to Vienna [Duffy (2000) 298]. Glatz surrendered on 26 July. [Duffy (1985) 119]

---

[2] The Knight Cross and Grand Cross of the **Maria Theresa Military Order** [*Militär-Maria-Theresien-Orden*] was founded on 18 June 1757 for meritorious and valorous acts by commissioned officers.

In 1761, the corps was reduced to 2 companies. At the defence of Schweidnitz, 10 out of the 24 sappers were killed with a further 11 wounded. Three officers were distinguished with the Maria Theresa Order. In 1772, the Sapper Corps was combined with the Engineer and the Miner Corps.

Sappers c1762

Pontoneer Corps

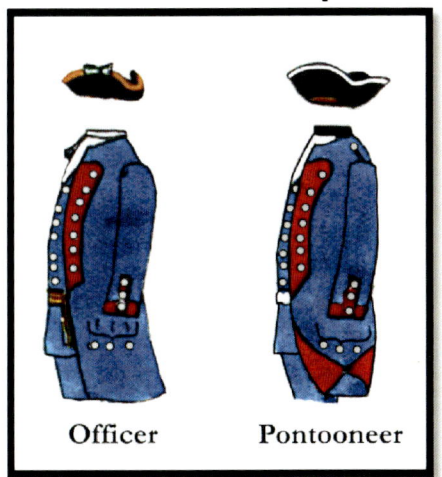

Officer   Pontooneer

In 1749, two companies of Pontoneer were formed. In the Seven Years War, the first company commanded by *Bruckhauptmann J.C. Paumann* was attached to the Austrian Main Army. The second company commanded by *Bruckhauptmann P.S. Gastl* was attached to the *Reichsarmee*.

HEADWEAR: Black tricorn with silver edging and silver cockade strap.

STOCK: Black cloth neck stock.

COAT: Ultramarine blue long-tailed

coat with poppy red green lapels, Brandenburg cuffs with three buttons and turnbacks. White buttons.

WAISTCOAT: Ultramarine blue double breasted waistcoat.

DISTINCTIONS: Officers had black tricorn with gold edge.

LEGWEAR: Ultramarine blue breeches, long white stockings and black long cavalry boots.

Pontooneer, 1762

EQUIPMENT: White leather sword belt.

SIDEARMS: Grenadier sabre with brown leather scabbard. Brass metalwork.

Each company had:
Staff–
1 Bruckhauptmann,
1 Brucklieutenant,
1 Feldpoter,
1 Felscher [surgeon],

Men–
1 Feldwebel [sergeant major],
2 corporals,
1 drummer,
15 pontoneers,
10 *Wasserer* [watermen]

Equipment –
60 wooden pontoons.
40 copper pontoons.

Pioneer and Pontoneer NCO in 1762
[Ottenfeld (1895)]

Pioneer Corps

The pioneers performed their work at the head of the marching columns, removing obstacles, repairing roads, and building bridges. *GFWM Lacy* in 1757 suggested that such a unit should be formed. The pioneers were recruited from skilled craftsmen, miners, fishermen and carpenters.

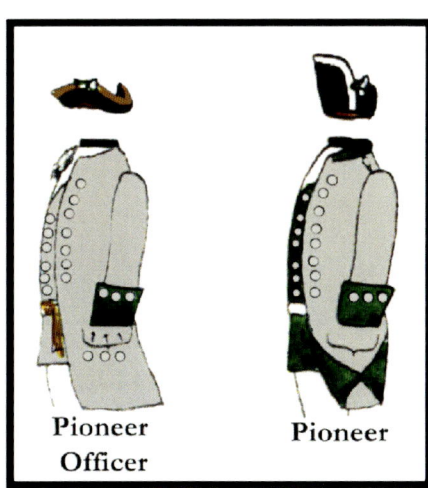

Commanders
1758 *Major Carl Frhr v Schmidburg*
1759 *Obrist-Lt. Carl Ludwig Montmartin*
1760 *Major Carl Frhr v Enzenberg*
1763 Disbanded

In January 1758, the Pionierkorps had four companies of 111 officers and men. Each Company had one corporal and 50 Jäger attached. The

Jäger were recruited from hunters and gamekeepers.

Pioneer Company (1758)
Staff – 1 Captain, 1 1st Lt, 1 2nd Lt,
Men – 1 *Feldwebel* [sergeant major], 4 Corporals, 3 drummers, 25 *Zimmerman* [sappers] and 76 pioneers.

In 1759, each company was increased to 261 officers and men.
Staff – 1 Major, 1 Adjutant, 1 *Proviantmeister* [quartermaster], 1 *Feldscher* [surgeon], 1 *Unterfeldscher* [assistant surgeon], 2 *Fourier* [clerks],
Four Companies – 1 Captain, 1 1st Lt, 1 2nd Lt, 1 *Feldwebel* [sergeant major], 4 Corporals, 3 drummers, 25 *Zimmerman* [Sappers] and 125 men.

Pioneer, 1762

Uniform
HEADWEAR: Plain black casket.
STOCK: Black cloth neck stock.
COAT: Cornflower blue long-tailed coat with apple green collar, cuffs and turnbacks.
DISTINCTIONS: Black tricorn with gold edge and black leather cavalry boots.
LEGWEAR: White breeches, black gaiters and black shoes.

Campaign
The pioneers proved themselves in 1758 at Hochkirch, in 1760 before Glatz, in 1761 at the siege and storming of Schweidnitz. The bridges were assigned to the Pontoneer. In 1762, the corps was dissolved by Kaunitz for reasons of cost against the will of the generals for cost reasons. An independent pioneer regiment was not again formed until 1867.

Jean Baptist Vicomte de Gribeauval (1715-89)

He was born in Amiens on 15 September 1715 to a middle class Amiens lawyer. In 1732 aged of 17, he entered the garrison Artillery School at La Fère where *Bernard Forest de Belidor* (1698-1761) famous for being the founder of the science of modern ballistics taught him. In 1735, he was promoted into the officer only *Corps-Royale de l'Artillerie* as *officier-pointeur* [Hennebert (1896) 22]. His first campaign experience was with the siege train in the 1743 csmpsign in Germany. Between 1744 and 1747, he served in Flanders with Marshal de Saxe's army and obtained the rank of *commissionaire ordinaire* in the *Corps-Royal de l'Artillerie*.

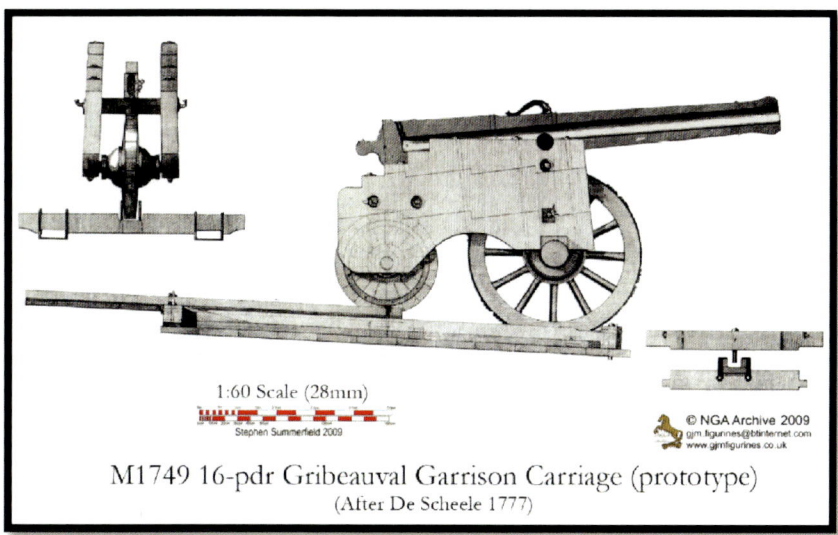

M1749 16-pdr Gribeauval Garrison Carriage (prototype)
(After De Scheele 1777)

In September 1748, whilst in the garrison duty in Cherbourg, he proposed a design for a Garrison Carriage based upon a modified naval carriage. In March 1749, the M1749 Garrison Carriage was constructed in Douai and tested. [Fave (1871) IV: 144-5, Dollaczek (1887) 335] This had a medium sized solid trailing wheel on the fixed trail end of the high carriage cheeks which were built-up in a series of steps. This carriage had the advantage of being able to fire over flat embrasures that were less likely to be damaged by fire from enemy siege guns. *Vallière* decided not to accept it for production so only one prototype was constructed. [Naulet (2003) 128-130

In 1752, he was promoted to *Capitaine* [First Captain] in the Corps of Miners [Nardin (1982) 44]. In 1755, still only a Captain in the Corps of Miners, he was chosen by *Comte Marc-Pierre D'Argenson,* the Secretary of State for War, to study the condition of the borders and fortresses whilst collecting a scale model of the new M1754 3-pdr Prussian battalion gun design by Dieskau. On 20 May 1755, *Gribeauval* arrived in Berlin and on 29

May was given full access to the battalion gun. On 9 June, *Gribeauval* returned to Paris with the model that had previously been requested. In his official report of the mission to Prussia, he liked the manoeuvrability but lacked sufficient hitting power. [Nardin (1981) 43-7]

The Royal Ordinance dated 20 January and February 1757 introduced one "Swedish" 4-pdr and one M1757 1-pdr Rostaing gun to each French infantry battalion. *Gribeauval* attributed the humiliating defeat at Rossbach (5 Nov 1757) to regimental artillery. [Hennebert (1896a) 30]

Soon after the outbreak of the Seven Years War, *Empress Maria Theresa* realised that the Austrian Corps of Engineers lacked expertise especially in conducting sieges so asked the *King of France* for the services of good engineer officers. As a consequence in June 1757, *Gribeauval* was promoted directly to *Lieutenant-Colonel* from *Capitaine* and was sent to join the French Ambassador, *César Gabriel de Choiseul, Duc de Praslin* (1712 –1785) in Vienna. *Gribeauval* had been recommended for this task by his patron *Victor-François, 2nd Duke de Broglie* (1718-1804) According to Passac (1816: 100) *Gribeauval* and *Choiseul-Praslin* advised *Marie Theresa* that the ineffectual *FM Charles-Alexander of Lorraine* (1712-80) should be replaced by *FM Leopold Joseph Daun* (1705-66) as commander in chief of the Austrain Army. As a consequence, *Daun* was able to arrange the transfer of *Gribeauval* to Austrian service.

Sapper Equipment and sidearms in 1760

On 10 March 1758, *Gribeauval* entered the Austrian engineers as *Obrist*. At the camp of Neustadt in Moravia, he demonstrated the latest siege methods. He initiated a much needed investigation and reform of Austrian engineering. [Duffy (2000) 293] He was attached to *FZM Ferdinand Philip Graf Harsch*. *Gribeauval* supervised the failed Austrian siege of Neisse whose key position was the modern star-fort named Fort Preussen during which he was promoted to *GFWM* [equivalent to brigadier-general in the British Army]. [Duffy (2008) 148-9]

In October 1759, *Gribeauval* wrote a memorandum in response to *Daun's* request for the improvement of the defences of the City of Dresden in order to allow it to hold out for 10-12 days. By 26 October, the programme of works had been agreed and the Saxon envoy, *Graf Flemming*, consented to provide the necessary labour, transport and materials. However, these were inadequate due to the parapets being excavated from inside rather than outside the works so making it an obstacle for the defenders as well as a high parapet.

In July 1760, he was attached to *FZM Gideon Ernst Frhr. von Loudon* who at the start of the campaign was in Königgrätz. *Gribeauval* was the technical director of the siege of Glatz which started on 21 July and was taken by storm on 25 July. [Duffy (1985) 119]

Whilst still in the Austrian Army in March 1762, *Gribeauval* was instructed by *Dubois* of the War Office to answers to his 18 questions on the Austrian Artillery. The answers so pleased *Duc de Choiseul* (who was Secretary of State for War) that *Gribeauval* was breveted *Marechal de Camp* [equivalent *FML* in the Austrian or to major-general in the British Army] on 25 July 1762. A copy of the Warrant dated 25 July 1762 can be found reproduced in Hennebert (1896) 511-2.

In August 1762, *GFWM Gribeauval* commanded the technical troops in the defence of Schweidnitz. Under his was *Major Frierenberger* of the artillery, *Obrist-Lt Steinmetz* of Engineers, *Captain Pabliczek* of miners and *Captain Eghels* of the newly raised Corps of Sappers. [Duffy (2008) 369-271]

Whilst still in captivity on 26 October 1762, *Gribeauval* was promoted by the Austrians to *FML* [equivalent to major-general in the British Army] and awarded the Grand Cross of the Maria-Theresa Order.

The Peace of Hubertusburg was signed on 15 February 1763 that ended the Seven Years War. In April 1763, he was released from captivity and returned to Vienna where he informed the Austrians that he wished to return to French service.

In 1763, *Gribeauval* wrote a response to the French Secretary for State for War's requesting suggestions for the improvement of the French Artillery. In April 1764, *Duc de Choiseul* chose *Gribeauval* as an *inspecteur de l'artillerie*. In 1764, he undertook tests at Strasbourg on the 18 calibre guns produced by Maritz II. [Picard (1906) 71-73]

However, on 24 December 1770, the *Choiseul* Ministry ended at the height of the Falklands Crisis between Britain and Spain. *Gribeauval* had lost all his political support with *Choiseul's* fall from grace. On 26 January 1771, *Marquis de Monteynard* (1720-82) replaced *Choiseul* as Secretary of State for War and decided to revert to the Vallière system by the Decree of 23 August 1772.

On 10 May 1774, *Louis XV* died. On 3 October 1774, the committee of the four Marshals of France after reviewing both systems recommended the re-instating of Gribeauval System. In 1 January 1777, *Gribeauval* was appointed *First Inspector-General of the Artillery* and died on 9 May 1789. [Fave (1871) IV: 160].

See (Dec 2010) *Smoothbore Ordnance Journal* Issue 2 for fuller biographical details on *Gribeauval* and a discussion of his Garrison Carriage.

Chronology of the Seven Years War

1756

29 Aug	Prussia invades Saxony.
9 Sept	The Saxon Army retires to the fortified camp at **Pirna**.
1 Oct	*Frederick* with 28,000 Prussians defeats 33,354 Austrians under *Browne* in the very hard fought battle of **Lobositz**.
7-19 Oct	Austrians fail to relieve Pirna and the Saxons surrender on 17 October.

1757

18 Apr	Prussia invades Bohemia.
21 April	The 14,550 Prussians defeat 15,000 Austrians at **Reichenberg**.
6 May	The 65,000 Prussians defeat 60,000 Austrians outside **Prague**.
18 June	At the battle of **Kolin**, the Austrians with 33,160 infantry, 18,630 cavalry and 154 guns defeat 34,500 Prussians.
24 June	**Prague** is relieved by *Daun* after the Prussian army withdraws.
14-15 July	The Austrians under *Macquire* and *Arenberg* storm and capture **Gable**. The Prussians surrender after running out of water.
23 July	The Austrians bombard the Lusatian textile town of **Zittau** and are forced to surrender after much of the town is destroyed by fire.
26 July	The French with Austrians from the Netherlands defeat the *Duke of Cumberland* during their invasion of Hanover at **Hastenbeck**.
13 Aug	The Austrians defeat the Prussians at **Landshut (1st)**.
16 Aug	*Frederick* declines to give battle at **Zittau**.
5 Sept	Austrians capture **Bautzen.**
7 Sept	The smaller Prussian Army of 13,300 commanded by *Winterfeldt* is defeated by 32,549 Austrians at **Moys**. *Prince Karl von Bevern* takes command of the remnants of the Prussian Army and *Winterfeldt* dies of his wounds the next day.
16-17 Oct	*Andreas Hadik* commanding 3,400 Hussars, Grenz, Dragoons and Infantry plus 2x 3-pdrs and 4x 6-pdrs raids **Berlin**
26 Oct	The Autrians start their siege of **Schweidnitz** by digging their first parallel.
5 Nov	The 30,000 French, 9,900 *Reichsarmee* and 3,850 Austrians are defeated by 22,500 Prussians under Frederick at **Rossbach**.
12 Nov	Prussian garrison in **Schweidnitz** surrender after the storm by the Austrians.
22 Nov	The 83,000 Austrians under *Daun* attack and defeat the prepared defences west and southwest of **Breslau** manned by 38,700 Prussians under the *Bevern*.
5 Dec	*Frederick* with 39,000 men severely defeats 50,000 Austrians and Saxons at **Leuthen.**
6-21 Dec	The Prussians besiege and capture of **Breslau**.
23-28 Dec	Then the Prussians besiege and capture of **Liegnitz**.

1758	
16 April	**Schweidnitz** is retaken by the Prussians.
15 May-2 July	The Austrian garrison of **Olmütz** with 8713 men and 324 artillery pieces holds out against the 8,000 Prussians supported by 31 guns, 16 mortars and 14 howitzers.
5-8 June	*Andreas Hadik* with 2,000 grenadiers, Hungarian Fusiliers and Grenz raids the Elbe.
28 June	The Austrians attack the Prussian supply train of 4,000 wagons bound for Olmütz at **Gundersdorf**.
30 June	The Austrians ambush the Prussian supply train at **Domstadtl**, capturing of 3,000 Wagons, 2,328 men and 58 officers. This forces *Frederick* to abandon his siege of Olmütz.
23 July	*Daun* forces *Frederick* to give up the planned attack on the Austrians at **Königgrätz**.
31 July	The *Reichsarmee* in fieldworks at **Sebastiansberg** beat off the Prussians of *Asseburg* after a 5 hour action.
9 Aug	Prussians complete their retreat from Bohemia.
25 Aug	*Loudon* captures the small fortress of **Peitz** garrisoned by Prussian militia.
14 Oct	*Daun* defeats *Frederick* at **Hochkirch**. The Prussians lose 9,907 men and 104 of their 140 pieces.
26 Oct-7 Nov	The Prussians defenders of **Neisse** are able to hold off the Austrians.
6-9 Nov	Prussian successful defence of **Dresden**
1759	
26 Mar	*GM Knobloch* drives an Austrian detachment out of **Saalfeld**.
26 Mar	A Prussian detachment of 16 officers and 700 men under *Oberst Dieringshofen* is forced to surrender at **Greiffenberg**.
15 Apr	A Bn of IR57 Andlau, a Bn of IR16 Königsegg with 1,000 Grenz and Hussars stand behind fieldworks and abattis at **Sebastiansberg** until their right flank is turned by the Prussians who capture 1,500 men, 2 colours and 3x 3-pdrs.
27 July	Unsuccessful attack by *Jahnus* against the Prussians commanding the heights at **Gottesburg**.
28 July	*Jahnus* attack at **Friedland** is beaten off and so is forced to return to Bohemia.
1 Aug	The 6,000 Austrians at **Goldenöls** under *Wolfersdorff* make a successful escape to Trautenau.
5 Aug	The Prussians withdraw from Leipzig.
12 Aug	The Austro-Russians defeat *Frederick* at **Kunersdorf**.
13 Aug	The Prussians withdraw from **Torgau**.
18 Aug	The small isolated Prussian garrison of **Grünberg** attempts a breakout and Land-Bn de Rege is caught at **Lawaldau** by two squadrons of the Bethlen Hussars.
21 Aug	The Prussians withdraw from **Wittenberg**.
27 Aug	Prussians retake **Wittenberg**
27 Aug	The small Prussian garrison of **Peitz** surrenders to one of *Hadik's* detachments and so opens up the direct route to the Elster.

30 Aug	**Torgau** is stormed by the Prussians and the next day the *Reichsarmee* garrison marches out.
4 Sept	Austrians liberates **Dresden**
8 Sept	The 14,000 Austro-Imperial Army is defeated by 5,000 Prussians at **Zinna** (Torgau).
13 Sept	Prussians recapture **Leipzig**
21 Sept	Action of **Meissen**
21 Sept	The Austro-Imperial under *Hadik* defeat a much smaller Prussian force at **Korbitz (Löthain)**.
25 Sept	The 2,500 Austrians under *Vela* is destroyed by Prince Henry at **Hoyerswerda.**
20 Nov	The 42,000 Austrians under *Daun* capture 13,000 Prussians under *Frederick von Finck* at **Maxen**.
29 Oct	The 16,000 Austrians is defeated by 15,000 Prussians at **Pretzch.**
2-3 Dec	The Austrians defeat the Prussians under *Diericke* at **Meissen**.

1760

20 Feb	*Czettau* is captured with his copy of Frederick (1753) *General-Principia vom Kreige* at **Kossdorf.**
15 Mar	Skirmish of **Leoschütz** and **Neustadt.**
23 June	*Loudon's* Austrians defeat a Prussian Corps at **Landeshut (2nd)**.
13-22 July	Prussians lay siege and destroy large parts of the **Dresden** but fail to take it.
26 July	Austrians capture the fortress of **Glatz**.
15 Aug	*Loudon* ignorant of the disposition of *Frederick* is severely defeated at **Liegnitz**.
20 Aug	The Austro-Imperial is defeated by the Prussians at **Strehla**.
17 Sept	Prussian indecisive attack upon **Kunersdorf, Hochfiersdorf** and **Bögendorf** lasts 16 hours.
27 Sept	The Prussians are forced to abandon **Torgau**.
2 Oct	The Prussians withdraw from **Leipzig.**
2 Oct	Attack by the *Reichsarmee* on the Prussians under *Hülsen* at **Dobien** that after a stubborn resistance withdraws into Brandenburg.
9-12 Oct	Austrians and Russians occupy **Berlin**.
13 Oct	Saxony is liberated after the Prussians withdraw from **Wittemberg.**
27 Oct	HR Széchenyi and Stab Dragoons is soundly defeated by the Prussian *Avant-garde* under *Kleist* at **Radis**.
29 Oct	The small Corps of Reid escape destruction at **Düben**.
2 Nov	*Kleist* with 2,000 Prussian cavalry clashes with 10 squadrons of Austrian cavalry of *Brentano* at **Staupitz.**
3 Nov	The 55,640 Austrians under *Daun* is defeated by the 48,000 Prussians in Frederick at **Torgau**.
7 Nov	The battered rearguard commanded by *Brentano* is able to resist the Prussian *Avant-garde* long enough to permit *Lacy's* artillery to withdraw to safety at **Meissen**.

	1761	
	15 Aug	4,000 Austrian cavalry attack a smaller Prussian cavalry force at **Kloster-Wahlstatt**.
	5 Sept	Near action at **Ronnenburg** where the Prussians under *Seydlitz* decide to call off their attack upon the *Reichsarmee*.
	9 Sept	*Frederick's* fortified camp of **Bunzelwitz** is surrounded but is not attacked.
	1 Oct	In less than four hours *Loudon* commanding 15,200 Austrians and 800 Russian Grenadiers storms and takes **Schweidnitz**.
	5 Nov	Skirmish of **Lerchen-Berg** and **Rosswein** where the Austrians defeat Prussian *Freikorps* in field defences.
	Dec	Reduction of the Austrian Army due to financial problems.
	1762	
	5 May	Russia renounce the Austrian alliance.
	12 May	Action of **Döbeln**.
	14 June	Skirmish of **Lampersdorf**.
	20-21 June	Skirmish of **Heidersdorf**.
	6 July	Battle of **Adelsbach**.
	7 July	Skirmish of **Johannesburg**.
	9 July	*Catherine* deposes her husband *Peter III* and Russia terminates the Prussian alliance.
	21 July	**Burkersdorf** Engagement.
	2 Aug	The Austrians defeat the Prussians at **Teplitz**.
	9 Aug	Prussians start their siege of **Schweidnitz**.
	16 Aug	Austrian relief of Schweidnitz is halted by Prussian *General Bevern* at **Reichenbach**.
	18 Sept	Second Austrian relief of Schweidnitz.
	29 Sept	Skirmish at **Dittersbach**.
	9 Oct	Prussians finally capture the fortress of **Schweidnitz** when the magazine blows up.
	29 Oct	The Austrians are defeated by the Prussians at **Freiberg**.
	7 Nov	Skirmish of **Lands-Berg**.
	30 Dec	Austro-Prussian peace negotiations opened at Hubertusburg.
	1763	
	10 Feb	Treaty of Paris between Britain and France.
	15 Feb	Treaty of Hubertsberg officially ends the Seven Years War leaving Silesia in Prussian hands.

Glossary

German	Definition
Abteilung	Detachment or section
Achselspangen	shoulder strap
Aufgebot	Provincial levies of cavalry and militia for home defence
Bataillon	battalion
Batterie	battery
Erblande	Hereditary Lands including Austria and Bohemia. This does not normally include Hungary.
Eskadron / Schwadron	squadron
Fähnrich	senior officer aspirant
Feldmarschall (FM)	*Field Marshal* would command an army. [Austrian and Prussian] and was equivalent to British *general* or a French *Marechal de France*
Feldmarschall-Lieutenant (FML)	[Austrian] *Major-general* who commanded a division of several brigades
Feldwebel	sergeant major
Feldzeugmeister (FZM)	[Austrian] *Lieutenant-general* of Infantry who would command a wing of an army.
Festung	fortress
Festungsartillerie	Fortress artillery
Freiherr [Frhr.]	Baron
Gala-Uniform	full dress uniform
gefallen	killed in action
General de Cavallerie (GdC)	[Austrian] *Lieutenant-general* of Cavalry who would command a wing of an army.
General der Infanterie (GdI)	[Prussian] Equivalent to a British *lieutenant-general*.
General der Kavallerie (GdK)	[Prussian] Equivalent to a British *lieutenant-general*
Generalfeldwachtmeister (GFWM)	[Austrian] Also known as *General de Bataille* commanded a brigade equivalent to a French *brigadier* or British *brigadier-general*
Generalkriegskommissariat	General War Commissariat: The supreme administrative authority for military finances (recruiting, budgets, mustering, inspections and audits).
General-Lieutenant (GL)	[Prussian] Equivalent to a British *major-general*.
General-Major (GM)	[Prussian] Equivalent to a British *brigadier-general*
Generalstab	general staff
Generalstabschef	chief of staff
Geschütz	gun
Geschützbatterie	gun battery
Graf	Count
Grenz	Border troops.
Grenz	border
Handschuhe	gloves

German	Definition
Hauptmann / Rittmeister	Infantry captain / cavalry captain
Herzog	Duke
Hofkammer	Ministry of Finance and the supreme agency for the administration of the crown lands.
Hofkriegsrat	Ministry of War (1556-1848)
Husar	trooper of hussars
Husarenregiment	hussar regiment
Infanterie	infantry
Infanterieoffizierssäbel	infantry officers' sword
Infanterieportepee	infantry sword knot
Ingenieuroffiziere	Engineer officer
Ingenieuroffizierskorps	Engineer Officer Corps
Inhaber	Also *Oberstinhaber, Regimentsinhaber* or *Chef* [from the French]. The proprietor of a regiment
Innerösterreich	Inner Austria including Styria, Carinthia, Carniola, Gorizia-Gradisca, Trieste and Fiume.
Insurrectio	Hungarian feudal levy.
Jäger	rifleman or rifle unit
k.k. [*kaiserlich-königlich*]	Lierally imperial-royal and was used to describe the Habsburg state and army (1745-1867).
Kadett	Cadet
Kamaschen	gaiters
Kämmerer	treasurer (court appointment)
Kanonier	gunner
Kavallerie	cavalry
Kavallerieoffizierssäbel	cavalry officers' sword
Kavallerieportepee	cavalry sword knot
Kompagnie	company
Kontribution	Military Tax in the Austro-Bohemian lands from 1620.
Korporal	corporal
Kragen	collar
Landrekrutenstellung	Provincial recruitment established in the 1680s in Austro-Bohemia where each province had a quota of recruits to provide supplemented by voluntary recruitment in times of war.
Leibgürte	barrelled sash
Lieutenant / Leutnant	lieutenant
Major	major
Mantel	greatcoat
Markgraf	Count
Militärgrenze	Military Border was a defence screen stretching from the Adriatic to present-day Romania to protect against Turkish incursions.
Mörser	mortar
Obrist	Colonel [*Oberst* in modern German]

German	Definition
Obrist-Lieutenant	Lieutenant-Colonel [*Oberst-Leutnant* in modern German]
Offizier	officer
Patronentasche	ammunition pouch
Pionier	pioneer
Pistolentasche	holster
Reich	Holy Roman Empire
Reichsarmee	Imperial Army was only mobilised in the case when *Reichskrieg* was declared by the Imperial Diet
Reichsgeneralfeldmarschall	Imperial Field Marshal was the highest rank in the *Reichsarmee*
Reichshofkanzlei	Imperial Chancellery in Vienna (1559-1806)
Reichskreig	Official war declared by the Imperial Diet and binding on the whole *Reich*.
Reichsstandschaft	Imperial Diet
Reichstände	Imperial Estates
Reithose	riding trousers
Rosspartie	Artillery transport
Sappeurkompagnie	sapper company
Staatkanzler	State Chancellery responsible for foreign policy established in 1742
Staatsrat	Council of State was the supreme advisory body for domestic affairs established in 1761
Stände	Estates
ungarischer Hose	Hungarian trousers
Unteroffizier	non-commissioned officer
Vorderösterreich or Vorlande	Further Austria: Habsburg possessions in southern Germany of Breisgau
Wachtmeister	Sergeant major
Zeughaus	Arsenal
Zug	platoon

References

Adye RW and Eliot GW (1813 rp2010) *Bombardier and Pocket Gunner*, Ken Trotman Ltd.

Albertini-Handschrift (1762) *Dessins des Uniformes des Troupes I.I. et R.R. de l'Année 1762*, [Depicts 102 different uniforms.]

Anon (1885) *Mittheilungen des k. k. Kriegs-Archivs*, Vienna

Anon (1974) *Austrian Uniforms of the Seven Years War*, Greenwood and Ball Publication.

Asprey R.B. (1999) *Frederick the Great: The Magnificent Enigma*, History Book Club,

Becher, Johann Christian (1757-60) *Wahrhaftige Nachricht derer Begebenheiten, so sich in dem Herzogthum Weimar by dem gewaltigen Kriege Friedrichs II., Königs von Preußen, mit der Königin von Ungarn, Marien Theresen, samt ihren Bundesgenossen zugetragen*, Weimar

Brauer, Hans (1926-62) *Heeres-Uniformbogen*, Uniformbogen No. 7 and 23, Berlin.

Schmidt-Brentano, Antonio (2006), *Kaiserliche und k.k. Generale (1618-1815)*, Österreichisches Staatsarchiv [Austrian State Archive.]

Camille Rousset, (1868) *Le comte de Gisors 1732–1758, Études Historiques*, Paris

Chandler, D. (1976) *The Art of War in the Age of Marlborough*, B.T. Batsford Ltd, London.

Cogniazzo J. (1780) *Freymüthiger Beytrag zur Geschichte des österreichischen Militärdienstes* [Frank remarks to the history of Austrian military service], Frankfurt and Leipzig.

Dawson AL & PL, and Summerfield, S (2007) *Napoleonic Artillery*, Crowood Press.

Dawson DL and Summerfield S (2008) *French Artillery to 1824: Gribeauval, AnXI System and Manual*, DP&G Publishing.

Dolleczek, Anton (1896 rp1970) *Monographie der k.u.k. österr.-ung. blanken und Handfeuer-Waffen, Kriegsmusik, Fahnen und Standarten seit Errichtung des stehenden Heeres bis zur Gegenwart*, Kreisel & Groger, Vienna, [reprinted by Akademische Druck- u. Verlagsanstalt, Graz]

Donath, Rudolf (1970) *Die Kaiserliche und Kaiserlich-Königliche Österreichische Armee 1618-1918*, Simbach

Dorn, G. and Engelmann, J.
- (1989) *The Infantry Regiments of Frederick the Great 1756-63*, Schiffer Publishing Ltd.
- (1989) *The Cavalry Regiment of Frederick the Great 1756-63*, Schiffer Publishing Ltd.

Duffy, Christopher
- (1974) *The Army of Frederick the Great*, David & Charles, London
- (1975 rp 2006) *Fire and Stone: The Science of Fortress Warfare 1660-1860*, Castle Books, Edison, NJ.

- (1977) *The Army of Maria Theresia*, David & Charles, London.
- (1985) *The Fortress in the Age of Vauban and Frederick the Great 1660-1789*, Routledge and Kegan Paul, London
- (1996) *The Armies of Frederick the Great*, 2nd Edition, Emperor's Press
- (2000) *Instruments of War*, Volume I of the Austrian Army in the Seven Years War, Emperor's Press
- (2003) *Prussia's Glory; Rossbach and Leuthen*, Emperor's Press.
- (2008) *By Force of Arms*, Volume II of the Austrian Army in the Seven Years War, Emperor's Press
- (2009) *The Wild Goose and the Eagle: A Life of Marshal von Browne 1705-57*. Tricorne Press, UK.

Drant, Will & Ariel
- (1965) *The History of Civilisation*, Volume IX: The Age of Voltaire, Simon and Schuster, New York
- (1967) *The History of Civilisation*, Volume X: Rousseau and Revolution, Simon and Schuster, New York.

Dwyer, P.G. (2000) *The Rise of Prussia 1700-1830*, Longman, London

Frederic, Jacques Andre (1759) *Des Troupes de sa Majesté Imperiale Royale comme elles se trouvent effectivement l'an 1759*, Augsbourg

Funcken, Liliane and Fred (1976), *The Lace Wars*, Volume 1 & 2, Ward Lock Ltd, London

Graeffer, C. (1797) *Oesterreichischer Militaer-Almanach: für das Jahre 1797*, Vienna

Grant, Charles Stewart (1987) *From Pike to Shot 1685 to 1720*, Wargames Research Group.

Grosser Generalstab (1901). *Die Kriege Friedrichs des Großen. Dritter Teil: Der Siebenjährige Krieg 1756–1763, Volume 1 Pirna und Lobositz*, Berlin.

Hausen, Heinrich Freiherr von (1861) *Allgemeine Militär-Encyclopädie*, Volume IV, p182

Haythornthwaite, Philip
- (1994a) *The Austrian Army 1740-80: Vol 1 Cavalry*, Osprey Publishing
- (1994b) *The Austrian Army 1740-80: Vol 2 Infantry*, Osprey Publishing
- (1995) *The Austrian Army 1740-80: Vol 3 Specialist Troops*, Osprey Publishing

Hennebert
- (1896a) *Gribeauval, lieutenant-général des armées du roy*, Paris
- (1896b) "Gribeauval: premier inspecteur général du corps de l'artillerie. Quelques pages inedites relatives a son se jour en autriche," *Revue d'Artillerie*, **47**, 598-623.

Hochedlinger, Michael (2003) *Austria's Wars of Emergence 1683-1797*, Longman.

Hollins, David (2005) *Austrian Frontier Troops 1740-98*, Osprey Publishing

Kemp A (1980) *Weapons and Equipment of the Marlborough Wars,* Blandford Press. Dorset.

Knötel, R. (1890-1921) *Uniformkunde,* Plates: IV:43; V:10; V:30; V:51; VI:12; VI:13; VI:44; XII:4 and XIV:59.

Langins J. (2004), *Conserving the Enlightenment: French Military Engineering from Vauban to the Revolution,* The MIT Press, London

MacLennan, Ken (2003) "Liechtenstein and Gribeauval: 'Artillery Revolution' Political and Cultural Context," *War in History,* **10**(3), 249-264.

Mollo, John (1975) *Uniforms of the Seven Years War 1756-63,* Blandford Press

Nardin, Pierre (1981) *Gribeauval, Lieutenant Général des Armées du Roi (1715-1789),* Paris

Ottenfeld, Rudolf von and Teuber, Oscar (1895 rp 2003) *Die österreichische Armee von 1700 bis 1867,* Verlag von Emil Berte, Vienna [reprint by Ken Trotman Ltd]

Passac, Chevalier de (1816) *Précis sur M. de Gribeauval, Premier Inspecteur de L'Artillerie de France,* In (May 1889), *Revue D'Artillerie,* 96-120.

Pengel R.D. and Hurt G.R.
- (1982b) *Austro-Hungarian Infantry 1740-1762,* On Military Matters.
- (1983) *Austro-Hungarian Hussars, Artillery and Support Troops 1740-1762,* On Military Matters.

Raspe Manuscript (1762) *Der sämtlichen Kayserlich Koeniglichen Armeen zur eigentlichen Kentnis der Uniform von jedem Regimente. Nebst beygefügter Geschichte, worinne von der Stiftung, denen Chefs, der Staercke, und den wichtigsten Thaten jedes Regiments Nachricht gegeben wird.,* Nürnberg.

Rickett, Richard (1983) *A Brief Survey of Austrian History,* 7th Edition, Georg Prachner Verlag, Vienna.

Rothenberg, Gunther E. (1982) *Napoleon's Great Adversary: The Archduke Charles and the Austrian Armmy 1792-1814,* B.T. Batsford Ltd., London.

Rubli, F. von (1749) *Artillerie Exercitia, und Experimenten, welche zu Moldau Thein Anno 1749 in Beysein des Feldt Marchal Fürsten Ioseph Wenzel von Liechtenstein, unter der Direktion des Feldt Artillerie Comendanten und Feldt Marchal-Lieutenant von Feuerstein bewürcket worden.* KA, Kreigwissenschaftliche Memoiren, 13/465.

Scott H.M. (2000) "Prussia's emergence as a European great power, 1740-1763," in P.G. Dwyer (2000) *The Rise of Prussia 1700-1830,* Longman, London, pp153-176.

Seaton A.
- (1973a) *Frederick the Great's Army,* Osprey Publishing
- (1973b) *Austro-Hungarian Army of the Seven Years War,* Osprey Publishing

Schirmer, Friedrich, (1989) *Die Heere der kriegführenden Staaten 1756-1763,* Revised New Edition, KLIO-Landesgruppe.

Schultz, Johann Gottfried (1757-60) *Abbildung Preußischer Kayser und Französischer Soldaten aus dem siebenjährigen Kriege*.

Showalter, D.E. (1996) *The Wars of Frederick the Great*, London.

Smith, Digby [Translator]
- (Aug 2010) "Wurzbach's Biography of Jean Baptist Viscomte de Gribeauval (1715-1789) written in 1859," *Smoothbore Ordnance Journal*, **1** (03)

Summerfield, Stephen
- (2009) *Saxon Artillery 1733-1827*, Partizan Press.
- (Dec 2010) "Part 1: Summary of Gribeauval's Life," *Smoothbore Ordnance Journal*, **2** (01), Ken Trotman Publishing
- Dec 2010) "Part 2: Gribeauval in France before the Seven Years War (1715-57)," *Smoothbore Ordnance Journal*, **2** (02), Ken Trotman Publishing
- (Dec 2010) "Part 3: Gribeauval in Austrian Service (1758-62)," *Smoothbore Ordnance Journal*, **2** (03), Ken Trotman Publishing
- (Dec 2010) "Part 4: Gribeauval Garrison Carriage," *Smoothbore Ordnance Journal*, **2**(04), Ken Trotman Publishing
- (2011a) *Austrian Seven Years War Infantry and Engineers Uniforms, Organisation and Equipment*, Ken Trotman Publishing.
- (2011b) *Austrian Seven Years War Cavalry and Artillery Uniforms, Organisation and Equipment*, Ken Trotman Publishing.

Susane, General (1874 rp 1992) *Histoire de L'Artillerie Francais*, Paris [Reprint by C. Terana]

Szabo, F.A.J. (2007) *The Seven Years War in Europe 1756-63*, Longman, London

Thümmler, Lars-Holger (1993) *Die Österreichische Armee im Siebenjährigen Krieg Die Bautzener Bilderhandschrift aus dem Jahre 1762*, Berlin

Thürheim, Andreas (Graf) (1880) *Gedenkblätter aus der Kriegsgeschichte der k. k. Österreichischen Armee*, Vol I-II, Vienna

Wilson P.H. (1998) *German Armies: War and German Politics 1648-1806*, UCL Press Ltd., London.

Wood, J. (2008) *Armies and Uniforms of the Seven Years War Volume 3 - The Coalition Forces: Austria, Sweden and Russia*, Partizan Press, Nottingham.

Wrede, Alphons Freiherr von (1898-1905), *Geschichte der K. und K. Wehrmacht. Die Regimenter, Corps, Branchen und Anstalten von 1618 bis Ende des XIX. Jahrhunderts*, Volume I-V, Vienna

Wurzbach, Constant von (1859-61), *Biographisches Lexikon des Kaiserthums Oesterreich, enthaltend die die lebensskizzen der denkwürdigen perosnen, wesche seit 1750 bis 1850 in den österreichischen kronländern geboren wurden oder darin gelebt und gewirkt haben*, K. K. Hof- und Staatsdruckerei, Vienna,

Regimental Index

In 1769, the Infantry and the Grenz were numbered sequentially for the first time. Below is given the regimental order as used in the book and in alphabetical order.

Infantry Regiments

1769	Regimental No.	Page	Alphabetical	1769	Page
IR1	Kaiser	63	Andlau	IR57	110
IR2	Erzherzog Karl	130	Angern (1758)	IR49	106
	Erzg Ferdinand (1760)	130	Arenberg	IR21	83
IR3	Lothringen	65	Baden-Baden	IR23	86
IR4	Deutschmeister	66	Baden-Durlach	IR27	91
IR7	Neipperg	68	Batthyány	IR34	136
IR8	Hildburghausen	69	Bayreuth	IR41	98
IR9	Los Rios	117	Bethlen	IR52	141
IR10	Jung-Wolfenbüttel	70	Botta	IR12	73
IR11	Wallis	72	Browne;	IR36	96
IR12	Botta	73	Clerici	IR44	113
IR13	Moltke	74	Alt-Colloredo, Anton	IR20	82
IR14	Salm	75	Jung-Colloredo, Karl	IR40	97
IR15	Pallavicini	77	d'Arberg	IR55	121
IR16	Königsegg	78	Alt-Daun, Heinrich	IR45	102
IR17	Kollowrat	79	Daun, Leopold	IR59	112
IR18	Marschall	80	de Ligne	IR38	120
IR19	Pálffy, Leopold	131	Deutschmeister	IR4	66
IR20	Alt-Colloredo	82	Erzherzog Ferdinand 1760	IR2	130
IR21	Arenberg	83	Erzherzog Karl;	IR2	130
IR22	Hagenbach	85	Esterhazy, Joseph;	IR37	137
	Sprecher (1757);	85	Esterhazy, Nicolaus	IR33	134
	Lacy (1758)	85	Forgách	IR32	133
IR23	Baden-Baden	86	Gaisruck [Gaisrugg]	IR42	100
IR24	Starhemberg	87	Gyulai	IR51	140
IR25	Piccolomini	88	Hagenbach;	IR22	85
	Thürheim (1757)	88	Haller	IR31	132
IR26	Puebla	90	Harrach	IR47	104
IR27	Baden-Durlach	91	Harsch	IR50	107
IR28	Wied-Runkel	92	Hildburghausen	IR8	69
IR29	Wolfenbüttel, Alt-	93	Kaiser	IR1	63
	Loudon (1760)	93	Kheul	IR49	106
IR30	Sachsen-Gotha	118	Kinsky (1761)	IR36	96
IR31	Haller	132	Kollowrat	IR17	79
IR32	Forgách	133	Königsegg	IR16	78
IR33	Esterhazy, Nicolaus	134	Lacy (1758)	IR22	85
IR34	Batthyány	136	Los Rios	IR9	116
IR35	Waldeck	95	Lothringen	IR3	66
IR36	Browne	96	Loudon (1760)	IR29	93
	Tillier (1759)	96	Luzan	IR48	114
	Kinsky (1761)	96	Maguire	IR46	103

IR37	Esterhazy, Joseph	137	Marschall		IR18	80
	Sikovics (1762)	137	Mercy		IR56	109
IR38	de Ligne	120	Moltke		IR13	74
IR39	Pálffy, John	139	Neipperg		IR7	68
IR40	Jung-Colloredo, Karl	97	O'Kelly (1761)		IR45	102
IR41	Bayreuth	98	Pálffy, John		IR39	139
IR42	Gaisruck (Gaisrugg)	100	Pálffy, Leopold		IR19	131
IR43	Platz	101	Pallavicini		IR15	77
IR44	Clerici	113	Piccolomini,		IR25	88
IR45	Alt-Daun, Heinrich	102	Platz		IR43	101
	O'Kelly (1761)	102	Puebla		IR26	90
IR46	Maguire	103	Sachsen-Gotha		IR30	118
IR47	Harrach	104	Salm		IR14	74
IR48	Luzan	114	Sikovics (1762)		IR37	137
IR49	Kheul	106	Simbschen		IR53	143
	Angern (1758)	106	Sincère		IR54	108
IR50	Harsch	107	Sprecher (1757);		IR22	85
IR51	Gyulai	140	Starhemberg		IR24	87
IR52	Bethlen	141	Thürheim (1757)		IR25	88
IR53	Simbschen	143	Tillier (1759);		IR36	96
IR54	Sincère	108	Waldeck		IR35	95
IR55	d'Arberg	121	Wallis		IR11	72
IR56	Mercy	109	Wied-Runkel		IR28	92
IR57	Andlau	110	Alt-Wolfenbüttel, Carl		IR29	93
IR59	Daun, Leopold	112	Jung-Wolfenbüttel		IR10	70

Grenz Infantry Regiments

	Regimental No.	Pg	Alphabetical		1769	Pg
GIR1	Likaner GIR	162	1st Banal GIR	GIR10	IR69	171
GIR2	Ottochaner GIR	163	2nd Banal GIR	GIR11	IR70	172
GIR3	Oguliner GIR	164	Broder GIR	GIR7	IR66	168
GIR4	Szluiner GIR	165	Grasdiscaner GIR	GIR8	IR67	169
GIR5	Kreutz GIR	166	Kreutz GIR	GIR5	IR64	166
GIR6	St. George GIR	167	Likaner GIR	GIR1	IR60	162
GIR7	Broder GIR	168	Oguliner GIR	GIR3	IR62	164
GIR8	Grasdiscaner GIR	169	Ottochaner GIR	GIR2	IR61	163
GIR9	Peterwardeiner GIR	170	Peterwardeiner GIR	GIR9	IR68	170
GIR10	1st Banal GIR	171	St. George GIR	GIR6	IR65	167
GIR11	2nd Banal GIR	172	Szluiner GIR	GIR4	IR63	165
-	Tschaikist Bn	173	Tschaikist Bn	-	-	173

Jäger-Korps (disbanded in 1763)

Regimental No.	Notes	Pg
Deutsches Feld-Jäger Korps	Est 1758 to accompany the Pioneers	174
Deutsches Frei-Jäger-Korps Otto	Est 1759	178

Freikorps (disbanded in 1763)

Regimental No.	Notes	Pg
Company de Lacy	Est 1758	179
Freikorps Bethüne	Netherland *Freikorps* est. 1757	179
Freikorps Kühlwein	Netherlands *Freikorps* est. 1762	179
Freikorps Le Bon	Netherlands *Freikorps* est. 1762	179
Green Loudon Freikorps	Est. 1758: also known as *Freiwilligen-bataillon Loudon,* Loudon Grenadiers, *Grün Loudon*	175
Korps Wurmser	Netherlands *Freikorps* est. 1762	179
Von Böck Freikorps	Est. 1759: *Voluntaires Silesiens, Voluntaire Böck* or *Vountaire Beck*	177

Engineering Corps

Regimental No.	Notes	Pg
Engineer Corps		180
Miners Corps		184
Pioneer Corps		189
Pontoneer Corps		188
Sappers Corps		185